IRISH N

From the international success of Neil Jordan and Jim Sheridan, to the smaller productions of the new generation of Irish filmmakers, the recent flowering of Irish cinema may be seen as a symbol of the nation's emergence from the backwaters of twentieth-century culture into the mainstream of the global economy.

In a country where the modern has been long regarded as a source of suspicion, cinema has occupied a fraught position within Irish society. Attacked by the Church for its detrimental influence on the faithful, regarded by the left as a tool of capitalism and by the Republican movement as a weapon of imperialism, it provided the battleground for the competing discourses within the emergent State during the early years of the twentieth century. At the same time, for the emigrant Irish, particularly of Britain and America, the cinema articulated, responded to and fashioned their experiences of departure and arrival.

Irish National Cinema argues that in order to understand the unique inheritance on which contemporary filmmakers draw, definitions of Irish culture and identity must engage with the cinema of the diaspora. In its discussion of contemporary Irish filmmaking, the book further reflects on questions of nationalism, gender, the representation of the Troubles and of Irish history, as well as cinema's response to the legacy of the 'Celtic Tiger'.

Ruth Barton is Research Fellow at the Centre for Film Studies, University College Dublin. She is the author of *Jim Sheridan – Framing the Nation* (2002) and co-editor of the forthcoming Irish film and television reader *Keeping It Real*.

NATIONAL CINEMAS SERIES
Series Editor: Susan Hayward

AUSTRALIAN NATIONAL CINEMA
Tom O'Regan

BRITISH NATIONAL CINEMA
Sarah Street

CANADIAN NATIONAL CINEMA
Chris Gittings

FRENCH NATIONAL CINEMA
Susan Hayward

GERMAN NATIONAL CINEMA
Sabine Hake

ITALIAN NATIONAL CINEMA 1896–1996
Pierre Sorlin

NORDIC NATIONAL CINEMAS
Tytti Soila, Astrid Söderbergh Widding and Gunnar Iversen

SPANISH NATIONAL CINEMA
Núria Triana-Toribio

Forthcoming titles:

CHINESE NATIONAL CINEMA
Yingjin Zhang

GREEK NATIONAL CINEMA
Maria Stassinopoulou

MEXICAN NATIONAL CINEMA
Andrea Noble

SOUTH AFRICAN NATIONAL CINEMA
Jacqueline Maingard

IRISH NATIONAL CINEMA

Ruth Barton

Routledge
Taylor & Francis Group

LONDON AND NEW YORK

First published 2004
by Routledge
11 New Fetter Lane, London EC4P 4EE

Simultaneously published in the USA and Canada
by Routledge
29 West 35th Street, New York, NY 10001

Routledge is an imprint of the Taylor & Francis Group

Typeset in Galliard by
Keyword Publishing Services Ltd, Wallington, Surrey, UK
Printed and bound in Great Britain by
Biddles Ltd, King's Lynn

British Library Cataloguing in Publication Data
A catalogue record for this book is available from the British Library

Library of Congress Cataloging in Publication Data
A catalog record for this book has been requested

ISBN 0–415–27894–5 (hbk)
ISBN 0–415–27895–3 (pbk)

FOR MY MOTHER,
ANNE BARTON

CONTENTS

ILLUSTRATIONS

Unless otherwise credited, all images appear courtesy of the Irish Film Archive of the Film Institute of Ireland.

ACKNOWLEDGEMENTS

Much of the research for this book was carried out under the Irish Research Council for the Humanities and Social Sciences (IRCHSS) doctoral and post-doctoral research fellowship schemes at the Centre for Film Studies, University College Dublin. Without the help of Sunniva O'Flynn and Eugene Finn at the Irish Film Archive, I could not have taken this project so far; they also kindly read and commented on early drafts of Part I. I am deeply indebted to the staff of the library at the Irish Film Centre, particularly Emma Keogh and Antoinette Prout. I would like to acknowledge the help of the staff at the National Library of Ireland, the British Film Institute library and the National Archive and also Madeleine Matz at the Library of Congress. I am grateful too to the local librarians who sent me details of cinema going and filmmaking in their areas. Particular thanks goes to Susan Hayward for her encouragement, to my 'anonymous' readers and to Alistair Daniel, Rebecca Barden, Lesley Riddle and Helen Faulkner at Routledge. Kevin Rockett, my PhD supervisor, has always been willing to help with time and advice.

Just as I thought I had viewed everything, Paul Balbirnie appeared in Dublin with a vast private collection of films, many of which now form the Balbirnie Collection at the Irish Film Archive. He generously allowed me to plunder his stash of videos and drew my attention to otherwise long-forgotten Irish films.

I am especially grateful to the network of fellow parents and relatives who, at a moment's notice have taken over the swimming run or picked up children from school and particularly to my parents-in-law, John and Clare Cremen for all their help. Finally, and most importantly, Willie, Conal, Eoin and Paddy lived with an automaton in their midst for sustained periods of writing. Their forbearance and support have made it all possible.

Permissions

An earlier version of Chapter 7 appeared in *Cineaste* (volume XXIV, numbers 2–3, pp. 40–5) under the title 'Feisty Colleens and Faithful Sons: Gender in Irish Cinema'. An earlier version of Chapter 9 appeared in *The Irish Review* (number 21, pp. 41–56) as 'From History to Heritage: some recent developments in Irish Cinema'.

Part I

FROM THE SILENT ERA TO THE 1960s: A HISTORICAL OVERVIEW

1

IRISH CINEMA – NATIONAL CINEMA?

From nationalist politics to identity politics – conceptualising Irish cinema

When, in 1993, the Irish government announced a series of measures designed to place Irish filmmaking practices on a secure, professional basis, it seemed at long last that Ireland would be able to boast a film industry of its own. After years of failed schemes, many of which foundered in the face of official hostility towards an entertainment form associated with loose morals and the corruptions of modernity, Ireland's choice was, in the words of the Labour minister, academic and poet, Michael D. Higgins, 'whether we become the consumer of images in a passive culture or whether we will be allowed to be the makers of images in an active culture, in a democratic society' (*Irish Cinema – Ourselves Alone*, 1995).

Underlying the minister's words lay an anxiety that was anything but new to debates around the cinema and Ireland. His concerns for the survival of indigenous cultural traditions in the face of the global mass-marketing of the image would have been met with a familiar nod from the policy-makers of the nascent Irish State of the 1920s onwards. If the issues are now less about protecting the good Catholic Irish from secular temptations than about gaining control of representation in the face of hegemonic multinationalism, the battleground is much the same. Caught between the two is the Irish public. Reported to be amongst the most enthusiastic cinema-goers in Europe[1,2], they have consistently sought out the pleasures of popular Hollywood film and have been aided in doing so by a trade that has viewed restrictions from above with little sympathy.

Threaded through Higgins' words is another supposition, that an Irish film industry will create an Irish film culture, and that this will, in some way, reflect, interrogate and enrich the national culture. We may now look back and question whether this indeed did occur in what we might call the 'Second Film Board years', namely the period following the re-establishment, after several years of dormancy, of the Film Board in 1993 under Minister Higgins. The chapters in the second half of this book are largely concerned with that period, one that saw the establishment of a commercial environment for multiple modes of filmmaking practice from Irish-language, to documentaries and short films to arthouse and commercial releases.

Writing on Australian cinema, Tom O'Regan proposes that:

> A national cinema is made of the films and film production industry of particular nations. National cinemas involve relations between, on the one hand, the national film texts and the national film industries and, on the other hand, their various social, political and cultural contexts.
>
> (1996: 1)

In the Irish case, the absence of a local film production industry for most of the twentieth century means that if we are to talk of a national cinema, or a national film text even, we have to engage in a series of acts of creative bricolage; that is, to see how an image of Ireland on screen emerged out of the national industries of other countries. This is not a new strategy – representations of Ireland created from both the British and Hollywood industries have been thoroughly explored in the seminal, though now out of print publication, *Cinema and Ireland* (Rockett *et al.*, 1987). This book proposes to build on that work by including in its frame of reference the films of the early twentieth century that fictionalise the experience of emigration and immigration (in particular the latter as seen from the point of view of the host countries of Britain and America) and by reappraising the work of directors such as Brian Desmond Hurst who attempted to make Irish films from within the British film industry (Chapter 3).[3]

It is now commonly accepted that the new desire to include the so-called 'diaspora' of Ireland within the parameters of the national may be dated from the moment of Mary Robinson's election as President of the Republic in November 1990. Obviously this is a simplistic rendering of a gradual shift in the concept of the nation but the president's announcement that she would be burning a candle in the window of Áras an Uachtaráin (the presidential residence) for those Irish abroad seemed to crystallise that development. This further coincided with an international embrace of all things Irish, from popular cultural artefacts (U2, Riverdance, 'boybands', Maeve Binchy and the many pretenders to her title) to high cultural representations: the plays of Brian Friel, the poetry of Seamus Heaney and the output of a younger generation of (mostly male) writers. The Irish 'imagined community', to borrow Benedict Anderson's classic formulation (Anderson, 1983), is not considered as being contained within one geographical space but as including the Irish within Ireland and those now domiciled elsewhere. Since many of these are now fourth or fifth generation immigrants and, as a consequence of interracial marriage, boast multiple ethnic affiliations (Alba, 1990; Byron, 1999) it is perhaps simplest to leave it that you are Irish, or 'hyphenated Irish', if you say you are (such à la carte ethnicity is not so acceptable in Ireland where new immigrants have yet to be incorporated within the national self-image). Many do indeed choose this option since, as Diane Negra wrote in 2001, 'it would be difficult to overstate the positive currency of Irishness in US popular culture .... As Irishness has surged into a globally marketed identity, Irish-American ethnicity has emerged as a particularly nostalgic point of connection with this phenomenon' (2001b: 229). An Irish national cinema is thus defined here firstly as a body of films made inside and outside of Ireland that addresses both the local and diasporic cultures. This is not to suggest that local and immigrant visions of Ireland are one: on the contrary, as Roy Foster discusses in the literary context, immigration entails erasing memories of the actual conditions that forced the initial act of emigration – famine, debt, lack of opportunity – and re-imagining the homeland as Edenic. Exile literature 'becomes more and more of a reflex-action, bearing less and less similarity to the emigrant existence as lived in the second and third generations, and simultaneously diverging more and more from life as lived in the old country' (Foster, 2001: 97).

It is common in definitions of national cinemas to stress the link between filmmaking and nationalism. The creation of a sense of national belonging, and its obverse, of exclusion, has traditionally taken place within the cultural domain. Timothy Brennan reminds us that, 'Nations ... are imaginary constructs that depend for their existence on an apparatus of cultural fictions in which imaginative literature plays a decisive role. And the rise of European nationalism coincides especially with one form of literature – the novel' (1990: 49). For all this, however, he is forced to recognise that:

> under conditions of illiteracy and shortages, and given simply the leisure-time necessary for reading one, the novel has been an elitist and minority form in developing countries when compared to poem, song, television, and film. Almost inevitably it has been the form through which a thin, foreign-educated stratum (however sensitive or committed to domestic political interests) has communicated to metropolitan reading publics, often in translation.
>
> (ibid.: 56)

Despite signs in the early years of the twentieth century (discussed in the following chapter) that cinema would play a vital role in the cultural dissemination of Irish nationalism, this was not to be. Irish nationalism followed the trajectory of so many other such movements, namely of starting out as a modernising project and ending up as a regressive and conservative force. We shall be discussing this in more detail in the forthcoming chapters, but for now it is enough to remember that cinema had little part to play in the nationalist agenda. This has primarily been the terrain of Irish literature.

It is only when we turn to the 'incomplete' project of Irish nationalism, the reintegration of Northern Ireland into the body politic, that we can see any sustained intersection between Irish cinema and politics. This brings us to a second question of terminology – the extent to which representations of Northern Ireland on film belong to the history of Irish cinema. Many of the films made about Northern Ireland have, as we shall be discussing, emerged out of the industries of other countries and operate on a generic basis that has little to do with understanding the politics of the Troubles and much to do with finding new turf on which to play out the tensions of the international political thriller. Local efforts to represent the Troubles are documented here but the wider history of filmmaking within Northern Ireland has only, regrettably, been touched on briefly.[4]

Arguably, Northern Ireland's screen history belongs equally to the annals of a British national cinema. This book is criss-crossed with references to films that have represented Irish nationalism from the point of view of a conservative British film culture, just as many more have been concerned with labelling the Irish as hilariously infantile and backward. Britain, Richard Kearney writes, emerged as 'a *narrated community* which invented itself in dialectical opposition to its "others" and most especially to Ireland, its first, last and most intimate rival' (2002: 98–9). Ireland being Catholic, a colony and an ally of revolutionary France, became the mirror into which Britain must look in order to establish its own identity which 'was in fact constructed upon the screening of its forgotten "other" in both senses of "screen": to conceal and to project' (ibid. 99). British popular culture's more recent embrace of Irish writers, broadcasters and comedians might thus be considered an antidote to the imperial mindset in a new era of regionalism and multiculturalism. It may equally be ascribed to an entrenched tradition of exoticising the Celt. Prompted by a viewing of *Into the West* (Mike Newell, Ireland, 1992), Robert McCrum in a *Guardian* article speculated:

> Partly it's because the Irish seem to the grim, colonising English altogether wittier, more charming and, yes, more likable. We are the oppressor, yet we envy the oppressed. They have been invaded, yet they remain, maddeningly, free . . . . Then again, our fascination is to do with the language, not merely the sense of words translated from another tongue but a rhythm and a music that takes us, in folk memory, back to the English of Milton and Pope. Shakespeare, we know, would have sounded Irish, as indicated by his rhyming of 'sea' with 'say' and 'stale' with 'steal'. It is hard, for instance, to explain the popularity of broadcasters such as Terry Wogan, Anthony Clare and Henry Kelly except in terms of their appeal to a style of speech that has been lost in the tide of Standard English and its thin, clipped, grey vowels.
>
> Partly, again, it's to do with Ireland's ability to seem in touch with an intense personal lyricism, a forgotten way of life, a past we desperately want to believe in, a place of storytelling and eternal verities, a country in which mother and father double with Mary and Joseph, where magic and prayer can change your life, and in which the truth is found in fire and water.
>
> (1992: 7)

Even if, however, the fictional construction of the Irish on the British screen belongs in part to the narration of British identity, in the absence of a history of indigenous, Irish counter-images, it has passed into the greater archive of the cinematic imaginary. This archive of images forms what I would like to consider the second constituent element of an Irish national cinema. Thus, the much used shot of John Wayne apparently holding Maureen O'Hara at arm's length in *The Quiet Man* (John Ford, USA, 1952) or of the father and son caught in silhouette in *Man of Aran* (Robert Flaherty, GB, 1934) enjoy an iconic value that far exceeds the narratives from which they arise. In the Irish context, the extraordinarily picturesque and photographic quality of the landscape has combined with an immigrant culture predicated on nostalgia and a history of tourism to endow the romantic vision of the landscape and its people with an enduring potency. Cinema has seized on this tradition, alternatively affirming it and negating it, replicating these visuals and subverting them with counter-images – of the corrupt city, the menacing countryside. Alongside this repository of images is a range of themes that recur within these films – of rebellion and sacrifice, of departure and return, of spiritual voyages, and these in turn are animated by a panoply of characters, many of them borrowed from the repertoire of early stage and vaudeville representations – the fighting Irishman, the buffoon, the long-suffering mother, the feisty colleen, the rebel son. Taken together, these images, themes and characters form the foundation of an Irish cinema and have, become, for each new generation of filmmakers, a way of defining their own work, whether they chose to reject them, incorporate them or rework them. As Thomas Elsaesser reminds us, 'a strong national cinema must feed on its predecessors and thus stand in a vampiric relation to what has gone before. Identity and pleasure in the cinema remain connected to questions of narrative, the art of repetition, and recognition' (1993: 60). Part of the process of creating a national cinema has been predicated on wresting the powerful practice of image-making from the control of other filmmaking traditions whether hostile or otherwise. This imperative formed the polemical basis of *Cinema and Ireland* which was conceived just as that process appeared close to being realised by the new wave of independent, deconstructive and avant-garde Irish films of the 1970s and 1980s.

Since the reformation of the Film Board, official policies and the greater availability of funding saw Irish filmmaking abandon low-budget practices in favour of participation in the international circuit of distribution and exhibition. More recently something of a strategic about-face has occurred with the Board committing itself to micro-budget digital production practices aimed primarily at a local market (see Chapter 6). This leads us to a third factor in defining an Irish national cinema – as an industry. Irish cinema circulates within a nexus of filmmaking practices that are now largely defined by multinational finance. Whether it can retain its own local cultural identity within this configuration is an all-embracing issue. In creative terms, the strategy of the periphery 'writing back' to the centre, discussed by Salman Rushdie in terms of the refashioning of the English language by post-colonial writers (Rushdie, 1982: 8) has given Irish producers the impetus to grasp the language of dominant cinema, tailor it to reflect a local idiom (through the appropriation of genres such as the gangster film, the road movie and the historical epic) and direct their product back at the home territories of that dominant cinema. Irish film and television have conventionally attempted to write back to two centres – Britain and Hollywood. This triangular relationship has provided the locus of much debate on how indigenous filmmakers in particular should orient their product – towards Hollywood, towards Britain, inwards, or in all directions at once. Indeed, this controversy has emerged each time it has seemed that a sustained period of filmmaking was about to occur. At a thematic as well as an industrial level, we find this 'writing back' complicating and underlining the practices of the early 'Abbey Films' of the late 1950s and early 1960s (discussed in Chapter 4) which positioned themselves within both the local and British film culture and attempted to address both audiences, and recurring throughout contemporary Irish cinema.

By the time of the publication of Martin McLoone's *Irish Film, The Emergence of a Contemporary Cinema* (2000), another key text in the academic critique of Irish cinema, the local versus the global debate had moved centre stage. McLoone's publication was informed by a considerable ambiguity, mirrored by Irish society at large and echoed in the minister's words quoted at the beginning of this chapter, over the Irish film and media industry's participation in global production practices.

For many commentators, the dynamics of funding have combined with a dilution of the local culture in the wake of its infiltration by global capital to create a new situation of cultural dependency. We need to be wary, however, of establishing a simplistic binary that offsets the local against the global, little Ireland battling against the giants of multinational enterprise. As Tim Bergfelder reminds us, as a matter of pragmatism Hollywood has always financed other national cinemas, including those of Europe (Bergfelder, 2000). Indeed, if one of the requirements of a national cinema is that it respond to the local culture, then the embrace of globalisation by certain sectors of Irish society has been well reflected in cinematic product. In other words, for large sectors of Irish society, globalism is a liberation from the old orthodoxies of nation and State.

This leads us to the fourth point of definition crucial to the understanding of an Irish national cinema, which is its dialogue with the national culture. Terry Eagleton has elegantly traced the concept of culture from a tool of enlightenment to a practice of self-definition: 'It [culture] now means the affirmation of a specific identity – national, sexual, ethnic, regional – rather than the transcendence of it' (2000: 38). 'Culture' is now 'cultures', most of them antagonistic in some sense or another. If the nation-state was constructed on the notion of a common culture, retrospectively established, so it is dismantled by the arrival of multiculturalism and cosmopolitanism with their supra-national links. But

> since transnational capitalism also breeds isolation and anxiety,
> uprooting men and women from their traditional attachments and

pitching their identity into chronic crisis, it fosters, by way of reaction, cultures of defensive solidarity at the very time that it is busy proliferating this brave new cosmopolitanism.

(ibid.: 63)

Culture in Ireland has thus evolved from being the articulation of an aspiration (revolution), to the expression of a collective identity (the stabilising of the nation-state) to a means of fracturing that identity (postmodern identity politics). Most of the films considered in this book reflect some stage in this process. The inherent drawback to the embrace of a collective culture is its rejection of 'deviant' identities, aspects of Irishness that do not seem to fit the formula, notably queer sexualities but also non-traditional interpretations of gender roles, non-Catholic religious affiliations, non-white skin colour and so on. When this apparent consensus is overturned, then a space emerges for the expression of those hitherto suppressed aspects of identity and these are in turn articulated through culture and through belonging to sub-cultures.

Cinema is so evidently situated within a transnational mode of circulation that it can offer a route out of restrictive national identity politics. It also behoves those responding to Irish cinematic texts that they bear in mind that they do not necessarily have to be interpreted via considerations of the national. This is not as easily achieved as might be imagined. Irish cultural production has long reflected a postcolonial imperative to assert the validity of a distinctive Irish identity, to become the subject rather than the object of description; hence the apparent national obsession with 'explaining ourselves to others'. This constant re-affirmation of a national identity has dictated that all cultural productions should in some sense reflect on what it means to be Irish. For a new generation of filmmakers, and other artists, this trope holds little interest and their work needs to be seen as the rejection of national identity politics in favour of other identity politics or as an expression of their internationalism, more part of youth culture, for instance, than Irish culture.

Homi Bhabha has written that 'counter-narratives of the nation that continually evoke and erase its totalizing boundaries – both actual and conceptual – disturb those ideological manoeuvres through which "imagined communities" are given essentialist identities' (1990: 300). Arguably, this is a process that is more likely to occur from within the given culture and one that a number of films discussed in the second part of this book attempt to do. Whether they achieve this with money garnered from international sources is not, as I argue in Chapter 6, particularly relevant, rather it is the manner with which they address their material that determines its outcome. Whether Irish cinema has achieved this at all is another question and one that needs to be raised.

The fifth ingredient in any definition of Irish national cinema is its distinctiveness as an artform. Irish cinema has struggled to find its own place in a critical environment dominated by the literary. The place of the novel, the play and the poem within the construction of an Irish national identity, and as part of its deconstruction, has been and remains the subject of a massive academic industry. It is thus doubly important that Irish cinema be viewed not just as another way of reflecting on the national culture but as a medium in itself that has established its own traditions of representation. Approaching it via literary theory is not adequate on its own and we must be sensitive to its visual and aural signifiers as much as to its referencing of international trends in filmmaking. Certainly, the absence of any notable local filmmaking culture has inhibited the evolution of a distinct Irish cinematic language; for some, however, this in itself has been an empowering experience. As Neil Jordan has expressed it, working in cinema has enabled him to escape from the language of the literary past and operate within a new idiom:

> What I found most liberating when I first started working in cinema was there was no set of assumptions and associations specifically related to being an Irish director. But having worked in it now for several years, I find the Irish thing is emerging.... The importance I give to the emotional articulation of my world and work is not something typical in British cinema. The attempt to imagine another state of living, another way of being, is I believe very Irish. It's difficult to say what exactly underlies this or why it should be so. It's something to do with the quest for another place, another manner of thinking. It's a dissatisfaction with the accepted and scientifically approved explanations of the world.... Our mistake was to assume that we could be at home in a single nation. We fed ourselves on ideologies of violence and instant salvation, the illusion that history is a continuum moving forward to its perfect destiny. We thus forgot that we can never be at home anywhere. Perhaps it is one of the functions of writers and artists to remind the nation of this. To expose the old ideologies. To feel in exile abroad and also when one returns home.
>
> (Kearney, 1988a: 198–9)

Again, we can detect in Jordan's words a reluctance to be tied by national labels tempered by that very desire to designate himself as an Irish artist. We can, however, find ways in which Irish cinema distinguished itself from other artforms and other national cinemas. As my final chapter will argue, an important element in this is the existence of identifiably Irish actors, at home with the parts they are playing, familiar to local audiences, and accustomed to working as an ensemble within a filmmaking context.

The final distinction that I would like to make in regard to the definitions that structure this book is to argue for a greater interest in Irish cinema culture. We should remember that if Ireland did not have a film industry of any kind until the 1990s, and even then a very minor one, it has always had a cinema culture. This I am interpreting in its widest sense to include not just the films that have been made in or about Ireland and that the Irish have watched, the works of primitive and amateur filmmakers and documentarists, or the writings that have grown up around these films, from the popular coverage accorded them in fan magazines to the academic literature that has analysed them, but equally the spaces in which they have been viewed: the parish halls and picture palaces and later the television screens that have brought Irish and other films to viewers' homes. The first part of this book attempts to do some justice to that history of viewing, paying particular attention (in Chapter 3) to the contested nature of the cinema space during the early years of the Irish Free State. Here, as we shall see, the divergent interests of the new State played out their respective dramas. A viewer attending a film might observe that what they were watching made little sense after the censor had voided it of all references to immoral or, in the war years, politically insensitive behaviour or they might find their afternoon or evening out broken up by protestors raiding the auditorium to proclaim that what they were viewing was an offence to the Irish character or had royalist sympathies. Alternatively, they could, if they should so choose, defy the hegemonic strictures of the State or the republicans and travel to Northern Ireland to watch films about the British royals or the Second World War.

By focusing on the contested nature of the filmgoing experience as well as the films that might be considered relevant to a study such as this, I have tried to do justice to the title of this book and the series in which it takes its place. As writers before me have discovered, the process of defining the national in an academic environment that eschews such overarching grand narratives is a daunting task. In the context of a society that has spent the greater part of the twentieth century in dispute over definitions of nation and State, it is particularly awesome. Although it is now, as so many other authors of books such as this have concluded, extremely difficult to identify what we mean when we refer to a national cinema, this does not mean that one should not exist and that the aspiration to create and maintain one is invalid. Directors, producers and actors are engaged in making films that in various ways challenge and augment the images and narratives of Ireland. Many who define themselves as Irish also work within the industries of other countries and there is little to be gained in arguing that, for instance the British ethnic comedy *East is East* (GB, 1999) is in any measure Irish because its director is Damien O'Donnell or that there is anything Irish about *Tigerland* (Joel Schumacher, USA, 2000) because its star is a rising Irish actor, Colin Farrell. Is it possible to consider that another film directed by Joel Schumacher, *Veronica Guerin* (USA, 2003), about the murdered Dublin investigative journalist, financed primarily with Hollywood money and shot to the standards of global filmmaking, is Irish? Eventually, the process becomes reductive and susceptible to simple list-making. The success of so many Irish actors across the generations has allowed them and their characters to infiltrate and even subvert the narratives of other nations. That the future of Britain appears to lie in the hands of a young Irish cycle courier,

Jim (Cillian Murphy) in the science-fiction film, *28 Days Later* … (Danny Boyle, GB, 2002), where the Cockney hero, Frank, is played by another Irish actor (Brendan Gleeson), is just another reminder of the subtle twists of the globalised, post-colonial identity game.

Ultimately, I have exerted my right as a deconstructed, decentred individual to identify an Irish national cinema as it occurs to me. Elsewhere I have argued for an escape from the new canon of Irish films;[5] in this book the reader will find the little-known rubbing shoulders with the long-established. One of the pleasures of writing a book such as this is the discovery of moments of significance within otherwise forgettable films and one of my intentions throughout has been to draw attention to works that might otherwise have been relegated to the margins of the story of Irish cinema.

The above is not intended as a general prescription for the study of national cinemas but as a way of rationalising my own approach to the subject. This book is divided into two parts, the first being a general history of the practices of cinema going, the development of an immigrant cinema and the various attempts to produce locally-made Irish films. The second commences with the evolution of an indigenous cinema in the 1970s and proceeds to examine the films of the Second Film Board years on a thematic basis. It covers fiction and some non-fiction films (though for an authoritative study of the Irish documentary, the reader is directed to Harvey O'Brien's forthcoming *The Real Ireland* [Manchester University Press]). I have tried to reflect not just my own thoughts but the opinions of others by referencing the works of my colleagues in this area and drawing on newspaper and other reviews of the films and topics. The latter, I have assumed, represent the response of their authors but also appeal to their readers and thus, to an extent at least, speak on behalf of a wider audience again. Ultimately, the intention of this book is to reflect the work on Irish cinema that has preceded it, those titles already mentioned as well as publications by Luke Gibbons (1996), Kevin Rockett (1996), Brian McIlroy (1998) Lance Pettitt (2000) and others referenced through this text, whilst opening up new areas and new approaches to an ever growing body of films.

2

A SILENT REVOLUTION

The reception and making of Irish-themed films in Ireland and America before and immediately after the Easter Rising of 1916

The early days of Irish cinema coincided with an incendiary period in Irish history that would eventually lead to the Easter Rising of 1916 and culminate in independence and civil war. As the Lumière Brothers' cameraman, Alexandre Promio shot images of Dublin's main thoroughfare, Sackville Street (1897)[1] Catholic nationalism was emerging as the dominant political force outside of Ulster. The rise of an educated merchant class in the wake of the successions of famines in the mid to late nineteenth century and the achievement of the Protestant landlord, Charles Stewart Parnell, in uniting this class under the Home Rule banner meant that from 1885 onwards nationalist politics moved into a new constitutional, democratic phase.

As discussed in the previous chapter, during this period, culture was the main conduit for the expression of nationalism and identity. From the late nineteenth century, the creation of an appropriate literary idiom became the preserve of an educated Anglo-Irish elite – W.B. Yeats, Lady Gregory, J.M. Synge and others. The revivalists' desire to construct a new national literature was in tune with similar movements such as the Gaelic Athletic Association (GAA, formed in 1884) with its opposition to English games, and the Gaelic League, established in 1893 as the intellectual counterpart of the GAA. The Gaelic League aimed at restoring the Irish language and fostering writing through the medium of Irish; it also encouraged people to buy home-produced goods and wear what was considered to be traditional Irish clothing. Membership of the GAA and the Gaelic League tended to be drawn from amongst Catholics whilst the Irish Literary Society was largely the preserve of the Protestant Ascendancy.

The Irish literary revival wove a myth of Irishness that was both antiquarian and revolutionary, that defined itself through its difference and superiority to Englishness, and made direct appeal to the sympathies of local and international audiences. Although their writings were inspired by the peasant tradition, their audience was metropolitan and middle-class. As Colm Tóibín reminds us, Lady Gregory classified the riots that took place in 1907 during the infamous first production of *The Playboy of the Western World* as 'the old battle between those who use a toothbrush and those who don't' (Tóibín, 2002: 65; Kilroy, 1971). The filmic medium may well have inspired Joyce when he was writing *Ulysses* (Gibbons, 1996: 165) and even led him to dabble in cinema exhibition as a career (setting up and briefly managing Dublin's first dedicated cinema, the Volta, in 1909). In general, however, the creation of a popular culture for the masses was, it seems, far from the Ascendancy agenda.

Film, on the other hand, was a genuinely proletarian cultural form. The audience for the early cinema silents was not confined to the metropolitan circle who frequented the Abbey but was spread throughout Irish urban and rural life. This popular audience was swift to embrace moving pictures as were the travelling showmen of the day to screen them:

> When animated pictures came on the scene, my father and his brother Bracey introduced the first gas-operated movie machine to Ireland. Later my father bought a steam-engine, with a dynamo mounted on front and became one of the first men in Ireland to travel and show electric pictures. In the development of cinematography, the big step from gas to electric movies was a step of major significance.
>
> In some of the areas visited, the locals had never before seen an electric bulb and when the engine arrived in the village, it was greeted with awe and amazement. Once the engine was started up, the coloured lights on the canopy illuminated the whole area and the numerous on-lookers loudly applauded ...
>
> Bob, my uncle, used to drive the engine and operate the machine for showing the pictures. After her marriage mother sang to song slides, while father took the money at the door. One must remember that there were no cinemas in most Irish towns or villages at that time, or, indeed, no electric light, unless privately owned. So the arrival of Bailey's Electric Pictures, with the name lit up in coloured bulbs on the canopy, was an event of major importance to many a country town. The local kids would follow the engine to the local river to collect water and then stand in sheer amazement as Uncle Bob switched on the lights ...[2]
>
> (Bailey and O'Shea, 1996: 279)

The first images of Irish life to appear on the screen were cosmopolitan and eclectic. The cameras of the Lumière Brothers and the British Warwick Trading Company revealed Dublin and Cork to be bustling, modern cities. As early as 1898 a Belfast doctor, Robert A. Mitchell, captured and exhibited scenes from the Bangor Yacht Race of that year. James T. Jameson of the Irish Animated Picture Company initiated a local newsreel tradition by filming a commemoration of the revolutionary, Wolfe Tone, held in 1913 in Bodenstown and showing it in cinemas throughout Ireland. Local entrepreneurs, such as Thomas Horgan of Youghal in County Cork, soon saw the commercial potential of regional news items and produced a variety of actualities and 'topicals'.[3] As O'Flynn (1996) has noted, *The Youghal Gazette* appeared to transcend political bias:

> with one issue showing great celebrations at the release of hunger strikers from Wormwood Scrubs prison – local men, who had been interned for their role in the 1916 Rising – and a later issue marking the glorious return of local men from the First World War where they had fought alongside British soldiers.
>
> (ibid.: 58)

Horgan also capitalised on the centrality of Church observance to Irish life at the time, focusing in particular on its pageantry and communality in footage (*c.* 1917) of the Corpus Christi procession and crowds spilling down the steps of the chapel after mass.

In 1917 Ireland's first regular newsreel service was set up by Norman Whitten, manager of the General Film Supply Company in Dublin, with Gordon Lewis, who also worked for Pathé Gazette, as his cameraman. According to Liam O'Leary, Whitten had worked in British films with the early pioneer, Cecil Hepworth, and later returned to England where he continued to operate until his death (O'Leary, 1990: 14). The programme, *Irish Events*, showed a mixture of sporting news, religious pageantry and political events. Whitten, for instance, filmed the Sinn Féin convention of 1917 and had it ready for the cinemas that evening. The release of Sinn Féin prisoners in July 1917 provided another opportunity to capitalise on the political events of the time and steal a march on Gaumont; where Whitten could deliver the newsreel to Dublin cinemas within hours, the Gaumont photographer had to send his film to England for development and printing. One of the company's taglines was 'Britain for the British, Irish Events for the Irish' and Whitten was quick to take advantage of a general desire for indigenous Irish news and, in particular, a sympathetic portrayal of the aftermath of the Easter Rising of 1916.

British newsreels of the day, such as those of Topical Budget, depicted the events of 1916 and the later Civil War (1922–23) as an assault on property and propriety, with the camera lingering on burning buildings and looted shops.[4] The defeat of the 'rebels' in 1916 was emphasised through footage of prisoners being marched off under guard and the subsequent British withdrawal represented as an act of goodwill. Sinn Féin prisoners held under martial law were, it was reported by the Pathé Gazette in 1920, treated as 'prisoners-of-war' whilst sympathy for Michael Collins in his battle against the 'irregulars' was expressed in a number of newsreels. In contrast, Whitten's footage, although technically more primitive, made direct appeal to the hearts of its Irish audience. The intertitles to images of barricades being built, walls daubed with the slogan, 'No Pope Here', Catholic evictions and children poised on top of piles of bricks and rubble in Belfast of

1922 announce 'The Agony of Belfast. Where civil blood makes civil hands unclean'. Such overt expressions of partisan opinion did not escape the attention of the British authorities. Kevin Rockett has described the consequences of Whitten's decision to show a compilation newsreel of images of the nationalist struggle, *The Sinn Fein Review* (1919) – following an investigation by the appropriate authorities, the film was seized by the police whilst it was being screened at the Boyne Cinema, Drogheda and Whitten was not permitted to show it again (Rockett, 1987: 34–6). As a consequence of this, *Irish Events* came to an end, although Whitten continued to shoot occasional newsreel footage such as the sequences in Belfast (above) and also turned his hand to fiction filmmaking.

The brief flowering of local Irish newsreels and topicals, many shot by local cinema owners such as Thomas Horgan, during the revolutionary events leading up to independence, reflects their makers' awareness of the importance of controlling news and other images in a climate of war. Their success with cinema audiences similarly indicates a popular desire to imagine the nation in a particular fashion. Joep Leerssen has written that,

> a demographic group defines itself as a nation, not by the criteria on which the national self-definition is *based*, but by its willingness to perform that self-definition. One ought to remain aware of the fact that a common heritage, interest or 'character' does not cogently constitute a 'nation' unless the people involved are willing to acknowledge it as such.
>
> (1996a: 17)

The variety of *Irish Events'* subject matter, from the activities of Sinn Féin to sporting occasions to British military displays, suggests that the demographic group of the time admitted to a wide range of allegiances and interests. Indeed, this willingness to subscribe to such an eclectic view of Irish contemporary life hints at the existence within the popular audience of a much more plural outlook than nationalist histories have allowed for.

Fiction filmmaking commenced in Ireland as it did in other countries with the move from recorded to staged events. Rockett suggests that the first fiction film with an Irish subject was a comedy, *Irish Wives and English Husbands*, made by the Englishman, Arthur Melbourne-Cooper in 1907 (Rockett, 1987: 7). No copy has survived of this film although its title indicates a re-working of the trope of the national romance that was to structure much of British-Irish cinematic representations and was already commonly applied in other fictional forms. The recurrence of the theme of the traumatic love affair between an Irish and an English character underlines its potency in an era of extreme political upheaval. *The Irish Filmography* (Rockett, 1996) lists several such films (none of which has survived). In the historical melodrama, *The Incomparable Bellairs* (Harold Shaw, GB, 1915) the affair is between an impoverished Irishman and a well-bred young English woman, whilst in another short film, *Ashtore* (Wilfred Noy, GB,

1917), the star-crossed lovers are an Irish woman of humble origins and an English nobleman. A variation on the theme is the intrusion of an Englishman into a peasant (native Irish) romance such as occurs in *The Wearing of the Green* (director unknown, GB, 1910).

The other favoured mode of representing the Irish in early cinema was by means of the comic stage Irishman. Typical of such films was the 'Mike Murphy' series, produced by Martin Films from 1913 onwards. Judging by what is probably the one surviving print, *Mike Murphy As A Picture Actor* (Dave Aylott, GB, 1914), the series draws heavily on traditional variety humour with its hero, Mike Murphy (Ernest Westo), portrayed as a naive and good humoured tramp whose credulity leads him into a succession of improbable misadventures.

In early American cinema, things were little better. By the turn of the century the Irish were the dominant immigrant group within America and, as Noel Ignatiev has chronicled, had taken control of their own representation to the extent of transforming themselves from 'black' to 'white' (Ignatiev, 1995). The new 'lace curtain' Irish 'wanted images that would somehow unite the Irish past with the American present; images that could inspire rather than embarrass' (Williams, 1998: 200). Without access to the production of films, they found themselves at the mercy of the general run of stereotypes that early cinema inherited from vaudeville. In this respect early British images of the Irish had much in common with their American counterparts. If WASP (White Anglo-Saxon Protestant) America had been forced to recognise the political nous of the new Irish democrats, symbolised by Irish-American domination of Tammany Hall, the new medium of cinema lagged far behind. The many short films of 1896 onwards that featured Irish characters insisted on portraying them as imbecilic, drunk and swift-tempered. Drawing on stage characters popular in nineteenth-century entertainment, these films returned over and again to the pratfalls of Bridget the dim-witted servant (played in drag) whose inability to master simple domestic chores invariably led to disaster (in, for instance, *The Finish of Bridget McKeen* (USA, 1901), and Happy Hooligan, the layabout tramp. Irish construction workers blew themselves up with dynamite (*Drill Ye Tarriers Drill* [USA, 1900]) and a 'corpse' rose from the dead as revellers 'wake' him (*A Wake in Hell's Kitchen* [USA, 1900]).

Charles Musser has suggested that this mode of characterisation enabled contemporary Irish audiences to distance themselves from these older stereotypes as well as from their non-assimilated compatriots through humour and condescension (1991: 49). The films' frequent descent into mayhem also sanctions a ludic disruption of class values. Audiences, Irish and otherwise, are invited to enjoy the pandemonium that ensues when Lady Bountiful visits the Murphys (*Lady Bountiful Visits the Murphys on Wash Day* [USA, 1903]) and the household baby feeds the upper-crust benefactor's dress into the wringer causing Lady Bountiful to end up in the tub. In the same vein, Happy Hooligan's unintended victims in *Happy Hooligan's Interrupted Lunch* (USA, 1903) are three well-heeled women whose discomfort on finding their meal scoffed by an Irish tramp may have left them with few sympathisers amongst early cinema audiences.

Irish-American tolerance of such images did not, in any case, last long and in 1907 Irish filmgoers in Providence, Rhode Island, threatened to destroy a local cinema showing another exercise in cultural stereotyping, *Murphy's Wake* (GB, 1906). Musser adds that, 'Although newly offensive film stereotypes faded only slowly, particularly in comedy, egregious representations were often followed by protest' (ibid.: 53). The Irish may have had little part to play in early American filmmaking but the value of their custom ensured eventual change.

Working-class Irish audiences congregated in neighbourhood clubs and picture houses and by the teens were being catered for by filmmakers with quite a different agenda. In 1914 Walter Macnamara[5] released *Ireland A Nation* (USA), a series of historical vignettes replicating with, as Irish historians were soon to point out, little accuracy, the heroics of Robert Emmet, Michael Dwyer and John Philpott Curran, amongst others. *Variety* reported that:

> In New York the audiences that have been viewing the picture are almost wholly Irish. One night late last week the big 44th street auditorium was practically sold out at 25 and 50 cents. The audience was an intensely enthusiastic one and applauded even the titles.
>
> (*Variety*, 10 October 1914: 25)

Born in Lismore, Co. Waterford in 1876, Macnamara had made his reputation with the scenario for Universal's controversial and hugely successful *Traffic in Souls* (George Loane Tucker, USA, 1913) which was misleadingly marketed as a sex movie and in which both Macnamara and Tucker took roles. In common with Olcott and Whitten, Macnamara's pro-nationalist cinema led him into open confrontation with the British military authorities charged with keeping civic order. Macnamara travelled to Ireland in 1914 where he was arrested on suspicion of importing arms. Although these were revealed to be props for the filming of *Ireland A Nation*, they were not returned and the director described with some relish his harassment by the authorities whilst he was on location (in the absence of a studio, he used a greenhouse for indoor episodes). He had his revenge, according to the press, by openly recruiting for the nationalist cause in London where he addressed audiences of three to five thousand people (Blaisdell, 1914: 1,245).

By 1916, the Lord Lieutenant was faced with the sight of the Irish Volunteers openly drilling and parading and took various, largely ineffective, measures to prevent such displays of force. The military censor was given the task of vetting film exhibition, although his decision was not always upheld by those in charge of maintaining civic order. Macnamara updated *Ireland A Nation* in 1917 with newsreel footage from the War of Independence including shots of Michael Collins and Eamon de Valera. Although passed by the censor, the film was withdrawn by the military authorities on the grounds that it might exacerbate the already contentious issue of recruiting. When the film was shown:

> sections of the audience cried 'Up the rebels!' 'Up the Kaiser!' and cheered at the suggestion in a message on the screen that 'England's difficulty is Ireland's opportunity.' More cheers were raised at the representation of the murder of an English soldier by an Irish rebel.
>
> (*The Irish Limelight*, February 1918: 19)

The first significant cycle of films shot in Ireland in the early years of the century was the work of the Kalem Company, under Sidney Olcott. Olcott was a colourful character whose parents had emigrated to Toronto from Cork. He started as a child actor and moved in his twenties to New York. There he was employed by the newly established Kalem Company, which went on to become one of the biggest producers of their day. Throughout his career, Olcott exploited controversy and a trail of anecdotes accumulated in his wake. His reputation was, however, grounded in his meticulous production practices and his then unusual approach of scripting his films in advance and shooting on real locations. In 1910 he travelled to Ireland with Gene Gauntier (the 'Kalem Girl') who acted as scriptwriter as well as starring in many of the films, and his long-time associate Robert Vignola. On arrival, they completed shooting *The Lad From Old Ireland* (USA, 1910), which had already been partially filmed in New York and on board ship. They returned over the next several years to County Kerry to make a succession of films on Irish themes (Foster, 2000; O'Conluain, 1953). In total Olcott is accredited with 29 such films (Rockett, 1996). Whether or not some of the early films were directed by Vignola remains a matter of dispute but it is clear that the production worked on an ensemble basis.[6] O'Conluain reports that Olcott ran up against the wrath of the local priest early during his 1911 stay in Kerry when he shot *The Colleen Bawn* (USA, 1911) and was denounced from the altar for 'making a mockery of all that Irish people held most sacred' and worse; according to this story, Olcott had the last laugh, taking his case to the local Bishop and the American consul in Cork and eventually obtaining an apology from the priest who was then transferred to another parish. Olcott followed this up by equipping the local Irish Volunteers with rifles from the prop cupboard to assist them in their training (O'Conluain, 1953: 97). Since Olcott was a master of self-publicity, such tales may or may not be apocryphal. Of the commercial success of his Irish films there is less doubt. In 1912 and 1914 he returned with Gauntier after they had broken with Kalem, although the last trip was cut short by the outbreak of war. In the United States he was a popular speaker in Irish clubs, 'I addressed eleven groups ranging from 50 to 1,000 in less than two weeks. As a result all the films made in Ireland were profitable. It seemed everyone with Irish ancestry wanted to see the old country again' (Foster, 2000: 997). Olcott was less popular with the British authorities who particularly objected to his glorification of the eighteenth-century Irish revolutionary, Rory

O'Moore in *Rory O'More* (USA, 1911), claiming that it was interfering with their recruiting drive (O'Conluain, 1953: 97).

The Kalem films established a tradition which later indigenous productions retained, of producing historical melodramas in rural settings. Other than the contentious political allegories, the films also include comedies and romances, many drawn from existing, popular stage-plays. Christopher Morash dates this cross-fertilisation as the beginnings of theatre's 'Faustian pact with cinema' (2002: 154), noting that melodramas with a 1798 setting enjoyed an upsurge in interest amongst the audience for popular theatre in the period around 1916. In fact, this is a somewhat disingenuous summary of the long history of interaction between filmmaking and the entertainment enjoyed by vaudeville audiences from the late nineteenth century onwards. Morash's comments are made in the context of early cinema's usurpation of many of the themes of popular theatre – notably Westerns, detective plays and staged tourist sights (ibid.: 156).

The melodramas and historical romances on which this chapter focuses are informed by romantic nationalism, as well as the expectations of emigrant and other overseas audiences. Olcott's decision to shoot on location is exploited throughout the films' narratives as a guarantor of authenticity as well as satisfying a secondary tourist discourse. Thus, for instance, the opening titles of *The Colleen Bawn* assure the audience that the entire film is shot in genuine Irish locations and that the inn featured in the prologue is over 100 years old. In the same film a bed is indicated as having belonged to Daniel O'Connell and been occupied by him. Authenticity is further claimed through references to the original Boucicault drama of the same name. When one of the characters lands his boat, we are informed that this is the identical landing to that described by Boucicault in his play. A key figure in the development of a popular dramatic idiom, Dion Boucicault (1820–90) himself laid claim to a new authenticity in location and character when publicising his melodramas and historical narratives, particularly for an Irish-American audience (Grene, 1999: 5). Luke Gibbons sees in plays such as *The Colleen Bawn* (1860), *Arragh-na-Pogue* (1864) and *The Shaughraun* (1874) the roots of many later cinema representations (Gibbons, 1987: 211–20) whilst both Nicholas Grene and Elizabeth Butler Cullingford underline the conciliatory message within the dramatist's construction of his Irish and British characters (Grene, 1999; Cullingford, 2001).

History in both the plays and films is consistently rendered as high melodrama. The story of Olcott's *Rory O'More* that was to so incense the British authorities, for instance, is set against the background of an unspecified rising.[7] The eponymous hero is on the run from the Redcoats (the British military) and is abetted by his sweetheart Kathleen (Gene Gauntier). However, when one of the Redcoats seems on the brink of drowning, Rory (Jack J. Clark) rescues him. In gratitude, the soldiers are about to let Rory go when the informer, Black William (Robert G. Vignola) intercedes and demands Rory's arrest. Eventually, the parish priest, Father O'Brien

(Arthur Donaldson) secures Rory's release on the scaffold and in doing sacrifices his own life. Rory and Kathleen escape to America and freedom. In this and his other films, Olcott creates a swiftly paced narrative that only slows down to deliver the expected scenery shots of the Lakes of Killarney. Both *Rory O'More* and the later *Bold Emmett Ireland's Martyr* (Olcott, USA, 1915) have as their heroes brave and noble peasant characters and both boast strong, interventionist female roles. The fact that Olcott virtually remade *Rory O'More* later as *For Ireland's Sake* (Olcott, USA, 1914) suggests that this formula was well-liked by audiences.

Although the 'political' films tend to end with the escape of the hero to the home of revolutionary tradition, the United States, emigration is otherwise represented with some ambiguity. If the closing titles of *For Ireland's Sake* declare, 'To the West! To the West! To the land of the Free!', the encounter with metropolitan capitalism is viewed elsewhere with some reservation. *The Lad From Old Ireland*, for instance, imagines the consequences for its hero of being forced to emigrate. In this narrative, Terry (Sidney Olcott) leaves his sweetheart to find his fortune in America. The film establishes the contrasts between what he has left behind and his new life through a series of edits that juxtapose Aileen (Gene Gauntier) and her neighbours working at the hay and Terry's employment in the construction industry. The action then jumps ten years forward in time to follow Terry's successful political career. Again, a sequence of edits contrasts his new milieu of elegant, well-heeled admirers with Aileen's life in the cottage where the priest comforts her. Fortunately, Terry follows the voice of his heart and returns home just as Aileen's family is being evicted by the iniquitous agent whom he sends packing.

The emphasis of Gauntier and Olcott's films is on displaying the communality of Irish life and the bravery of certain individuals within it. Like the later indigenous films, those representatives of the British who appear are not demonised to the extent that we might expect from films with an overt nationalist agenda, and in this respect, we can also see Olcott as a successor to Boucicault. The tendency is to portray the English as simply out of place, as foreigners who might be better advised to remove themselves elsewhere. Unlike the informers and land agents, the British play by the rules and show respect for their enemy. The local Irish are able to recognise this quality as Olcott demonstrates at the end of *Bold Emmett Ireland's Martyr* when the woman of the cottage cries out, 'Long live the Major and the Lord Lieutenant'. The appeal of such a polemic is evident; the Irish position is based on rationality and understanding, not on fanaticism; these are a people who can reason and negotiate. On commercial grounds, it further pre-empts alienating those audiences who might not have any particular bone to pick with the English. Nor do the films even envisage the end of the social or political order, opting instead for heroes who triumph through escape. The aristocracy, when represented, as in Olcott's rendering of Boucicault's melodrama, *The Colleen Bawn*, are capable of redemption by marrying out of their class. In this version of a much-adapted narrative, Hardress Cregan (J.P. McGowan) falls in love with Eily, the Colleen Bawn (Gene Gauntier). Despite being warned by the priest, Father Tom (Arthur Donaldson), about her 'highborn lover', Eily consents to a secret marriage even though Hardress is honour bound to wed a rich heiress and save the family estate. After an array of misunderstandings and general skulduggery, the twosome are reunited by the resourceful priest and all ends happily. In another highly improbable romance, adapted by Gauntier from a poem by Thomas Moore, *You Remember Ellen* (Olcott, USA, 1912), the young couple are forced to roam through the countryside together when they realise they cannot make their living on the land. Eventually they arrive at a castle where it turns out that he is its lord and she will now be its lady. The film ends with the couple dancing together amongst the lavish surroundings of the castle.

Since dramatic narrative structures such as those employed by Olcott and Gauntier require a villain, this figure was relocated to within the Irish camp, in the person of the informer or the land agent. These are visually signified as evil by virtue of their dark clothing, malevolent expressions and a level of physical deformity. They operate on their own and are not pictured against the background of family and friendship. The character of the informer or go-between will irrupt later, as we shall see, in the dramatic works of the Film Company of Ireland where it also functions to critique internal dissent. The informer traduces the image of the idealised peasant or self-sacrificing priest of these narratives and, like the land agent in *Knocknagow* (below), illustrates the perils of placing self-interest before participation in the idealised community and of prizing financial gain in the place of frugality and devotion to the cause of freedom.

The key members of this society are the young hero and his sweetheart whose union is threatened by the intrusion of politics, economic circumstances or class. Stability is present in the figures of the homely Irish mother and her staunch ally, the local priest. The latter is generally configured within a domestic environment whilst being prepared, when occasion demands, to take an active part in the revolutionary activities of the young hero. Indeed, under circumstances that force the young men into in hiding, the priest becomes the visible head of the community.

Olcott's achievement, apart from simply making the films, was to create a body of work that reflected multiple aspirations. His portrayal of an inherently conservative, rural society was unlikely to cause offence either at home or abroad. This society's heroic young men had their own place within nationalist ideology, suggesting a glorious history of resistance and revolution. Then again, as WASP America re-aligned itself with the British in the face of German imperial hostility, Olcott purged his film of an overt anti-Englishness and reintegrated the Protestant aristocracy into the national narrative. The simplistic stage-Irish characters of early American cinema are replaced by individuals with considerable agency within these new, more sophisticated dramas.

Olcott retired from filmmaking in 1927, returning to Ireland in the 1930s to holiday and also to erect a chapel in County Cork to the memory of his parents.

When the first indigenous Irish film company, The Film Company of Ireland (FCOI) was launched in March of 1916, just before the Easter Rising, its work was deeply indebted to the tradition established by Olcott of alternating comedies and historical melodramas. Its founder, James Mark Sullivan, a successful lawyer, journalist and diplomat, had emigrated to the United States as a boy and was now determined to establish an Irish film industry. The FCOI, like many indigenous Irish filmmakers to follow, initially drew on the actors of the Abbey Theatre and most of the performers associated with these films were already familiar from their stage work. Sara Allgood, Fred O'Donovan, Joe Kerrigan and Nora Clancy (wife of O'Donovan) were all members of the Abbey Theatre Company, known as the Irish Players. Fred O'Donovan had gained a reputation for his romantic acting style after his acclaimed interpretation of Christy Mahon in *The Playboy of the Western World* during the Irish Players' 1911 American tour. Interviewed during this tour, O'Donovan, explained that the purpose of the Players was to present an authentic image of Irishness:

> They [the Players] felt that the romantic Irish dramas of Dion Boucicault were not a truthful reflection of Irish life and character. They reflected the sentimental Irishman as the English and those who wrote for English consumption liked to imagine him.
>
> The Irish Players wanted to put on the stage the real Irishman of today – to reveal real Irish conditions and real Irish character. Now, to reach the real Irish character, the poets and dramatists had to deal with the life of the peasantry, those who lived close to the soil and obtained their subsistence from it. The upper classes are veneered with English thought and manners, hence few of the plays which the Irish Players have presented deal with life in the cities – with business and social circles.
>
> (O'Donovan, 1988: 101)

O'Donovan was manager of the Abbey Company between 1916 and 1919, during which time he played a succession of leading parts in the FCOI films.

As *The Irish Limelight* put it, the FCOI's first three months' work was wiped out in the 'Dublin fire' (the Easter Rising) (January 1917: 3) and the company was forced to begin again; this it did, producing nine films in less than a year. In the absence of a studio, the FCOI could only film during the summer months and then only when light permitted. Their early films, shot and set like so many of the Kalem films in Kerry, were predominately comedies, most of them directed by Joe Kerrigan. Although none of these films has survived, their popularity with audiences and critics suggests that they managed to provide comic entertainment whilst also avoiding the pitfalls of the Irish stereotype. Their address was clearly to a local audience and they reflected the aspirations of O'Donovan and the cultural mood of the moment by focusing on rural, peasant characters and settings.[8] The *Limelight* noted approvingly of *Rafferty's Rise* that, 'The humour of the film is native at its source and provides a refreshing contrast from much of the imported buffoonery too often labelled as comedy' (May 1917: 4). The local press was equally enthusiastic and the films performed well in Irish cinemas where their Irishness was as promoted as it was lauded.

In the wake of this success, the FCOI moved into making longer features, releasing the six-reel, *When Love Came to Gavin Burke* and eight-reel *Knocknagow*, both directed by O'Donovan, in 1917. *Knocknagow* marks the beginning of a more overtly politicised indigenous cinema. By choosing to adapt Charles J. Kickham's popular novel of the same name, the FCOI invited their audiences to locate the revolutionary movement within an historical perspective and, in particular, reminded them of the long history of injustice suffered by the Irish people under colonialism.

Charles J. Kickham was born in 1825 in Tipperary and became involved in nationalist politics from an early age. *Knocknagow* draws on events of the period, making particular reference to the insecurities of the tenant farmer system. Since the 1820s, Daniel O'Connell had mobilised popular and educated Catholic opinion in his campaign for Catholic emancipation and, subsequently, the repeal of the Act of Union. The Young Ireland movement articulated much of the mood of the moment through its popular journal, *The Nation*, and the 1830s were marked by outbursts of agrarian unrest. However, in 1845, the first of a succession of potato blights led to widespread famine as the staple diet of the burgeoning rural population failed with catastrophic results. In 1848 an uprising engineered by the Young Irelanders came to nothing and many of their leaders joined the famine dispossessed in emigration to America. By this stage, the Repeal movement had foundered in the face of the new Peel administration of 1841 onwards and the internal economic crises engendered by famine. Kickham had taken an active part in the 1848 Rising and was jailed for Fenian activities in 1866. *Knocknagow* was published in episodes from 1870 onwards, shortly after his release.

Kickham's writing is rambling and diffuse, an effect that the film does not manage to dispense with entirely. O'Donovan's production retains much of the episodic nature of its source and most of Kickham's characters. The greatest alteration is to abandon the device of having the local Irish characters explain their country and its customs to a visiting Englishman, in this case, Mr Henry Lowe, nephew of the absentee landlord. Lowe is central to Kickham's novel and his induction into the iniquities of the landlord system and its effects on the simple but kindly Irish peasantry supplies his main raison d'être. The film also tones down Kickham's critique of the larger tenant farmer, Maurice Kearney, who now emerges as a righteous intermediary between the absentee landlord and the peasantry on his lands.

The opening titles of *Knocknagow* promise its viewers a journey back to the Ireland of 1848, 'when Irish smiles broke through every cloud of oppression'. The choice of date is curious, since, in fact, the events of the uprising are not included in the book or the film. A second departure from the original material is to create specific connections with Thomas Davis, one of the leaders of the Young Ireland movement, and its most eloquent chronicler, by quoting from his poetry, 'Yet meet him in his cabin rude/ Or dancing with his dark haired Mary./You'd swear they knew no other mood/But mirth and love in Tipperary'.

Rockett suggests that the catalyst for *Knocknagow*'s making was the screening of D.W. Griffith's *The Birth of A Nation* (USA, 1915), in Dublin in 1916 (1987: 19), yet the intertitles warn that, 'there are waiting for you neither soul stirring thrills nor sensational climaxes'. It seems more likely that the film was intended to be read not as an epic triumph of nation-building but as a tale of simple folk whose innate goodness enables them to overcome injustice. It is redolent of the cult of the peasant that imbues Irish cultural representations of the period, displacing onto the country people of its central narrative the values of the imagined nation. Further, by asserting a line of descent from the Young Ireland movement, the film accedes to popular nationalist rhetoric that saw ideological victory in military failure. Easter 1916 had already become another instance of Irish right foundering in the face of British might, as had happened before in the rebellion of the Young Irelanders.

The film's theme of violated pastoralism is an accurate reflection of Kickham's concerns, but neither text is willing to commit itself to a radical political solution. In the final moments of the book, the central characters survey the fields of Knocknagow, now stripped of its homes and tenants. 'The divil's cure to the landlords', comments Wat Murphy. 'An Irish Parliament wouldn't thrate 'em that way. An' still they're agin their counthry' (Kickham, 1988: 616–17). Salvation, they conclude, lies in education for the people of Ireland alongside retention of the core values of the peasantry. Neither book nor film can envisage the complete overthrow of the landlord system, arguing instead for its reformation under Home Rule.

The FCOI's *Knocknagow* paints a picture of a stratified but harmonious community. The peasantry, exemplified by Mat Donovan or Mat the Thresher (Brian MacGowan, whose name is also spelt 'Magowan'), are industrious, working hard at their fields and living in cramped but clean cottages. The Kearney family is relatively prosperous, the womenfolk engage in charitable activities and spend their leisure hours conversing and doing needlework. Life 'below stairs' is equally convivial as the servants and their friends share jokes together. Knocknagow is owned by Sir Garrett Butler (Charles Power) a benevolent if careless landlord who spends much of his time abroad in Italy, and only Mat owns his own property. The unity of this small community is underlined by an early scene showing all its members happily coming together at Knocknagow to celebrate Christmas. Despite the story taking place during the Great Famine, the only mention of starvation occurs when Kearney accuses the landlord and his class of 'starving the people in the middle of plenty'.

The film expresses no interest in breaking down these class differences; rather it reinforces them through a series of romantic sub-plots. Both the aristocrat, Sir Henry Lowe and a local lad, Arthur O'Connor (Fred O'Donovan), are in love with Mary Kearney (Nora Clancy). Given the relative differences in background, neither relationship is initially realisable and the film must enable its romantic hero, Arthur, to become a member of the middle-class so that his affair with Mary may succeed. Arthur's mother wants him to join the Church but, recognising his love for Mary, the priest advises the young man to take up medicine and offers to fund his study.

The true villain of the piece is the land agent on the Butler estate, Pender (J.M. Carre). Physically and morally repugnant, Pender plays an almost identical role in this film to that of Kalem's informers and land agents. It is he who is responsible for violating the natural order of the countryside, robbing the rents, evicting the peasantry and burning their cottages. He is to be found lurking behind hedgerows and listening in on conversations. He operates alone, outside the humanising influences of home, family and neighbour. His is an ideology of self before community, money before morality.

Pender's early victims are impoverished peasants such as the Brians who are driven onto the road when their home is burnt to the ground; later we learn that he evicts the Hogan family despite their son having distinguished himself fighting in the British army. It comes as some surprise then when the agent attempts to evict the Kearneys. Before this can happen, Sir Garrett Butler appears as a *deus ex machina* and steps into the breach, disposing of Pender and enabling the sundry lovers to be reunited. The film concludes with the admonition that, 'We are a moral people, above crime, and a clean-hearted race must eventually come into its own no matter how long the journey, no matter how hard the road.'

The message here is that violent intervention is not worthy of the Catholic Irish – to underline this, Mick Brian is tempted to kill Pender but changes his mind when he witnesses the dying Nora Leahy (Kathleen Murphy) reciting the rosary – and that natural justice will save them. The film establishes the shortcomings of the absentee landlord system and at moments it seems to come close to inciting revolutionary action only to reaffirm the moral authority of the upper classes at the end.

The film's own internal contradictions, its ability to critique and endorse the landlord system with one breath suggest that the contemporary ideologues of a socialist revolution were out of step with popular cultural expectations. *Knocknagow* does not anticipate any serious disruption to the system, rather it makes overt appeal to a Catholic trust that God will best reward those who suffer most. Just as it rehearses the evils of a colonial culture in its depictions of evictions and involuntary emigration, so it displaces the blame for these onto the rogue Irishman, Pender. Frantz Fanon has written that the idea of compromise is central to the process of decolonisation. It appeals in particular to the nationalist bourgeoisie who are afraid of being swept away by the revolt of the masses and try to distance themselves from it in the eyes of the settlers (Fanon, 1967: 48–9). By positioning themselves as honest brokers between the colonisers and the masses, they attempt to deflect violence by explaining to the 'enemy' the reasons for the revolt of the peasantry, inviting them in so doing to intervene before blood is shed. Compromise or conciliation – the difference is one of terminology. The recent academic stress laid on Boucicault's politics of compromise is uttered in approving tones, yet he, Olcott and the emergent Irish filmmakers of the FCOI had in common a fear of inciting revolutionary action or seeming to condone violence. The same prerogative echoes through the history of Irish filmmaking, reappearing in the conciliatory films of the recent Troubles.

The intervening years since the publication of Kickham's opus had witnessed the gradual dismantling of the old landlord system. The depletion of the lands following the famines had emptied them of their poorest inhabitants and a succession of acts, starting with Gladstone's Land Acts of 1881 and 1882 and culminating in Wyndham's Act of 1903 saw rents decrease and tenure become assured with purchase eventually assisted by the State. By the time of the film's making, the Irish landlord class was increasingly composed of educated Catholics, many of them Sinn Féin supporters. This is reflected in the altered characterisation of Kearney. In the original novel, the tenantry is as likely to suffer from the effects of his poor husbandry as from the machinations of the absentee landlord. The film's propensity to sanitise Kearney's record suggests that it actively endorses the position of the rising Catholic bourgeois farmer who had emerged in the wake of the Famine and the land acts. Pender in turn symbolises one direction the indigenous Irish can take, the route of self-interest and rampant materialism. When contrasted with the self-sacrificing Kearney and the solid freeholder, Mat, the parable is clear and points with remarkable perspicacity to the post-Independence Free State with its ideologies of benevolent paternalism and anti-consumerism.

From about 1918 onwards, the FCOI seems to have aligned itself more with the Irish Theatre Company than with the Abbey. The Irish Theatre Company had been founded by Edward Martyn, Joseph Plunkett and Thomas MacDonagh in 1914 as an alternative to the Abbey and its work drew more closely on the amateur tradition than did the theatre of Yeats and Lady Gregory. Plunkett and MacDonagh had met in 1910 when the latter was taken on to tutor Plunkett in Irish. Both, like Patrick Pearse, were poets and associated with mysticism and the cult of blood sacrifice; as well as their theatrical work, they collaborated on the politico-literary journal, the *Irish Review*. Along with Pearse and the other 1916 martyrs, they were executed by the British on the grounds of their participation in the Easter Rising. Martyn was also a prominent public figure, a playwright who had been associated with the founding of the National Theatre. Thomas MacDonagh's brother, John MacDonagh directed another melodrama for the FCOI that, like *Knocknagow* invited audiences to draw associations between past injustices and contemporary politics. The shooting of *Willy*

Reilly and His Colleen Bawn (John McDonagh, Ireland, 1920) was inter-rupted by its principal cast and crew's political activities. According to one writer, two of the actors, George Nesbit (Squire Folliard) and Jim Plant (Sir Robert Whitecraft) were arrested and imprisoned during its making and used false names in the credits to escape identification (Downing, 1979–80: 43). McDonagh has recalled how, when he was shooting *Willy Reilly* in the grounds of St Enda's (the building used by Patrick Pearse for his experi-ments in a progressive education for Irish boys and the fictional home for both the O'Reillys and Folliard in the film) it was decided to make a quick promotional film around the flotation of the 1919 Republican Loan. The finished result shows Michael Collins presiding over the event and a number of luminaries of the moment signing up:

> In those dangerous and exciting times no cinema owner would dare risk exhibiting the republican Loan films so it was planned to visit certain cinemas, rush the operator's box, and, at gun-point, force the operator to take off the film he was showing, and put on the Loan Film. On the appointed night, all went smoothly as arranged, and the volunteers got safely away before the British forces discov-ered the plot.
>
> (McDonagh, 1976: 11)

Willy Reilly and His Colleen Bawn again drew on a literary source (a novel of the same title, published by William Carleton in 1855). The story is set in the eighteenth century and concerns the relationship between Catholic and Protestant landowners during the Penal Laws of the seventeenth and eight-eenth centuries. Aimed at maintaining Protestant supremacy, these laws curtailed rights of land and property ownership and, in 1729, removed the right to vote from Catholic freeholders. On the one hand is Willy Reilly (Brian MacGowan), a disenfranchised Catholic and, on the other, Squire Folliard (Dermot O'Dowd), 'a high-tempered crusty old Protestant gentle-man'. Folliard is father to the Colleen Bawn, Helen (Frances Alexander), with whom O'Reilly falls in love after rescuing Folliard from the desperate bandit, Red Rapparee (Barrett McDonnell). Helen is to be married to Sir Robert Whitecraft (Seamus MacBlante) who, the intertitles inform us, 'was a notorious Catholic hunter during the Penal Laws'. The film is less about love across the social divide than about the differences of religion that keep O'Reilly and Helen apart. Folliard insists that O'Reilly convert to Protestantism in order to marry his daughter, the latter refuses.

The message, that Protestant and Catholic are not as different as they might think, is underlined by its County Cavan setting. Cavan is one of the three Ulster counties that were ultimately to be part of the Free State and would have had, at the time of the film's setting, a substantial Protestant population.[9] Throughout, the film is keen to emphasise the mutual respect with which Folliard and O'Reilly hold each other. Thus the former can say of O'Reilly, 'although you are a Papist, you are a brave man and a gentleman'.

Figure 2.1 Willy Reilly and his Colleen Bawn (l-r): Whitecraft (Jim Plant), Helen, the Colleen Bawn (Frances Alexander), the Squire (George Nesbit) and Willy Reilly (Brian Magowan).

The Reverend Mr Brown is introduced to O'Reilly as, 'a noble Protestant clergyman' who is opposed to sectarianism. O'Reilly lives in a substantial home as does Folliard (in reality, two sides of St Enda's) and the two men are, in all respects other than religious, equals. When Whitecraft continues to run amok, engaging in acts of violent sectarianism and burning down O'Reilly's home, the 'decent Protestants' agree that he has gone too far. Ultimately, the court dispenses justice and Whitecraft and his ally, Red Rapparee, are arrested.

The romance between Helen and Willy is signalled as bringing together the past and the future. As the success of the affair between Arthur and Mary in *Knocknagow* suggested a union between the classes, so this film appeals for a bridging of the religious divide. The couple meet on the ivy-clad ruins of a castle in Folliard's grounds, a new future promised in the ruins of the old. The film naturalises the sweeping away of the old (Protestant) order, contrasting the energetic interventions of the Catholic Willy with the helplessness of Folliard and his wan, swooning daughter.

From a technical point of view, both *Knocknagow* and *Willy Reilly* suffer from overloaded narratives and a tendency to intersperse the action with lengthy explanatory intertitles. Although they are not completely unaware

29

of the possibilities offered by camera and editing, in comparison with the Kalem films and other films of the period they are difficult to follow. On occasion, O'Donovan displays a sense of cinematic effect, such as in the use of flashback in *Knocknagow* to re-enforce Henry Love's words when he informs Butler what is happening to his tenants, and an extended sequence where the camera cuts between the dying Nora and Mick Brian's discovery of the rifle. Editing is used in *Willy Reilly* to heighten dramatic effect as occurs in the build-up to the Colleen Bawn's planned wedding with the duplicitous Sir Robert, an event that is only stopped thanks to a last minute intercession by Hastings. In prison, Willy Reilly has a vision of Helen which fades away as he reaches out to her.

The amateur nature of *Knocknagow* proved problematic for the American trade reviewers who found the acting and set design unsophisticated and its grip of contemporary filmmaking practices weak: 'It's the combined crudities, one piled on top of the other, that bring the picture so far below present day standards' (Bell, 1921: 35). The reviewer continued to lament the fact that, with so much drama taking place in contemporary Ireland, the film had to be a period piece.

As we have seen, this appeal to the past was in keeping with the ideological imperatives of a nationalist movement that sought legitimacy through an implied continuity with previous insurgents. It also added historical depth to contemporary grievances by reminding viewers of the long history of agrarian dispossession and injustice associated with colonial rule. Further, these films insisted on the necessity for internal unity in the face of an almost invisible aggressor. Boundaries of class and religion are put aside time and again as the narrative drive seeks to isolate those internal elements, such the landlord's agent, who threaten the organic whole of the community.

The cumbersome plotting of *Knocknagow* in particular, would almost certainly have been less off-putting for a local audience well-versed in the ramifications of Kickham's novel and *The Irish Times*, in an approving notice of the film's fidelity to its source, reported that it was playing to crowded houses (*The Irish Times*, 23 and 24 April 1918: 3).

In both films, there is a certain disjunction between narrative and spectacle. As we have discussed, the outcomes of their plots seek to contain any revolutionary aspirations within a conservative social structure. However, both films are interspersed by a number of set-pieces that function outside of the narrative to trigger associations with non-diegetic events. Thus, for instance, when Mat the Thresher decides to leave for America, the intertitles exclaim, 'What curse is on this land of ours when men like Mat are forced to leave its shores.' Mat, in turn, calls out, 'Good bye Ireland. You are a rich and rare land although poverty has been forced upon you.' In fact, Mat is leaving Ireland because of a failed love affair and, by virtue of being a freeholder, is in a more stable financial situation than his neighbours. As a straightforward dramatic ploy, Mat's departure and its accompanying rhetoric are reminders of the continuing trauma of emigration. Similarly in *Willy Reilly* there is a chilling sequence in which Sir Robert leads off the priest with a noose around his neck following the break-up of a clandestine gathering of Catholic worshippers. The occasion takes place virtually outside of the unfolding of the central intrigue but is again resonant of a history of anti-Catholic practices. The narratives of these two films are further disrupted by moments in which the audience is invited to enjoy the spectacle of traditional rural pastimes. *Knocknagow*'s celebration of peasant life is underscored in a number of set-pieces, such as the hurling match, the country wedding and the travelling peep-show, all of which betoken its communality and reflect the revival (and invention) of gaelic games and cottage industries by the nationalist project.

We can assume that the FCOI's films were influenced by the earlier Kalem works but they also diverge from them in a number of interesting respects. If we compare the more politicised films, we can see that whilst both employ incidents from the past as analogies for the present, they bring contrasting perspectives to bear on them. The Kalem films tend to be confrontational, their narratives set in motion through a conflict that ends in victory of some kind; the indigenous films are largely consensual, their objective being to achieve resolution by ejecting the disruptive element in order to create unity. The American films, such as *Rory O'More* and *Bold Emmett Ireland's Martyr* present a narrative resolution that conflates escape to the United States with escape to freedom. In *Knocknagow*, Mat travels to America to 'rescue' Bessy and they find true happiness in the simplicity of an Irish setting, whilst in *Willy Reilly*, the hero returns from deportation to marital contentment in Ireland. Emigration in the indigenous films is a temporary condition, with return its desired correlative; in the American 'political' works it is the solution to the problem. Visually, the 'American' films make much of the Irish landscape, playing on the emigrant nostalgia for 'home', a strategy entirely absent in the FCOI works. Likewise, there are noticeable differences in the filmmakers' approach to female roles. In *Rory O'More*, for instance, Kathleen plays a key part in the drama, alerting Rory and acting as a decoy to the Redcoats whilst in *For Ireland's Sake* Eileen is an active participant, showing no hesitation in wielding a gun when events call for it. These strong female parts may well be ascribed to Gene Gauntier's status at Kalem and her later decision to establish her own production company. Gauntier played both these roles and the later film was produced by Gene Gauntier Feature Players. In comparison with these vigorous characters, the women in *Knocknagow* and *Willy Reilly* appear limp and affectless. Helen, particularly, has little to do within the narrative but be rescued by Willy Reilly, nearly married off to Sir Robert, and finally to lose her mind, as the film puts it, when Willy Reilly is deported. Only his return can cure her. Given the commitment of individual Irish women to the Rising and later to Sinn Féin, it is a shame that they should have been so thoroughly sidelined by film history.

If *Willy Reilly* is remarkable for its spirit of ecumenism, Norman Whitten's first fiction film, made in the same year, is imbued with Catholic reverence. *In the Days of Saint Patrick* (1920) is a reconstruction of the life of the patron saint from birth through slavery to his return to Ireland as Christian missionary. The film ends with an epilogue showing relics of Saint Patrick in County Down and footage of the 1919 pilgrimage to Croagh Patrick, shot possibly for *Irish Events*. The final sequence is a study of Cardinal Logue, then Archbishop of Armagh and a successor to St Patrick.

In the Days of Saint Patrick alternates between pious reconstructions of early Christianity and moments of high drama. In common with the FCOI films, much of the narrative information is conveyed through wordy intertitles, written in this production in Irish and English. Like the films of the FCOI too, Whitten's work is informed by the cult of the peasant. St Patrick (Ira Allen) is a simple rural dweller and his most faithful converts come from the same milieu. The static imagery of much of the establishing sequences is offset by the occasions when a miracle occurs. Water springs from a well, flames erupt from a slab of ice, an angel appears. With the encounter between the slaves and the heathen Irish of Antrim, the visual register changes remarkably. As the slaves are driven to market, so the screen is filled with shots of horse-drawn chariots charging across the sands. It is certainly no coincidence that the paganism of Ulster is insisted on within the film's narrative. Patrick's first owner, King Milcho (Eddie Lawless) resides there, his halls decorated with columns, his entourage one of decadence and splendour.

Figure 2.2 In the Days of St Patrick. Alice Keating as Lupita.

After his (religious) conquest of Ulster, Patrick proceeds to the Hill of Slane where he lights the flame that will kindle the fire of Christianity throughout Ireland. As the intertitles proclaim, 'he who kindled it will vanquish the kings of Ireland'. The army of Christ and the army of Satan are then locked in deadly combat over the Hill of Tara until the will of God triumphs.

Whitten's film is clearly designed as a celebratory freedom narrative, reworking and anticipating the triumph of the Catholic faith in a subjugated country. It relishes the theme of the revenge of the slave on his master, particularly when this takes place in Ulster. At the same time, it indulges its expected audience's love of religious ritual, including a lengthy consecration scene set in Rome as well as the present-day scenes of pilgrimage.

The new Irish cinema, like so many others, posed a contradiction between technological innovation and regressive discourses, reproducing for its audiences the most antiquated of gags, stereotypes and eventually narratives. Its pioneers were an eclectic band of entrepreneurs and idealists who found their readiest clients amongst the working classes, immigrants and the dispossessed. In the Irish context, we may choose to view its output in Gramscian terms as a consensual tool of hegemonic institutions (in America the WASP establishment, in Ireland the Catholic bourgeoisie) or a counter-hegemonic weapon (expressing anti-colonial ideologies), or indeed both simultaneously. What is clear, looking back over the early history of images of Ireland and the Irish, is that we can discern a movement from diversity to containment, from a celebration of modernity and an acknowledgement of the multiple allegiances within the emergent State to an assertion of religious and cultural unity. Given the process of decolonisation taking place during these years, this expression of a united front ought not to surprise us, as much as it may disappoint. As the next chapter will discuss, in the immediate post-revolutionary period and later, cinema found itself at the receiving end of the coercive policies of the new State whilst much of its production was left to the diasporic filmmakers.

3

CONTESTED IMAGES

Filmmaking and viewing in the early days of the Free State; immigrant narratives of exile and assimilation

By the early 1920s cinema was institutionalised as a mass-market industry based around Hollywood. The disruptions of the First World War had seen Europe swiftly lose ground to its American rivals in film production; furthermore this period cemented a narrative approach to filmmaking based around the three-act structure, an adherence to psychological realism and a strong teleological drive.

Audiences too had become increasingly sophisticated, demanding ever higher standards of verisimilitude and professionalism from their viewing fare. The generation of primitive filmmakers who had guaranteed an eclecticism of styles and narratives in early filmmaking practices were gradually forced out of the industry in favour of more market-oriented professionals. Cinema now required capital and, particularly with the advent of sound in 1929, studios and the latest equipment. Without State subsidy or quota schemes that favoured domestic product, it became virtually impossible for countries outside of America to sustain a national film industry.

The alternative was to continue to produce works on a non-industrial, *ad hoc* basis that would draw on familiar local themes and utilise non-professional talent. The years after independence, as this chapter discusses, were peppered with such films, as they were with rumours of schemes to launch a properly capitalised industry. For all such entrepreneurs, the greatest barriers to the creation of an indigenous industry were government and Church hostility to the making and viewing of films; linked to this was a blanket cultural inertia that, for multiple reasons, lay over the new Free State for the first decades of its existence.

The opening years of the 1920s in Ireland were amongst the most violent in the evolution of the State. The first Irish national assembly, Dáil Éireann, had been convened in 1919 and was dominated by Sinn Féin, despite the fact that many of its members were in jail or on the run. The failure of the British to provide an adequate response to nationalist demands for a Republic led to the outbreak of the War of Independence shortly afterwards. The activities of the Volunteers were initially confined to arson, arms raids and intimidation, but the often brutal response of the Crown forces, in particular the notorious 'Black and Tans', ex-soldiers who acted as special constables in the Royal Irish Constabulary from 1920 onwards, saw the Irish side engage in increasingly violent guerrilla warfare. The Crown lost 525 of its forces in 1920–1 and at least 707 civilians were killed between January and July 1921 (Lee, 1989: 47). The Treaty that followed in December 1921 recognised the existence of the Irish Free State but cemented partition. In general, the country appeared to support this and the Dáil narrowly passed it in January 1922. The animosities engendered by the Treaty debate continued, however, with the pro-Treaty side led by Michael Collins and its opponents by Eamon de Valera. In Northern Ireland, violence broke out almost instantly, 'with atrocities that sound gruesome even in permissive retrospect. During the first six months of 1922, 171 Catholics and 95 Protestants were killed, often in the most revolting circumstances' (ibid.: 60). In June 1922, civil war broke out between the 'Free Staters' and the 'Irregulars' and the ensuing conflict has since been regarded as laying the foundation for the years of violence that erupted most disastrously with the beginnings of the 'Troubles' in Northern Ireland in 1969. Thousands of lives were lost in the Civil War with family member pitted against family member and neighbour against neighbour. In May 1923 de Valera instructed his followers to lay down their arms. By this stage Michael Collins had been assassinated and the new peacetime government was led by W.T. Cosgrave's Cumann na nGaedheal. De Valera left Sinn Féin in 1926 to found Fianna Fáil and formed his first government with Labour in 1932.

The events leading to independence form the backdrop to several of the indigenous films made during the early years of the Free State. However, as we shall see, Irish filmic narratives were most consistently produced outside of the State from this point onwards until the resurgence of the Irish film industry in the latter half of the century. Before turning to these, we will look more closely at the interplay between cinema and Irish society during this period.

The society that emerged out of independence has been characterised as rural, introspective and dominated by a rigid adherence to Catholicism:

> Occupying a role in Irish life that made it [the Roman Catholic Church] an integral part of that life, it enjoyed the unswerving loyalty of the great mass of the people. In the 1920s it used that authoritative position in Irish society to preach a sexual morality of severe restrictiveness, confirming the mores and attitudes of a nation of farmers and shop-keepers, denouncing all developments in society that might have threatened a rigid conformism in a strictly enforced sexual code.
>
> The Hierarchy was much distressed in the 1920s by the threats posed to what it sought to confirm as traditional Irish morality by the cinema, the English newspaper and the cheap magazine, by the new dances that became fashionable in Ireland as elsewhere in the post-war period, by provocative female fashions, and even by the

innocent company-keeping of the countryside at parties and cei-
lidhes.

(Brown, 1981: 39)

The response of those in power to such ecclesiastical anxieties was to
introduce a policy of rigid censorship, starting with the censorship of
films. The Censorship of Films Act was one of the first to be passed by
the Cumann na nGaedheal government in 1923 and empowered the censor
to keep from the public films that were, 'indecent, obscene or blasphemous'
or 'would tend to inculcate principles contrary to public morality or would
be otherwise subversive of public morality'(Censorship of Films Act, 1923).
This was to be just one of many legislative measures taken by successive
post-independence governments to counter external influences, particularly
those that filtered through by way of the English popular ('gutter') press.
Between 1930 and 1939, the censors banned some 1,200 books and 140
periodicals (Adams, 1968: 71); in the same period, they banned 164 films
out of a total of approximately 1,118 submitted and imposed cuts on a
further 301 (Rockett and Collins, 1980: 24). The State's first film censor
was James Montgomery who 'quite happily stated that he knew little about
films, but "took the Ten Commandments as his guide".' (Rockett, 1980:
12). Montgomery was succeeded in 1940 by Richard Hayes who had to
contend not only with the problem of protecting the morality of the Irish
populace but of defending them from the evils of wartime propaganda.
Article 52 of The Emergency Powers Order of 1939 had given the censor
the power to ban any film whose exhibition might be 'prejudicial to the
maintenance of law and order or to the preservation of the State or would
be likely to lead to a breach of the peace or to cause offence to the people of
a friendly foreign nation'. The latter was on occasion taken to be the
Germans and the Italians and films or newsreels suggesting sympathy with
the Allied cause were summarily banned (Ó Drisceoil, 1996: 30–58).
Otherwise, as Ó Drisceoil recounts, Hayes maintained the policy on foreign
entertainment established by Montgomery:

> He frowned particularly on 'lascivious dances' in American musicals
> and on all forms of 'Anglicisation' and 'Americanisation'. He was
> very careful not to allow 'any light or frivolous treatment of mar-
> riage to appear on the screen'; abortion and birth-control were
> forbidden subjects, though 'illegitimacy' and divorce were permis-
> sible provided they were presented in a suitably unfavourable light.
> On one occasion Hayes obliged a distributor to change the title of a
> film from *I Want a Divorce* to *The Tragedy of Divorce*.
>
> (Ibid.: 35)

The Free State's censorship policies were much admired by the clerical
establishment of Northern Ireland whose members spoke out on a number
of occasions in favour of a similar course of action at home.

Film censorship was not just a question of a repressive government impos-ing rigorous restrictions on a vulnerable public. Much of the impetus for the control of cinema images came from the Catholic church and allied groups, individuals, and newspapers such as the Fianna Fáil mouthpiece, the *Irish Press*. The Eucharistic Congress of 1932 was the occasion for mass expres-sions of religious devotion and in this atmosphere an organisation styling itself An Rioghacht (League of the Kingship of Christ) launched a new crusade for the reform of the cinema.[1] In America in 1932 Joseph Breen became involved in the campaign to apply 'moral' standards to Hollywood filmmaking and by 1933 was running the Studio Relations Committee (SRC), the code adopted by the trade association the Motion Picture Producers and Distributors of America (MPPDA) under its (Protestant) president, Will Hays. Breen's views on self-regulation of the industry were very much in line with his peers in the Catholic Church in America, notably the layman, Martin Quigley and the Jesuit, Father Daniel Lord: 'Breen was ... in almost constant conspiratorial correspondence with Quigley and other prominent Catholics, attempting to involve the Church hierarchy in a demonstration of Catholic cultural assertiveness.' (Maltby, 1996: 243). Breen and Quigley drew the Legion of Decency into their campaign with enormous success, ensuring that censorship or 'self regulation' was dictated by Catholic standards of morality (Black, 1994). The fact that the ensuing 'clean cinema' campaign in the US was fronted by a number of Irish-American clerics such as the Rt Rev. Dr Cantwell, Bishop of Los Angeles, who regularly paid visits 'home' (Tipperary in Cantwell's case) added impetus to the censorship drive in Ireland.

Members of the Church hierarchy exhorted the faithful to boycott films they perceived to be detrimental to national morality. At the same time, they recognised that film could serve their own purposes if put to educational use. Their crusade was endorsed by the leading Catholic newspaper, *The Irish Catholic*, who looked to the success of the American censorship campaign for inspiration:

What we need is literature and pictures which inspire noble deeds, and leave unsung and unhonoured the sordid and criminal side of life. The tendency of human nature is downward and, therefore, it should be the aim of all to combine to lift it on the wings of innocent joy and gladness – the joy of noble art and the elevation inspired by unstained beauty. The splendid example which has now been set on the other side of the Atlantic is one that can be followed here in order to ensure the best use of films for educational pur-poses. Hollywood's Augean stables may not perhaps be cleansed in a single day; but it is pleasing to reflect that a noble and inspiring movement has been inaugurated by the Catholic Church and is being pushed forward with an energy and determination that should have the happiest of results.

(*The Irish Catholic*, 21 July 1934: 5)

Anticipating censorship, many distributors cut their films themselves before submitting them to the Irish censor.[2]

It is perhaps surprising that the construction of new, lavish cinemas continued apace throughout the first decades after independence. The Theatre Royal in Dublin's Hawkins Street, built in 1935 at a cost of £250,000 and seating 4,000 people, was claimed at the time to be the most up-to-date theatre in Europe (*Kinematograph Weekly*, 26 September 1935: 3). It was opened with full honours by Sean Lemass, then Minister for Industry and Commerce, in a ceremony attended by a host of dignitaries. Equally, whilst the government showed no interest in the many projects for founding an industry put before it, ministers were quick to be associated with the public enthusiasm for Irish films or Irish-themed films, turning out in numbers for premieres of Victor Haddick's *Voice of Ireland* (GB, 1932), *Man of Aran* and *The Informer* (John Ford, US, 1935).

A high entertainment tax and a levy on imported films (in other words, nearly every film) provided a steady flow of revenue into the government's coffers; the budget of 1932 even introduced a tax on publicity materials. In the years 1933–4, income from the film trade amounted to nearly £80,000 in exchequer receipts (*Kinematograph Weekly*, 17 May 1934: 7).

Even if the Irish were not the most frequent cinema-goers of Europe, picture palaces such as the Theatre Royal must have provided the dwellers of the notorious city slums with one of their few affordable moments of escapism and luxury. As one letter to the *Dublin Evening Mail* suggests, in a deeply prudish society, they were beacons of intimacy and privacy:

> Personally I consider a nice cushy seat in a nice warm cinema a very appropriate place to do one's cuddling and kissing, and surely the fair lady deserves it after a strenuous day's work in a stuffy office, or behind a counter. She leaves her work at 6 o'clock, rushes home for a hurried supper and then off to meet her lover. They can't kiss in Ma's and Pop's presence, that demands too much nerve. If they stop on a street to kiss they are considered a public nuisance. So when they leave their love-making until they reach the inviting cosiness of cinema seats, they do so from necessity, not by choice.[3]
>
> ('Golly Gosh', 1935: 3)

The very popularity of the cinema-going experience left it at the mercy of a multiplicity of interest groups determined to protect the ignorant populace from its insidious pleasures. Not only did the State, through its agent, the censor, control the viewing habits of audiences, cinemas also became the target of parties from all aspects of the political spectrum eager to establish hegemonic control over the cinema-going nation.

In 1930 a group of university students, numbering amongst them future film historian, Liam O'Leary, the actor, Cyril Cusack, and a future president of Ireland, Cearbhall Ó Dálaigh, raided the Savoy Cinema in Dublin to protest against the screening of the film, *Smiling Irish Eyes* (William A.

Seiter, USA, 1929) which one stated was 'a travesty of the Irish life and an insult to the Irish people' (*Kinematograph Weekly*, 20 February 1930: 31; Rockett, 1987: 55). Their protest was against a romantic comedy that was constructed around the popular Irish stereotypes of the nineteenth century and needs to be seen as part of a wider intellectual movement associated with the Frankfurt School of the 1930s to the 1950s, particularly Theodor Adorno and Max Horkheimer's critique of American mass culture, and the corresponding American grouping of mass culture critics. This conglomeration of left-wing and liberal thinkers articulated a commonly held belief that the industrialisation of culture was a threat to traditional folk practices, to aesthetic values and to political life. For such intellectuals, cinema, with its roots in mass production, encapsulated the worst of the culture industry, leaving the masses open to control and manipulation. Individuality was being stamped out in the rush to conformity and standardisation.

Coming from an alternative political perspective but influenced by much the same reasoning, others denounced cinema as an insidious tool of British imperialist propaganda. In the early 1930s local brigades of the IRA took to 'requesting' cinema managers not to show any material that depicted the British royalty or British military or naval events. On one such occasion, a travelling showman, William Walsh, was raided in his caravan in Co. Galway by a gang of IRA men who demanded that he hand over his copy of the British film, *Tell England* (Anthony Asquith/Geoffrey Barkas, GB, 1931)[4] that he had been showing around the county. The armed men also held up one of Walsh's employees who was travelling by tractor and whom they suspected of being in possession of the contentious film print. The men appear to have been easily identified and were tried in Galway Court. After being remanded in custody, they were led away by the gardaí to cheers and shouts of 'Up the Republic' from the crowd outside. As the local paper reported,

> On Friday night last, about sixty young men marched from Eyre Square to Galway prison where the six men charged with being identified with the alleged larceny of the film 'Gallipoli' had been detained. The procession was headed by a man carrying the tricolour and placards with inscriptions 'Join the I.R.A.' and 'Help the Prisoners' were carried by other members of the parade. After having marched as far as the prison gates the parade returned to the Square and thence through the main street before dispersing. The men who are stated to be members of the I.R.A were afterwards told that the six prisoners had been removed to Limerick prison earlier on Friday evening.
>
> (*The Galway Observer*, 30 September 1933: 3)

The State's desire to distance itself from such activities was demonstrated by the severity with which this breach of law was treated. In November of the same year, the protestors were tried by the Military Tribunal in Dublin and sent to prison.

The screening of the film of the Royal Wedding (between Princess Marina of Greece and Prince George, Duke of Kent) in December 1934 was met with equal antagonism. When it was shown in the Savoy in Dublin's O'Connell Street, a gang of 'intruders' wearing slouch hats and trench coats stormed the cinema and attacked the screen. *The Irish Times* commented pointedly that, 'there was a notable absence of police, and it was not until the trouble was virtually over that the Guards arrived' (*The Irish Times*, 4 December 1934: 7). Questions were, however, raised in the Dáil over the incident, again suggesting an official desire to contain this kind of subversion.

The response of republican groups to the coronation film (of King George VI and Queen Elizabeth) in May 1937 was inevitable. Although there was no official ban attached to its screening in the Free State, a group of interested parties met with film renters to 'discourage' them from showing the news item in their cinemas. An outraged *Irish Times* correspondent fulminated in response to this news that,

> the ordinary citizen has had a legal right filched from him by an anonymous group which claims, without any previously-received authorisation, to speak for him. The business is so fantastic that it makes the Government's claim to speak in the name of 'a sovereign, independent, and democratic state' quite ludicrous.
>
> (*The Irish Times*, 11 May 1937: 4)

In the event, the ordinary citizens took matters into their own hands by travelling *en masse* on specially organised trains to see the film in Belfast and the border towns. This was not to be the only occasion where Belfast cinemas gleefully offered audiences south of the border the opportunity to see newsreels and films otherwise denied them by the censor and his surrogates. In 1941 special trains were laid on again to enable Irish audiences to see *The Great Dictator* (Charlie Chaplin, US, 1940) which was banned in the Free State. This time the censor banned the Southern newspapers from advertising the Belfast screenings, a further infringement on civil freedom of choice that was widely reported in the North.

A few indigenous Irish films were made in the immediate post-Independence period and, despite their relatively unsophisticated nature, they were invariably successful at the box office. The first of these was a series of light comedies produced in 1922 by Norman Whitten, directed by John MacDonagh and starring the Irish variety artist and comedian, Jimmy O'Dea. None of these has survived and judging by reviews, their appeal was more to a local audience familiar with O'Dea's stage act and willing to overlook the films' primitive production values. In fact, the films (*The Casey Millions, Cruiskeen Lawn* and *Wicklow Gold*) seem to have attempted to place O'Dea in the part of the romantic lead whilst retaining his comic persona, which, if his later films are anything to judge by, was straining the limits of the performer's range.

Sweet Inniscara (Emmett Moore, Ireland, 1934), a sentimental rural tale financed by the Cork publishing dynasty, the Crosbies (Power, 2001), is generally credited with being the first all-Irish talking film. Although rumoured to have had a successful US release, it is doubtful if the film made it any further than a handful of Irish clubs. The British trade paper *Kinematograph Weekly* dismissed it as crude, colourless and unconvincing (22 February 1934: 23). Whimsy continued, however, to characterise one strand of indigenous filmmaking, emerging in O'Dea's later border comedy, *Blarney* (Harry O'Donovan, Ireland, 1938). Like so many local productions, *Blarney* was warmly reviewed in the Irish press whilst on its limited British release it was more commonly described as modest and unsophisticated and deemed just about adequate for the (undiscerning?) working classes. Whimsy was also central to the Northern Ireland comedies directed by Donovan Pedelty and featuring the local singer and comedian, Richard Hayward, *The Luck of the Irish* (Ireland, 1935), *The Early Bird* (Ireland, 1936) and *Irish and Proud of It* (Ireland, 1936). Although the strong accents and certain details of *mise-en-scène* signal the regional distinctiveness of the Pedelty/Hayward collaborations, their titles and use of stock characters (the impecunious titled country gentleman of the first film, the wily rogues of the second) belong to the general repertoire of Irish stereotypes. Their production values are notably more sophisticated than those of their counterparts in the South and they attracted substantial audiences in the Free State as well as in their home territory.

With its play on female middle class aspirations and snobbery, and the petty impositions of Protestant moralism, *The Early Bird* rises above its limitations in an often provocative manner. Of necessity, such subversion is reined-in at the film's finale which returns the small community in which it is set to an atmosphere of harmony. Financed through the British quota system (discussed below), Pedelty's films seemed to betoken the potential for a regional filmmaking tradition that was in fact unrealised for many decades to come.

Aside from comedies, indigenous Irish filmmaking of this period focused on two themes, the heroics of the War of Independence and the virtues of a simple rural life. In doing so, it was merely reflecting the ideological climate of the time, specifically the tenets of cultural nationalism. Much has been written about the Irish version of cultural nationalism in the late nineteenth through to the early to mid-twentieth centuries and its influence has reverberated through Irish society to the present.[5] Mention of it has already been made in the previous two chapters and we have seen how the revivalists – Lady Gregory, Douglas Hyde, W.B. Yeats – and their contemporaries in the GAA and similar bodies sought to bring the nation into existence through aspects of culture, notably literature but also sporting activities, craft-making and so on. In the aftermath of independence, the new State followed the classic trajectory of post-colonial entities by declaring its nationhood to be the consummation of generations of struggle and thus confirming its legitimacy. At the same time, it was obliged to clamp down on perceived competing internal rivals to power by naturalising its existence. In this manner, the revolutionaries of one generation became the conservatives of the next, sti-fling opposition, intent on maintaining the status quo. New states, such as the Irish one, tend to be paternalistic and autocratic to the extent that for their subjects it may seem that little has changed since the evacuation of the earlier imperialist regime. The existence in Ireland of the border was a reminder of unfinished nationalist business and lip service, at least, was paid to this blight on the body politic by most forms of official cultural expression over the next few decades. The 'national question', it has been argued, dominated official policies at the expense of social development so that, 'the politics of identity, precisely by locating division and difference at the border of the Irish state, has tended to obscure another internal political reality: class difference' (Lloyd, 1993: 18).

Cultural expression, or the lack of it, was closely linked to post-indepen-dence nationalism; the severity of internal censorship is one testament to the new State's determination to exert control over artistic output whilst restricting the importation of contaminating influences from more modern cultures. Approved contributions to the national self-image included works that eulogised the founders and ideologues of the new State and those that dwelt on the virtues of self-sufficiency and rural plenitude. We do, however, need to remember that Ireland was not the Soviet Union and that artistic dissent was not a life-threatening position. Critics of the new Free State (Éire after 1937) might find their books or plays banned and lose their livelihoods but not their lives. Many such oppositional voices chose to live in exile, others moved between home and abroad, whilst some remained in the country. In terms of the emergent Irish film culture, as we shall see, few filmmakers chose actively to critique the politics of the new State or to question the official history of Republicanism. Indeed the local success of the home-produced works that echoed the tenets of cultural nationalism suggests that there was a substantial level of popular acceptance of its core ideologies. It is to these that we now turn.

If the elliptical *By Accident* (J.N.G. Davidson, Ireland, 1930) suggested the influence of the continental surrealists in its depiction of a self-pro-claimed cowardly young man contemplating his death, the general thrust of filmmaking was to eulogise the masculine ideals of the new Ireland. Declan Kiberd, amongst others, has critiqued the inability of the State to move beyond the fetishisation of the heroes of independence, 'those who had begun with the claim to have invented new forms of politics almost all ended as conservatives; and it was the military heroism, rather than the creative and critical thought, of the 1916 rebels which they celebrated' (1996: 389).

This comment is borne out by the narratives of two locally produced films about the War of Independence, *Irish Destiny* (George Dewhurst, Ireland, 1926) and *The Dawn*[6] (Tom Cooper, Ireland, 1936), both portraying the war as a testing ground for honour and masculinity. Given the intervening events of the already unmentionable Civil War, this consensual nationalism

Figure 3.1 Irish Destiny.

may be regressive but it is hardly startling. Indeed, within the terms of the films, Republicanism represents a forward-looking ideology. Of the two, the earlier film is the most ambitious, moving between the O'Hara family home, the poteen distillery ('a vile and ruinous alcoholic concoction', according to the intertitles, 'the distilling of which is prohibited by the Irish Republican Army'), the IRA headquarters in Dublin and the Curragh prisoner camp in Kildare. Poteen becomes the symbolic poison of those backward natives who have not embraced Republicanism and it is to their surreal and highly threatening hideout that Denis O'Hara's (Paddy Dunne Cullinan)[7] kidnapped fiancé is brought and treated with some considerable menace.

In common with the films of the earlier period discussed in the previous chapter, the informer is central to both works. In *Irish Destiny* it is the poteen distiller; *The Dawn*, by contrast hinges on retrieving the reputation of a family whose past has been tainted by the false rumour of having produced a traitor in 1866 (presumably the failed Fenian Rising of 1867). In this film, the framing of Brian Malone leaves a slur on the family name that can only be redeemed at the end of the film when his grandson, Billy (Donal O'Cahill), is revealed upon his death at the hands of the Black and Tans to be an undercover IRA intelligence officer whose work has saved many Irish lives. The film echoes with the rhetoric of nationalism – 'Sinn Féin now stands for the whole policy of self-reliance', Billy's father explains

43

at one point, while in the closing frames he turns and addresses the camera declaring 'The fight must go on!' More than that, the redemption of the family through the death of their son literalises the ideology of blood sacrifice associated with the 1916 Rising.

The Black and Tans appear as somewhat abstract villains, particularly in *Irish Destiny*, although the interchanges between them and the IRA, the ambushes and the daring escapes provide the films with some extended action sequences. Laying aside the films', particularly *The Dawn*'s, makeshift aesthetic, these bring a sense of excitement to the events. To be in the IRA is viewed as being thrilling, particularly for young men; their sisters and girlfriends support them and only their mothers are left to fear for their safety. It is interesting to compare this enthusiasm with the later, more jaundiced response to the old IRA evinced in recent works, especially those such as *Broken Harvest* (Maurice O'Callaghan, Ireland, 1994) and *Korea* (Cathal Black, Ireland, 1995) that very belatedly acknowledge the trauma of the Civil War. Such films, as we shall see, filter their critique of cultural nationalist values through a problematising of masculinity, even if ultimately they reassert its validity as a symbol of national identity. Also of note in the films of the 1930s is the impression of a society comfortable with its middle-class rural identity. That the IRA leaders should be the scions of elegant country houses, their interiors suggesting generations of wealth, their members waited on by servants, presents a view of an indigenous way of life now little represented in Irish cinema of any kind. Both films demonstrate a strong sense of locality and the local. Tom Cooper, who was a cinema owner in the Munster region, employed old IRA men as extras on his film. Kerry is the centre of these men's world and their fight is with those who have invaded the 'Kingdom'.[8]

The Dawn was received with equal eagerness by cinema-goers and critics, the latter lauding its eschewal of commercial filmmaking practices and its re-creation of local Kerry life. It was not, however, to be 'the dawn for which most Irish cinema-goers have been anxiously waiting when we shall be released from the bondage of Hollywood' (*Evening Herald*, 22 August 1936: 71) not least because of those very characteristics which recommended it to its home audience. 'Acting is generally bad, even amateurish. Film is painfully slow in the development and telling of its story. Chief recommendation, and just about the only one, is the loveliness of the outdoor locale' moaned *Variety* (23 February 1938: 15) whilst *The New York Times* concluded that 'Erin will go broke, if it doesn't quit producing the likes of either [*The Dawn* and *The Luck of the Irish*]' (19 February 1938: 19).

In contrast, when Irish-American John Ford made *The Informer* (USA, 1935), a film that covered the same time frame as *Irish Destiny* and *The Dawn*, the finished product was something of a *cause célèbre*. Ford's film, with its much greater resources, attempts to achieve a sense of the universal whilst drawing once more on the theme of the informer. In this instance, he is played as a tragic fool, a misfit who, as the characters in the film repeat, did not know what he was doing. Gypo Nolan (Victor McLaglen) informs because he is outside the capitalist system, not because he is part of it. The money that he receives for betraying his friend Frankie McPhillip (Wallace Ford) leads him into a menacing underworld of false companions, pubs and brothels. *The Informer* is, as Pat Sheeran has discussed, indebted to the aesthetics of German expressionism, in particular the films of Murnau (Sheeran, 2002). The scene of Nolan's 'trial' by the IRA recalls Fritz Lang's *M* (Germany, 1931) and has in common a sense of entrapment and suspicion. If the tensions raised by the errant individual's simultaneous rejection and need of the community are essential to Ford's worldview, the depiction of Dublin as the locus of decay is a far cry from his sentimental vision of rural Ireland, expressed most famously in *The Quiet Man* (see next chapter).

Dublin as it appears in *The Informer* is a city demoralised by war and policed by the embodiments of the colonial power, the British soldiery. Colonialism has spread itself insidiously throughout the social fabric whose citizens have lost their moral bearings. They are a lumpenproleteriat who alternately insinuate themselves into Gypo's affections when he appears to have money and, like the biblical horde who turned against Christ referenced in the film's opening quotation from the New Testament ('Then Judas repented himself – and cast down the thirty pieces of silver – and departed') they abandon him when he has nothing left to give them. The debauched wealthy continue to drink and dance and declare their allegiance to the Crown as the people of the slums starve.

Only Mrs McPhillip (Una O'Connor), the prostitute/Mary Magdalene figure, Katie Madden (Margot Grahame) and the IRA leaders aspire to some level of probity. For Gypo there is no escape and in the end he falls dying at the foot of the crucifix and McPhillip's mother in a final profusion of imagery that performs the rhetorical elision of mother, Church and country in the suffering icon of Mother Ireland/the Mother of God and her sacrificed son. 'Frankie, Frankie, your mother forgives me', Gypo declaims, arms outstretched. As the death of the son in *The Dawn* recalled the rhetoric of blood sacrifice associated with Pearse and romantic Republicanism, so Gypo's dying is a kind of personal and national purgation. Ford's heroic vision of Gypo's self-sacrifice and his elevation of the film's characters to religious allegories is a considerable departure from Flaherty's original novel which is in any case set in the Civil War not during the War of Independence.

Liam O'Flaherty's novel *The Informer* (first published in 1925) is a disenchanted account of the Dublin slums during the Civil War. It is a tale without heroes or, indeed hope. In it, Frankie McPhillip is a criminal and a murderer who, on a drunken night out with Gypo, killed the secretary of the Farmers' Union and was, along with his friend, expelled from the Organisation. Gypo informs on Frankie for the money, not to rescue his prostitute-girlfriend who, in the book is described as 'a drug fiend, a slattern, an irresponsible creature' (O'Flaherty, 1971: 34). When the police come to arrest Frankie, he does not die a hero's death but accidentally shoots himself. The Organisation is not the disciplined IRA brigade of Ford's imagination but a communist cell, its leader, Dan Gallagher, a fanatic who spouts the jargon of communism whilst admitting he does not care for people. The book is scathingly dismissive of politics, describing Frankie McPhillip's father as 'a Socialist and chairman of his branch of the trade union, but a thoroughly respectable, conservative Socialist, utterly fanatical in his hatred of the status of a working man' (ibid.: 51).

Gypo moves through the book, as he does through the film, like a man already dead and the two narratives come together at certain junctures, notably the end where he achieves some kind of redemption in the church. The suggestion that Gypo and Katie, the film's Mary Magdalene figure, will use the £20 to buy their passage to America is Ford's invention and explicitly links the film into his wider oeuvre, discussed in greater detail later. Sheeran speculates that the massive success of *The Informer* in the United States, where it won four Academy Awards and a number of other prizes, may be explained by 'the appeal of a down-at-heel hero to radical intellectuals and cinemagoers during the latter end of the Great Depression' (Sheeran, 2002: 7). In Ford's re-working of the story, *The Informer* becomes a failed emigration narrative and, we might speculate, equally functioned to reassure those who had taken that boat that theirs was a justified decision.

In Ireland, where *The Informer* was initially banned before being passed on appeal, the national press was as enthusiastic as the public who broke all records at the Capitol cinema in Dublin when the film opened. Again, it is not difficult to see why a fiction that refashions a history of shame into a triumph of heroism should find local resonances, particularly when it is visually and thematically imbued with a reverential Catholicism.

The sole film of the period to question the prevailing orthodoxies of heroic nationalism was a silent adaptation of Frank O'Connor's short story of the same name, *Guests of the Nation* (Denis Johnston, Ireland, 1935). The playwright Denis Johnston's only film is certainly the most amateurish of the independence films, with lights visibly being reflected on players' faces, and those partaking in it made no secret of their limited resources. As Johnston recollected, they learnt as they went along: 'practically every problem in the growth of the silent movie from Griffith to Pabst cropped up in some form or other during the two leisurely summers we spent on this fascinating task' (Adams, 2002: 132). Like the story on which it is based, it is a reminder of the loss of human values in war. The narrative describes the capture of two British soldiers and the common ground they and their IRA guards discover. When the guards are ordered to shoot their prisoners, all must suffer, if only two fatally. The title plays on the Irish reputation for hospitality and the choice of a simple but picturesque cottage for their captivity underscores the film's sense of irony.[9] As a Protestant playwright and someone who was part of a group of artists who circulated outside of the ambit of cultural nationalist influence, Johnston was perhaps best positioned to offer a more critical view of the War of Independence. He remained interested in cinema, taking a role in *Riders to the Sea* (Brian Desmond Hurst, GB, 1936) and becoming briefly involved in writing the screenplay for *Ourselves Alone* (Brian

Figure 3.2 The Informer. Victor McLaglen (Gypo Nolan) and Una O'Connor (Mrs McPhillip).

Desmond Hurst, GB, 1936) but he directed no further films. Johnston moved instead to television (he was appointed Director of Television Programmes for the BBC after World War Two) and continued to write fiction and non-fiction.

The alternative to comedies and IRA dramas was to represent Ireland as the last repository of a simple, primitive culture. The most influential of these films was Irish-Canadian Robert Flaherty's *Man of Aran*. Flaherty's singular images of an isolated island community locked into a life-or-death struggle with nature have been widely analysed for their influence on the documentary movement and in the context of Irish cinema and culture. The ethics of staging events such as the shark hunt which by the 1930s was already an anachronism on the island, the film's use of archetypes and its celebration of an essentialist virility are well documented (Barsam, 1988: 58–71; Pettitt, 2000: 77–80). Flaherty's documentary/travelogue is part of a tradition of envisioning Ireland, for which the Aran Islands function as a palimpsest, as the bearer of an authenticity otherwise lost in Western culture. No wonder, therefore, that the première of *Man of Aran* was 'the most brilliant film function that has ever taken place in Ireland' and was attended by the President, Eamon de Valera, members of his cabinet and the Diplomatic Corps (*Kinematograph Weekly*, 10 May 1934: 25). Of course the film chimed perfectly with the ideals of cultural nationalism; more worryingly, with its emphasis on the values of folk customs and its love of the strong, 'savage' body, it echoed the aesthetics of fascism. Martin McLoone confronts this association, which may seem justified in the light of the decision to award Flaherty's film the Mussolini Cup at the Venice Festival of 1934, by arguing that Flaherty did no more than reflect a particular aesthetic strand of the time whilst remaining innocent of its political implications. Indeed McLoone considers it more disturbing that contemporary Irish critics such as de Valera's close supporter, Dorothy McArdle, viewed the film as a salutary form of realism, an antidote to other, more sullying images of Irishness (McLoone, 2000: 38–44).

The film follows the supposedly representative Man of Aran (Colman 'Tiger' King) and his child and his wife as they move between their small, sparse cottage, their daily routine of hefting stones, clearing ground, spreading seaweed and their participation in the communal activity of fishing, finally culminating in the dramatic shark hunt amidst the Atlantic storm. It has an unobtrusive circularity, bringing the viewer from its opening sequences of the hens and farmyard animals gathered around the house, taking us through the drama of the hunt and returning us at the end to the cottage. Aesthetically, Flaherty's film, in common with his earlier *Nanook of the North* (Canada, 1922), is a magnificent work of art. He positions his subjects so that they seem engulfed by the mass of land and sky. Man, in Flaherty's world, is part of nature but subordinate to it, always in danger of being crushed by forces greater than his own. The family is central to this vision and the father-son lineage a guarantor of its endurance. However, most controversially, Flaherty did not merely observe the primitive peoples he so loved to document, he actively intervened in their depiction to present them at their most noble. He wanted 'his films to ennoble mankind, to reveal tradition and culture, and to foster human understanding' (Barsam, 1988: 58). This was to be undertaken on a mythic level and, therefore, at the expense of any exploration of the economic background to his subjects' lives.

Man of Aran now occupies a troubled position within Irish cultural life, representing for many the falsification of Ireland by the many cultural invaders who plundered it for its transformative powers, and of local Irish willingness to collude in this process. Since its release, it has become a marker of both artistic excellence and compromise. Denis Johnston had met Flaherty on the island when he was filming *Man of Aran* and observed with some disapproval the latter's manipulation of reality for the shoot. In his own play *Storm Song* (1934) he 'set out to dramatize the process of film-making and the dilemmas of the documentary director' (Adams, 2002: 135). Later, Martin McDonagh in *The Cripple of Inishmaan* (1997) wove the making of *Man of Aran* into the dramatic events of his Aran islanders, for whom the arrival of a Hollywood film crew (not that Flaherty's film crew was from Hollywood) is an opportunity for escape if they are 'discovered'. It is also a validation of their own importance to the world. When they finally see the

Figure 3.3 Man of Aran. Maggie Dirrane (Man of Aran's wife).

film, they dismiss their cinematic alter-egos as, 'wet fellas with awful jumpers on them' (McDonagh, 1997: 60). Visual artist, Dorothy Cross' 1997 video installation, *Storm in a Teacup*, featured an extract from *Man of Aran* projected on to a willow-patterned cup of tea placed on a lace table-cloth. The work entraps the mythic within the domestic, suggesting that it is all indeed just a 'storm in a teacup'.

An alternative view of the Aran Islands from a short film made just slightly before Flaherty's, the documentary *Aran of the Saints* (GB, 1932) released by the Catholic Film Society of London, reminds us that Flaherty's was not the only way to represent the islands. *Aran of the Saints* presents their culture as vibrant and youthful and, of course, deeply religious, a remarkable absence in Flaherty's version. With its recurrent images of children playing, its emphasis on arrivals and departures, and its brief exploration of the economics of rural/ maritime life, *Aran of the Saints* has little investment in suggesting that there is anything archaic about island life. Simple, it certainly is, but otherwise it is future-oriented and linked to mainland culture.

That Flaherty's vision of the West of Ireland was not forced upon a resistant audience is borne out by the release in 1938 of *The Islandman* (Patrick Heale, Ireland 1938).[10] More technically accomplished than its indigenous predecessors, the film's thrust is to elevate the culture of the remote, Irish-speaking Blasket Islands over that of metropolitan Dublin. This it achieves through its device of creating a central character, Neal (Cecil Ford) who travels between the two. A medical student, he can treat a local fisherman, Liam (Brian O'Sullivan) when he is injured, but his own psychological healing can only be achieved through a return to the island and the young woman he has met there (that she is also Liam's betrothed leaves the film in some structural difficulty which can only be resolved by a series of dramatic coincidences). Visually, *The Islandman* reveals its indebtedness to *Man of Aran* although it keeps its commercial options open by including highly sentimentalised sequences of native singing and dancing that dilute an otherwise stark aesthetic. If *Man of Aran* embodies what Luke Gibbons, after Panofsky, has discussed as 'hard primitivism' (1987: 200), *The Islandman* veers between a display of the natural but barren beauty of the island and a celebration of communality that might more readily be categorised as 'soft primitivism'. As Neal, whose outsider's perception of the island is established as the ideal viewing position for the film, explains to Eileen (Eileen Curran), 'This isolation from the outside world is the principle charm of your people and you.'

The Islandman was released in Britain by Butcher's Film Service who were responsible for many of the Irish-British immigrant films (discussed below). In its self-conscious display and exploration of a vanishing way of life, it further conforms to an established trend within indigenous cultural productions of 'explaining ourselves' to what is perceived as the outside world. In this case, its anticipated metropolitan viewer, the vicarious traveller, is not just the English or American visitor, so common in post-war narratives (and discussed in the following chapter) but the deracinated Dublin intelligentsia who have become separated from their true cultural origins.

Censorship was just one aspect of a culture that, for many, was narrow and stifling. The economic ideal of rural self-sufficiency discouraged industrialisation and it has been widely agreed that civil society achieved balance only as a consequence of emigration. The outflow of the population that had followed the famines of the nineteenth century continued throughout the first half of the twentieth. Between 1841 and 1961 the Irish population fell from 6.5 million to 2.8 million (Tansey, 1998: 11). Remarkably, even this was blamed on the cinema, with the Bishop of Ardagh and Clonmacnoise declaring in a Lenten pastoral that Irish girls emigrating to Britain were being, 'lured, perhaps, by the fascination of the garish distractions of the city, and by the hectic life of the great world as displayed before their wondering eyes in the glamorous unrealities of the films'. He added that, 'It is not the least of the sins of the kinema to breed a discontent that is anything but divine with the prosaic placidity of rural life' (*Kinematograph Weekly*, 18 February 1937: 22).

Only in the late 1930s did emigration decline, this probably as a result of the overall decrease in opportunities in the countries most affected by the

Depression. Emigration peaked in the late 1950s when it reached an annual average of 60,000 (Mjoset, 1992: 269). Such figures include not just economic emigrants, they also account for the outflow of writers, artists, actors and filmmakers in search of more conducive conditions for creative work.

These migrants joined an international movement of displaced artists and intellectuals, many of them the victims of fascism or other repressive regimes. For a considerable numbers of these individuals, Hollywood offered opportunities and a community of fellow exiles which they both embraced and despised; certainly, their contribution to mainstream film culture during this period was enormous (Nowell-Smith and Ricci, 1998; Phillips, 1998).[11]

One of the most influential of these émigrés was Rex Ingram (1893–1950). The son of a Church of Ireland rector, Rex Hitchcock, as he was then known, left Ireland permanently in 1911. In 1913, he entered the film industry, still centred in New York, and over the course of his career created some of the greatest films of the silent era, notably *Four Horsemen of the Apocalypse* (US, 1921) starring Rudolph Valentino and Alice Terry, *The Prisoner of Zenda* (US, 1922), *Scaramouche* (US, 1923) and *Mare Nostrum* (US, 1925–6). Descriptions of Ingram's personality insist on his Irish charm, and his passageway into Universal Pictures was assisted by its co-founder, P.A. Powers, who came from County Waterford (O'Leary, 1993: 60). There was clearly never going to be any scope for someone of Ingram's ambitions in Ireland, nor was his subject matter likely to win him any admirers within the Catholic-State hierarchy. As his biographer Liam O'Leary describes it, *Four Horsemen* ... 'reached Ingram's native Dublin in January of 1923 where a savage attack by a narrow-minded sectarian press did not lessen its popularity' (ibid.: 82).

Ingram's cinema might have scandalised the Irish press but it is his slightly older fellow exile, Herbert Brenon (1880–1958) who is notoriously alleged to have made one of the first 'sex films', *Neptune's Daughter* (US, 1914) anywhere in the world (Graham, 1995: 24). Brenon worked in Hollywood, London and Italy and was nominated for an Academy Award in the inaugural 1927/28 awards. Unlike Ingram, he made one Irish-themed film in the United States, *Kathleen Mavourneen*, in 1913. Another director, Herbert Wilcox, was in his own words, 'as Irish as the Blarney Stone itself' 1967: 2). He also made several Irish-themed films, notably a version of the Peg Woffington story, *Peg of Old Drury* (GB, 1935) but he is now so closely associated with the British industry that it is hard to extract him from its history.

The emigrant director who moved most successfully between Irish and other material was born in Belfast in 1895. Brian Desmond Hurst's Irish films make a useful study for what they reveal about the position of the exiled artist when she or he chooses to engage with native material. Hurst left Ireland for Canada in 1921 after active service and enrolled in art college. He continued to study art in Paris where he moved in a circle of French and émigré intellectuals and artists. In 1928, Hurst was introduced to John Ford who, according to Hurst's unpublished autobiography, was delighted to meet an Irishman and 'soon adopted me as his cousin' (Hurst, undated: 73). Ford also appears to have been responsible for finding Hurst his first job in Hollywood in the art department at Warners as well as his first film role, leading a donkey along a road in *Hangman's House* (John Ford, USA, 1928). Brian Desmond Hurst's opportunity to make a film himself came when a wealthy mentor, Henry Talbot de Vere Clifton, offered him the finance. The result was *The Tell-Tale Heart*,[12] (GB, 1934) adapted from a supernatural tale by Edgar Allan Poe and made with amateur actors for £3,000. Selling it on as a 'quota quickie' (see below), Hurst made a small profit and garnered an array of positive press notices on both sides of the Atlantic. Somewhat presciently, the *New York Herald Tribune*, after favourably comparing Hurst with Ernst Lubitsch and Rene Clair, wrote, 'Here is a picture that will not fit into a pigeon-hole, even at the top of the pile' (quoted in Sykes, 1942: 4–8).

Hurst went on to become a prolific but uncategorisable director, working mainly out of the British film industry in the 1930s and 1940s (McIlroy, 1994). Although he seems to have functioned as 'director-for-hire' on many projects, his Irish films reflect a desire to explore popular narratives as well as drawing on key stage productions and recent historical and political events. The first of these was *Irish Hearts* (GB, 1935)[13] also financed by Clifton. A romantic melodrama adapted from the novel, *Night Nurse* (1913), by J. Johnson Abraham, the viewable portion of this film suggests an Ireland of some modernity where the characters, both male and female, worry that marriage will interfere with their careers. Hurst's film shows an awareness of local detail, for instance, Pip (Patric Knowles) a friend of the hero, Trinity medical student Dermot Fitzgerald (Lester Matthews) exclaims, 'He ought to be making love to her [Norah] ... for all the notice he takes of her she might as well have a red nose and a Belfast accent.' For at least one contemporary reviewer, the mere fact that Ireland was being represented on screen by an indigenous production was good enough. After noting that the picture was produced almost entirely in the country, the writer then proceeds to list with approval the depiction of notable Dublin landmarks, adding that, 'Clogher Head, near Dundalk and Monasterboice will also be recognised easily by anyone who has visited these noted beauty spots' (*Dublin Evening Mail*, 12 March 1935: 3). This figure of the Trinity medical student was to recur in Irish films, often occupying a position of some ambiguity. In *The Islandman*, for instance, he stands for an Anglo-Irish intelligentsia that must be retrieved for national belonging by the purity of the West of Ireland, while in *Shake Hands With the Devil* (Michael Anderson, GB, 1959), he is again challenged to express his commitment to a 'real' Irish identity, this time by joining the IRA.

An encounter with Gracie Fields led to her financing Hurst's next Irish film, an adaptation of J.M. Synge's *Riders to the Sea*. Drawing as did the FCOI on the Abbey Actors, Hurst shot the film's exteriors in Connemara. Aesthetically, the film reflects the disparity between the two, with the actors delivering their lines in a highly theatrical manner whilst the camera revels in the bleak, natural beauty of coastline and sky. Hurst's visuals are invariably compared with those of his mentor, John Ford, and the opening shots of *Riders ...* are markedly Fordian in their elemental quality. They also illustrate the widespread acceptance of the kind of Irish images associated with *Man of Aran*. Arguably we may read the film's depiction of an isolated, dying, island community mourning its young men as an analogy for the wider state of Irish society in the 1930s.

Hurst failed to sell his film as a 'quota quickie' and notes ruefully in his autobiography that, 'Gracie never got her money back' (Hurst, undated: 105). Irish reviews on this occasion were a little more guarded, the *Dublin Evening Mail* critic warning readers that, 'if one is in a state of depression and is seeking something of a cheerful nature, it would be inadvisable to remain in the theatre during the showing of this picture' (14 July 1936: 7). Graham Greene, never a fan of 'Synge's incantatory style', found the film dreary and stage-bound, suggesting that it had missed an opportunity to display, rather than have its characters recall, the deaths that occur through the drama (1993: 56–7).

Hurst's next film, *Ourselves Alone*,[14] is the most challenging of his Irish productions. A War of Independence drama, it is distinguishable from works such as *The Dawn* and *Irish Destiny* by virtue of its ambition to balance

Figure 3.4 Ourselves Alone (l-r): Maire O'Neill (Nanny), Clifford Evans (Commandant Connolly), Antoinette Cellier (Maureen Elliott) and Paul Farrell (Hogan).

audience sympathy between the IRA men and the local RIC and British army. This is achieved by characterising the film's two main protagonists, secret IRA leader Terence Elliott (Niall MacGinnis) and his sister's fiancé, County Inspector John Hannay (John Lodge) as men of equal honour. This is tested throughout the drama as each side is faced with a series of moral dilemmas and ends with Hannay assuming responsibility for Elliott's death in order to facilitate the true love affair between Elliott's sister and the army intelligence officer, Captain Wiltshire (John Loder). Otherwise, *Ourselves Alone* conforms in many respects to the format of the indigenous dramas, locating its action primarily in rural Ireland and representing the IRA leaders as members of the middle classes, indeed possibly even in this case, of the Anglo-Irish ascendancy (Terence's family lives in Castle Elliott). At certain moments, the film's divisions appear to reference covertly the impending Civil War, in particular during the stand-off between Elliott and Hannay: 'I hate no one. It's love that I have been fighting for. I love my country. I love the things that Ireland should stand for and doesn't' Terry declaims, to which Hannay responds with a reminder that he is as Irish as Terry. Otherwise, the message that independence was a tragedy not a triumph lends weight to the sense that Hurst was keeping a close eye on his British market whilst attempting to put Irish narratives on the screen.

In his analysis of the contrasting responses to *Ourselves Alone* displayed by the British Board of Film Censors (BBFC), the Northern Ireland Ministry of Home Affairs and the Irish Free State Film Censor to the film and its public reception, John Hill concludes that the film's ideological indeterminacy was ultimately its downfall:

> while the film pushes in the direction of a preferred reading, its concern to extend sympathy to both 'sides' of the conflict also makes it a text which was liable to diverse interpretations when circulated in an Irish context. To put it crudely, by striving for a degree of 'balance' (or equivalence) in its representation of characters and events, the film also provided everyone (in Ireland at any rate) with something to object to.
>
> (2000: 330)

Hurst returned to literary adaptations for his final two Irish films, *Hungry Hill* (GB, 1947), jointly adapted by Daphne du Maurier from her novel of the same name, and *The Playboy of the Western World* (Ireland, 1962). The former is essentially a formulaic historical melodrama bookended by references to Ireland's tragic divisions. The latter is another Synge adaptation, the energies of the original dissipated by leaden acting and highly stylised visuals.

Hurst was a filmmaker of some skill (his wartime propaganda piece for the Ministry of Information, *Miss Grant Goes to the Door* [GB, 1940], is a classic of the genre). Whenever possible, he slipped Irish characters into his dramas – in another of his propaganda films, *A Call for Arms!* (1940) the forewoman of the munitions factory, played by Colleen Nolan, is a sympathetic, motherly Irishwoman. In his most successful wartime drama,

Dangerous Moonlight (GB, 1941), Hurst seems to come closest to expressing his own ambivalent situation. An exile, Stefan Radetzky (Anton Walbrook) explains, is 'a man without a country of his own'. Stefan must further decide to lay aside his value to society as an artist, in his case an international concert pianist, and join the war as a fighter pilot (conveniently a member of a different élite). In this he is influenced by his friendship with Irishman, Mike Carroll (Derrick De Marney) who fights, and ultimately dies. In an exchange between Carole (Sally Gray), Stefan's wife and Mike Carroll, she protests, 'I can't understand you. After all you told me about what Cromwell did to your ancestors in Ireland, and what you saw in the English, doesn't it seem funny to be going back to fight for them?' To which the reply is:

> The English are all right, some of them. I don't mind the Irish taking a crack at them. That doesn't count. But when someone else butts in, that's different ... beside you must preserve the English so we've got someone to fight against when this war's over.

This very closely echoes an exchange in another wartime drama, again about the need to commit to engagement. In *Halfway House* (Basil Dearden, Alberto Cavalcanti, GB, 1944) an Irishman finds himself in England under attack from German bombs and undergoes a change of heart: 'I won't be the first Irishman to ask is this a private fight or can anyone join in?' Terence (Pat McGrath) calls out before asserting, 'there isn't a family in all Ireland that hasn't got someone fighting in this war'.

Dangerous Moonlight might also interestingly be read against Desmond Hurst's own portrait of his bi-sexuality (in his unpublished memoirs). The camera lingers on the soft-focus features of Anton Walbrook, feminising him and presenting him as an object of desire. In the same way, Desmond Hurst's inclusion of extended scenes of young men stripped to the waist in changing rooms in *Irish Hearts* and *A Letter from Ulster* (GB, 1942) echo his fascination with the male body.

Of the expatriate directors, he also showed the most persistence in making Irish films and in canvassing for the establishment of an Irish film industry, though references in his autobiography suggest that his Northern Irish provenance did little to endear him to the authorities in Dublin. He happily spelt his name in Irish when the need arose and seems to have played up his Irish identity. His ability to raise studio and private financing permitted him to make films that were considerably more sophisticated than those of his peers in Ireland. It may have been personal preference, but it is also possible it was this very reliance on British goodwill and funding that drove him to sacrifice passion for balance. This is particularly evident in *Ourselves Alone* but also undercuts the political and artistic integrity of *Hungry Hill*. In this case, the film's suggestion that old enmities can be buried and that Catholics and Protestants can live side by side is offset by a final analysis that, in the words of one of the characters, 'only the unexpected can ever be hoped to work in Ireland'. In denying any rational solution to the religious and historical differences that have characterised Irish history, Hurst was merely allowing himself to be blown along by the prevailing winds of popular British political thought, and his film's message is little different to that of the classic British works on Irish subject matter of the time, particularly the 'Troubles' films such as *Odd Man Out* (Carol Reed, 1947) and *The Gentle Gunman* (Basil Dearden, 1952). Hurst clearly identified himself strongly with the British film industry, making a number of key British films, including a section of Alexander Korda's wartime rallying cry, *The Lion Has Wings* (Michael Powell, Adrian Brunel, Brian Desmond Hurst, GB, 1939). He also made one of the few propaganda films to address Northern Ireland's contribution to the war, the somewhat schematic *A Letter from Ulster*. Conveniently the film was long enough to become eligible as a quota release, guaranteeing it greater exposure than it might otherwise have merited.

Viewing Hurst's Irish films, their evident sympathy for Irish characters and locales always seems mitigated by a desire to present their themes in a way that British audiences will relate to, whether through an emphasis on literariness or conciliation. We might see in Hurst himself, a Northern-Irish working class, bi-sexual Protestant artist, making films that associated Irishness with Catholicism and the Free State out of the British (read English) film industry, a classic example of that indeterminate Northern Irish hybridity that has dogged internal issues of national identity.

If the dynamics of emigration provided Irish cinema with a generation of British and Hollywood-based directors who were able to put the resources of their respective industries to the service of their cinematic visions of Ireland, another kind of immigrant cinema addressed the concerns of the working-class Irish communities of Britain and the United States.

In Britain a cycle of films was produced between 1933 and 1942 that referenced, both through their titles and their performance, popular Irish ballads. They are sentimental and nostalgic, particularly in their depiction of Ireland and Irishness. Between them they rehearse narratives of departure and return, of rupture and reunion, and of success against the odds. Entrenched as they are in working class traditions of parlour entertainment and the music hall sing-along, these films may be placed in what Peter Bailey has termed a 'culture of consolation' (1986: xv).

Films such as *Father O'Flynn* (Wilfred Noy, Walter Tennyson, GB, 1935), *Kathleen Mavourneen* (Norman Lee, GB, 1937), *Mountains O'Mourne* (Harry Hughes, GB, 1938 and *My Irish Molly* (Alex Bryce, GB, 1938) respond, through song and performance, to two overlapping drives within British society at that moment. They address, on the one hand, the massive, working-class Irish immigrant population who had settled in urban areas such as Liverpool in the wake of a series of famines of the nineteenth century and earlier, and whose numbers were constantly being added to, as the economy of the Irish Free State stagnated. They also played to a general sense of nostalgia for an idealised rural simplicity and sense of rootedness.

The history and ethics of assimilation remain contested. On the one hand, it is argued that assimilation was imposed by the dominant culture in the interests of social stability and political consensus. On the other, it is true that it was to the benefit of the incoming population to obtain access to the existing infrastructure of education and opportunity. It is generally agreed that the Irish in Britain were never fully integrated nor fully separate and that many types of Irish immigrant co-existed, some achieving high position, others living in destitution. Many would have occupied both positions, holding on to their cultural identity whilst availing themselves of the opportunities on offer in the new society in which they found themselves (Swift and Gilley, 1999).

It is this equivocal situation that these films mirror. Through their display of collective cultural rituals, in particular, the ceilidh or celebration of song and dance, they reinforce a cohesive Irish ethnic identity that was linked to a strong sense of Ireland as a homeland. At the same time, their narratives mostly allowed for at least one character to 'do well' in British society.

The production of these films was enabled by the introduction on the one hand of sound recording in 1929, and by the more contentious and slightly earlier Cinematograph Films Act of 1927, which gave rise to the so-called 'quota-quickies'. Academic considerations of the 'quota-quickies', which were made under the requirements of the Act, have undergone a change in recent years. In *The Age of the Dream Palace*, Jeffrey Richards considered the films to be 'a truly awful flood of cinematic rubbish' (1984: 3). Rachael Low argued that the quota legislation 'had a profound and damaging effect on the structure of the British film industry' (1985: 33). While the larger and better financed British production companies continued to make films that were distributed by indigenous companies and therefore outside of the quota system, a number of smaller companies were put in place solely for the purpose of supplying quota films to the American distributors.

Recently, the quota system has come under revisionist scrutiny and found not to have been quite as worthless as earlier commentators have claimed. H. Mark Glancy, for instance, has argued that, 'The low-budget British films, like Hollywood's "B" films, provided early opportunities for young or developing directors and actors. The film careers of directors such as John Baxter, Adrian Brunel, Michael Powell and Carol Reed began with "quota quickies", as did the careers of actors Errol Flynn, Vivien Leigh, James Mason, John Mills and Laurence Olivier' (1998: 62).

Lawrence Napper has posited that the 'quota quickies' spoke to and for a working-class audience largely based outside London and in areas where cinemas showed such films:

> I would argue that as a direct result of their stringent finances and the limited release pattern open to them, the quota producers sought to portray England for two specific markets: the lower-middle class and the older generations of the working class. Both were defined by their reluctance to partake in the optimistic visions of a consumerist society embodied in Hollywood and 'quality' British films. The lower-middle classes were ambivalent about

consumption, as they were about the cinema. The 'cloth-cap' working class looked back nostalgically to music hall. As a result of their portrayal of sections of British society which identified themselves not through processes of consumption but through British notions of class and community, the 'quota quickies' produced for these markets responded exactly to the intentions of those who had created the Films Act of 1927.

(1997: 40)

As we have seen already, a small number of Irish directors, such as Richard Hayward and Brian Desmond Hurst, exploited the quota system to pursue their filmmaking ambitions. Like the Old Mother Riley comedies, the films discussed here seem to have all been designed to fill the British quota. They were made by studios devoted to quota production, generally Butcher's, were cheap and designed as second features. They fit well Napper's analysis of the quota films with their very specific address and their positioning outside the general conventions of mainstream musicals and other generic forms of filmmaking.

These films are not musicals in the conventional sense, however they are punctuated by the performance of musical numbers, specifically ballad singing, and displays of Irish dancing. To take a typical example, *Kathleen Mavourneen* which the trade paper reviewer pronounced to be a 'sound two-feature programme booking for the masses and provincial audiences' (*Kinematograph Weekly*, 11 February 1937: 35) opens in a Liverpool café where an Irish family is being sent off to America. The waitress and heroine of the narrative, Kathleen O'Moore (Sally O'Neil) watches them with envy commenting, 'I wish we were all going along with them in the morning. Away from this noise and bustle forever'. Her chance soon comes as she moves to Ireland with her young brother and sister to stay with her aunt. She leaves behind her the 'singing stevedore' Michael (played by Tom Burke[15] who had already performed in *Father O'Flynn* and was to take a similar role in *My Irish Molly*). In Ireland Kathleen falls in love with a neighbour, Dennis O'Dwyer (Jack Daly), whose well-to-do family opposes the match. A number of melodramatic interludes, double-crosses and daring rescues take place. Meanwhile, Michael is 'discovered', his voice trained and he becomes a celebrated singer in Britain. In common with Paddy (Niall MacGinnis) in *Mountains O'Mourne*, Michael's voice offers him an escape from poverty, as he announces, 'I won't be a stevedore any more. I won't be a lackey any more and I won't be indebted to anyone'. This newfound strength also enables him to stand back and bless the eventual marriage between Kathleen and Dennis.

Throughout the film singing functions as an expression of nostalgia and communality. In the opening sequences, Michael performs the song from which the film takes its title, *Kathleen Mavourneen*, and the group of Irish immigrants at the American wake[16] sits silent and moved. In a sequence that bears a strong similarity to the later *My Irish Molly*, also produced by John

Argyle, Michael performs the closing number over a montage of shots of Irish scenery. In *My Irish Molly* this sequence occurs in New York as the tenor, Danny (Tom Burke) realises that he will never succeed in America. Accompanied by another immigrant, the Italian accordion player, and watched by a policeman who must surely be Irish, Danny sings the ballad, *Mother Ireland*. As the lyrics interchange love of mother and love of place, so Danny also mourns the loss of his own lover whom he knows has found her place in the big city. Images of New York give way to idealised Irish scenes as Danny sings, wooing and mourning land, lover and mother.

'I could go for them Irish colleens in a big way', one of the Liverpool dockers comments in *Kathleen Mavourneen*. Sexually attractive as the women in these films may be, they can only find true love back home in Ireland, although their male counterparts may achieve fame in Britain after being discovered by a travelling impresario.[17] Love leads invariably to marriage and by implication to settling down in the perfect Irish cottage. These are strictly female spaces presided over by benevolent matriarchs, Mother Ireland incarnate. Ireland is thus doubly home, a country of origin and dream of return. More than that, it is England's better 'other', its natural beauties and home comforts ceaselessly compared with the grim, industrial Liverpool ports and London's threatening streets. As a fantasy, it belongs centrally to the British working-class 'culture of consolation' and also responds to an exilic sense of loss, centred around, as Hamid Naficy reminds us, 'house' and 'home':

> *House* is the literal object, the material place in which one lives, and it involves legal categories of rights, property, and possession and their opposites. *Home* is anyplace; it is temporary and it is moveable; it can be built, rebuilt, and carried in memory and by acts of imagination. Exiles locate themselves vis-à-vis their houses and homes synesthetically and synecdochically. Sometimes a small gesture or body posture, a particular gleam in the eye, or a smell, a sound, or a taste suddenly and directly sutures one to a former house or home and to cherished memories of childhood ... Sometimes a small, insignificant object taken into exile (such as a key to the house) becomes a powerful synecdoche for the lost house and the unreachable home, feeding the memories of the past and the narratives of exile.
>
> (1999: 5–6)

The ballad singing that is central to such films can be thus argued to function synesthetically, triggering an emotive response; the cottage synecdochically, a reminder of the real. This sense of loss, as Lawrence Napper suggests, is as much the property of an alienated working-class as of an exilic sub-culture. Like *Man of Aran* and *The Islandman* these films exploit a metropolitan nostalgia for a pre-industrial society whilst also expressing an immigrant yearning for home.

If the ballad films are reluctant to admit to the possibilities of assimilation, the popular variety hall husband and wife duo of Arthur Lucan and Kitty McShane were defined by it. In immediate pre- and post-war Britain, their Old Mother Riley stage act was one of the staples of the variety circuit and, like many such performers, they transferred it, with little alteration, to the screen. The *Old Mother Riley* films were also quota fillers and their address was certainly to the same audience that turned out in such large numbers to see them on stage. With its relish in knockabout humour and its subversion of middle-class mores, the series is typical of the cross-over between established music hall artistes and 1930s British cinema (Sutton, 2000). Lucan was English[18] and little of his act was identifiably Irish; at the same time, the films discreetly proclaimed their ethnic affiliations through devices such as the inclusion of shamrocks in the titles. Only in occasional films, such as *Old Mother Riley's New Venture* (John Harlow, GB, 1949) where, in an extended set-piece, McShane and an unidentified tenor perform well-known Irish ballads for the residents of the hotel which Old Mother Riley (Lucan in drag) has found him/herself managing, was his/her ostensible ethnicity cited. Although McShane retained her Irish accent, their stage personae suggest a high degree of assimilation. Lucan and McShane's performance of Irishness is perhaps symptomatic of the double bind of ethnicity in a hostile culture. Performance, in this case and in the ballad films, reflects on the experience of immigration. It reinforces ethnic identity through cultural enactment, it trades in a deep sense of nostalgia, it encourages a feeling of community, and it also makes Irishness palatable outside of the immigrant audience. Indeed, it suggests that performance is an intrinsic part of the immigrant experience, as individuals rehearse the collective aspects of the culture of origination whilst passing themselves off as assimilated members of their new communities. Equally, films such as the Lucan/McShane cycle disavow their Irishness by emphasising its artificiality – Lucan, as his audience well knew, was no more Irish than he was a washerwoman.

By virtue of ignoring the political strand of the Irish ballad in favour of the love song, these films negotiated a space for Irishness within popular British culture that seems to have appealed to immigrants and non-immigrants alike. It is doubtful that they would have been made without the requirements of the quota legislation and, with its passing, so their production stopped.

At first glance, the equivalent American cycle of Irish immigrant narratives, although dating from slightly earlier, seems to cover similar ground. Productions such as *Little Old New York* (Sidney Olcott, US, 1923), *Kitty From Killarney* (Arthur Rosson, US, 1926), *Finnegan's Ball* (James P. Hogan, US, 1927) and *Abie's Irish Rose* (Victor Fleming, US, 1929)[19] also foreground female characters, are melodramatic in structure, are interspersed with song and dance and incorporate narratives that move between the 'old country' and, in this case, America. As we have seen, initially images of the Irish on screen lagged behind the aspirations of the 'lace curtain' Irish. By the 1920s, Irish-themed films of this period had been transformed into an endorsement of immigration and assimilation, placing them at odds with their British counterparts. Many of these works are about the redemptive qualities of traditional Irish culture and their potential to redress the decline in American values occasioned by modernisation. Quite a number relive the experience of emigration, representing Ireland less, however, as an idealised motherland than as a troubled and deprived culture.

Finnegan's Ball, for example, opens in Killarney where the Finnegan family is making a staunch stand against poverty and the landlord.[20] Molly Finnegan's (Blanche Mehaffey) betrothed, Jimmy Flannigan (Cullen Landis), has already emigrated and is able to spare the Finnegans from eviction by sending them their fare to America. Molly's parents are unreconstructed comic stereotypes. As the intertitles inform us, 'every time Danny Finnegan [Charles McHugh] was about to make both ends meet, somebody came along and moved the ends'. Finnegan is shortly afterwards seen falling off his stool whilst attempting to milk his goat whilst his wife, Maggie (Aggie Herring) is viewed up to her elbows scrubbing clothes in their outdoor tub. She, we are informed, is addressed by Dan as his better half, 'to keep her from thinking she was the whole thing'. The family arrives in New York with their cockerel in a suitcase and instantly starts a fight with the Flannigans. The case is, however, dismissed when it comes to court upon the judge proclaiming 'sure it's no crime for a Flannigan to fight a Finnegan'. As Jimmy Flannigan proceeds to blunder through the obstacles that greet the country greenhorn on arrival in the big city, Molly is set up in a finishing school by Jimmy, enabling her to enter the fast track towards gentrification and assimilation. A series of misunderstandings result in her being expelled and return her to her pious Catholic origins (such films routinely associate Irishness with Catholicism) expressed in a scene where, observed by her sympathetic mother, she clasps her statue of the Virgin Mary and implores the holy figure to remember what a good young woman she is. By dint of a further plot twist common to filmmaking of this era, Finnegan mistakenly inherits a mansion and the family swiftly adapts to a life of high living. Here they hold the eponymous ball before being ejected on foot of the truth (that in fact a Denis not Danny Finnegan has inherited the property) about the bequest emerging. The narrative ends with Pa Finnegan recognising that he is just a hod-carrier after all before becoming a business partner of Flannigan's.

At each plot twist the Finnegans are offered the easy way into assimilated citizenship but, like a game of snakes and ladders, soon find themselves sliding back to where they started. Only when they learn to capitalise on their inherent qualities as sound, moral, hard-working individuals can they start up the ladder in safety. Under its ludic veneer, this and the other films offer a stern message about the importance of retaining the familial and moral structure of traditional Irish Catholicism in a culture where sinful veniality is always lurking.

Through a study of the star persona of Colleen Moore, Diane Negra has demonstrated that as the 'New Woman' gained cultural ascendancy,

American popular representations invested in Irish femininity a perceived stability and sexual conservatism:

> it would seem that these two female stereotypes were positioned on opposing sides of an economic divide, with the vamp announcing herself as finished product of her own labor in a way that foreclosed the shaping influence of patriarchy and the Irish girl as a raw resource to be acted upon by patriarchal and capitalistic influences.
>
> (2001a: 26)

This analysis holds good for the general depiction of the young Irish woman in 1920s Irish-American cinema, where she is defined by her charm, her inventiveness and her sexual innocence.

The central message of both *Lights of Old Broadway* and *Little Old New York* is that the key to assimilation is the female character. In both cases this is helped by the casting of Marion Davies in the central role. Davies brings with her an extra-textual sophistication that underpins her performance (although the *Variety* reviewer noted that this is 'probably the single Marion Davies picture not characterized by "clothes"' [9 August 1923: 26]). She is simultaneously ingénue and sophisticate, and her roles enable her to lift her family from its impoverished origins to a level of integration into mainstream New York culture.[21]

In *Lights of Old Broadway,* the family moves literally from the periphery to the centre as they make good and abandon their home amongst the immigrant squatters who have erected timber shacks on waste ground just outside the city; in *Little Old New York*, they are leaving an Ireland characterised as 'the most distressful country that ever yet was seen'. The films do not entertain the idea of return to Ireland and, unlike their British counterparts, focus on negotiating a space for their protagonists within the New York immigrant community. Rather than demonise the city, they regard it with warmth, celebrating its chaos. As an early intertitle from one of the Irish-Jewish romances, *The Shamrock and the Rose* (Jack Nelson, US, 1927) declares, this is 'the East Side of New York where the melting pot often boils over'.

In fact, the cinematic melting pot is never allowed to simmer too long and potential inter-ethnic strife is invariably contained by marriage and general pragmatism. Mari Kathleen Fielder argues that the ubiquity of these Irish-Jewish comedies and romances on screen and stage in the opening decades of the twentieth century reflects the familiarity of both Irish and Jewish ethnic figures within popular cultural entertainments and thus their usefulness as symbols of the efficacy of the melting pot theory – despite initial antagonism, love inevitably prevails and harmony between the two groups is cemented by friendship between the older generation and marriage between the younger (Fielder, 1985). The Irish race comedies of this period suggest a general will to integrate new arrivals into their host society; doubtlessly they were not just made to appeal to an Irish audience, although, with their clubs and neighbourhood cinemas, these guaranteed the films a level of commercial success. Astutely, they manage to appear both specific and universal. They play on suspicions that the new 'lace curtain' Irish of the 1890s onwards have abandoned their earthy roots, but offer the timeless fantasy of social advancement. Through their knockabout comic farces they articulate fears of the consequences of inter-racial marriage only to conclude with a harmonious resolution. To this extent, they too reflect the principles of assimilation then current within the American political and social establishment.

Modernisation (when accompanied by morality), in particular is viewed as integral to assimilation, hence the rejection of Ireland as a locus of backwardness and feudalism. Whilst it ran the risk of rehashing discredited stereotypes, the appearance of the bucolic, fighting Irishman in these films is a reminder of what the Irish must leave behind, even if they do so with what appears to be some regret. It is through the forward-looking female characters that the family will make the transition into contemporary American culture, whether through marriage or professional success, or both.

The films boast only minimal Irish creative input, instead they draw on and temper stereotypes inherited from popular song and stage. When *Abie's Irish Rose* found its way to the screen, it was simply exploiting the success of Anne Nichols' long-running stage play of the same name (first performed in 1922). Indeed so ubiquitous were comic figures of the Jew and the Irishman that when Nichols attempted to sue Universal Studios for plagiarism on foot of their release of *The Cohens and the Kellys* (Harry Pollard, US, 1926), the Judge dismissed the case on the grounds that these characters had been in the public domain for decades. Irish themes were generally popular in this era to the extent that films such as *The Little Irish Girl* (Roy Del Ruth, US, 1926) were made that had no apparent Irish content other than the title (Dooley, 1957: 213–14).

By the 1930s, levels of immigration had substantially decreased and this phase of filmmaking was over. Narratives of the trauma of arrival are replaced by stories that assume a relatively high degree of assimilation. Increasingly, although with some notable instances of backsliding, the atavistic portrait of the Irish was replaced by one that emphasised their social agency. As *Variety* commented:

> Plenty of producers have made the mistake of including pigs for background in plays and films concerning Ireland. There is no sorer spot with the race than association with porkers. Rowdiness, uncouth manners, drunkenness, etc., have all had their part in aggravating Irish audiences.
> (review of *The Luck of the Irish*, 20 January 1937: 15)

The influence of pressure groups such as the Ancient Order of Hibernians (AOH) and the Knights of Columbanus in civic life deterred producers from replicating the stereotypical portraiture of the Irish of the early decades of the century and, in any case, the high level of integration evidenced by Irish individuals made them, in WASP eyes, models of assimilation, a perspective likewise adopted by the largely Jewish producers of Hollywood cinema.

The Irish brawler was transformed into the professional soldier (*The Fighting 69th* [William Keighley, US, 1940]); more controversially, in the cycle of Cagney films, he turned into a small-time gangster whilst his nemesis, the Irish priest, enjoyed a new visibility. Joseph Curran has argued that, 'by defending the downtrodden and outcast, while at the same time upholding the law and basic social values, the Irish priest both reflected and confirmed the public perception of the Irish as mediators between old-stock Americans and ethnic minorities' (Curran, 1989: 52). The contribution of the Irish entertainer to American culture became the subject of a number of celebratory productions including another Cagney film, Michael Curtiz's *Yankee Doodle Dandy* (US, 1942)[22] and *Irish Eyes are Smiling* (Gregory Ratoff, US, 1944).

Representations of Ireland, as we have seen, in the period between Independence and the Second World War threw up a diversity of images and narratives. If indigenous filmmaking seems more easily identified as a national cinema by virtue of its popularity at home and its restriction to that home audience, it certainly did not amount to anything approaching an industry. Still, the critical and commercial success of the few films made in Ireland, however primitive they were, suggest that they gave people a picture of local Irish life that they could relate to. They appealed to the specific and the personal, and with their use of regional accents, literally spoke in a manner that directly addressed local audiences. Those working from within the industries of other countries, such as Brian Desmond Hurst, had to contend with the conflicting expectations of Irish and non-Irish audiences. Yet, popular British and American cinema of this period produced a panoply of representations of Ireland and the Irish that described and responded to the wider Irish immigrant community. As Ireland gradually moved out of its self-imposed cultural and economic isolation, it became increasingly important, as the next chapter will chronicle, to develop an infrastructure, if not an industry, that would facilitate Irish filmmakers to tell stories and produce narratives of life 'at home' that were of a comparable standard.

4

NEGOTIATING
MODERNISATION

From the Second World War to the 1960s:
the beginnings of an industry and the
influence of John Ford

The swift modernisation experienced by the European nations, the United
States and the Japanese in the wake of the Second World War largely passed
Ireland by. Although the country received some Marshall Aid, the continued
dominance of the inward-looking, regressive alliance of Church and State
delayed its abandonment of fiscal and cultural protectionism until the end of
the 1950s. Emigration ensured that energy and ambition were rewarded
with a ticket to America, Australia or Great Britain.

Since Independence, rumours of the investment in and even public
commitment to an Irish film industry had surfaced with regularity. In
most cases these involved individuals with alleged financial backing; occasionally it was suggested that the government was behind the scheme.
Certainly as time passed, official attitudes towards the establishment of a
national industry seemed to have gradually shifted from outright rejection
of the concept to an acceptance that this was one way of counteracting
damaging foreign influences imported from outside. As Fr Devane, one of
the most officious spokespersons of the Catholic Church with regard to
the cinema expressed it:

> The cinemas are the secondary or continuation schools – the uni-
> versities in which our youth complete their education and acquire an
> up-to-date knowledge of the world and life as it is lived by the
> modern neo-pagans. ... Will their impressionable minds be any
> more able to resist the seductive lessons of the screen than African
> primitives armed with bows and arrows can oppose a modern
> mechanised army with aeroplanes and tanks?
>
> (1942: 4)

The other safeguard remained censorship and that continued to dictate
what people watched well into the 1960s.

During the war film production was largely limited to the activities of the Irish Film Society, which made a series of short films including *Mannon's Acre* (Peter Sherry, 1944). The Department of Defence produced a series of army recruiting shorts that were included in the Irish edition of Movietone News (O'Flynn, 1996: 60), suggesting a certain level of military preparedness. The Film Society had already sponsored the production of the experimental *Foolsmate* (Brendan Stafford, 1940) and the following year established its own School of Film Technique. The Society published the magazine *Scannán* and its members met regularly to watch foreign language and experimental films. Over the next few decades, this was to provide a forum for intellectual debate that attracted academics, professionals and film devotees from across the country.[1] Also in 1941 the first indigenous fan magazine for cinemagoers, *The Screen*, was launched and, whilst its primary concern was reviewing films and purveying Hollywood gossip, it also allocated regular space to Irish film news.

In 1944 a resolution advocating a national film industry was passed at the Fianna Fáil annual conference on the basis that an industry entirely controlled by outsiders was an enemy of the national culture. In 1945 the government made an initial grant of £2,000, with provision for annual funding thereafter, to the newly founded National Film Institute, run by lay people on behalf of the Catholic hierarchy. This funding was to go towards the cost of producing films for government departments and acquiring educational films in the Irish language. Paradoxically, much of the credit for the emergence of a film culture in Ireland during this period must go the educated, often middle-class clergy. In the pages of *The Furrow*, Fr Kelly's film criticism was required reading for anyone with an interest that went beyond plot and stars, whilst the Institute was responsible for a number of publications for its members, for running training courses and for showing educational films in schools. Priests had the time and the resources to make amateur films of all aspects of Irish rural and urban life to which their clerical collar guaranteed them privileged access. These films now constitute a remarkable, in many cases unique record in moving images of Irish life in the mid-century.[2] One particularly enterprising priest, Fr Turloc O'Reilly, was responsible for making a fiction film, *Mulligan's Millions*, in 1963 with members of the local Cavan community. A comedy involving a Nazi saboteur, a local tramp and the discovery by the hapless Mulligan (Mel Doherty) of the fraudulent millions, the film was shot in sound and colour and used as a fund-raiser for the Cavan boy scouts.[3]

The first of the productions funded by the National Film Institute, *A Nation Once Again* (Brendan Stafford, 1946) seemed a vindication of the State's new and limited engagement in filmmaking. Even the title of this short documentary is affirmative, celebrating as it does the notion of a return to statehood after many centuries of colonisation. The film charts the career and dramatises the writings of Thomas Davis one hundred years after his death, inviting the viewer to see them as stages in a revolutionary tradition that was to lead directly from Wolfe Tone, through Padraig Pearse to the incumbent regime. Davis is positioned as the harbinger of independence, the ideologue of economic self-sufficiency and the inspiration for cultural nationalism. 'History has vindicated Davis', the voice-over declaims, 'His wild dreams have become hard realities.'

A Nation Once Again is a classic instance of the use of history as a legitimating discourse. As the camera pans across an Ireland of gleaming new schools and industrial buildings, the voice-over reads aloud passages from the writings of Thomas Davis that foreshadow every development. The suggestion is further made that such advances have occurred as a consequence of official intervention at policy level. Where the film is interesting is in the manner it chooses to represent Ireland and its aspirations at that particular moment in time. Not surprisingly, it lingers on its youthful population, including shots of children flicking through books in a bookshop and at their desks. It also pays the kind of lip service that the various regimes had adopted towards the learning of the Irish language that the English-speaking voice-over celebrates. Perhaps a little more surprising is the positioning of Eire as outward looking and part of a European intellectual tradition. Much is made of the newly constructed Dublin airport, rightly indeed, as the Terminal Building (designed by Desmond FitzGerald) was one of the earliest examples of modern architecture in the country. It is, we are told, 'the symbol of the new Ireland' and gateway to the wider world. In an earlier shot, passages from Davis' journal, *The Nation*, are highlighted. One of these reads: 'Every great European race has sent its stream to the river of Irish mind [*sic*].' This clearly reflects Davis' own ambitions to be part of the cultural and revolutionary tradition of mainland Europe but suggests a desire to overturn Ireland's self-imposed isolation and to re-insert the State into a wider European framework in the wake of the Second World War. Rural Ireland is drawn into a discourse of modernisation with footage of turf (peat) burning power stations and gleaming new hydro-electric power plants arising out of the natural landscape. The film also celebrates Ireland's military tradition and includes several sequences of soldiers drilling, yet it discreetly fudges the objective of such a display of force, merely suggesting that 'we' look forward to the realisation of a complete nation. The existence of Northern Ireland otherwise does not figure and the narration glosses over the awkward fact of Davis' Protestantism.

Given its provenance, Stafford's film may be taken to speak on behalf of an official re-casting of the national self-image that allows for a movement towards modernisation on the understanding that this will arise out of indigenous conditions. De Valera is cast as a kindly father figure to this new Ireland, reading in his precise, scholarly manner into the microphone whilst a mother and her children gather around the wireless listening to his words. Modernisation is thus cast as a conduit for the traditional, just as film itself has been harnessed to the discourse of hegemony.

Kieran Hickey has argued that the value of this and similar films made by a small pool of production personnel was that their inclusion of dramatic reconstructions provided crew and actors with their only opportunity to practise fiction filmmaking techniques (*Short Story – Irish Cinema* [documentary], 1986). As the Film Institute and various government departments produced a steady flow of short, educational films on issues such as road safety (*Next Please* [William Moylan, 1948]), food hygiene (*Everybody's Business* [Gerard Healy, 1951]), immunisation (*Stop Thief!* [Gerard Healy, 1953]) so the technical quality of the dramatic enactments of the central propagandist/educational message improved. Many of the makers of these documentaries and instructional films, including Liam O'Leary and Colm Ó Laoghaire, were members of the Film Society and attempted to adapt the techniques of the filmmakers they had admired to their own use. As one review of Ó Laoghaire's 1960 short film enthused:

> *Our Neighbour's Children* is a success simply because it was made strictly according to Pudovkin. It is not, like most documentaries made everywhere, a lantern lecture with a recorded commentary. This Ó Laoghaire film is conceived as a whole. The pictures mean nothing until they are put together. For me the high moment of the film was a simple shot showing a shop counter with some jars of bullseyes and sixpenny hair-clips. This shot had meaning only because it was spliced in after a close-up of a little crippled girl. The jars of sweets and the trinkets were (for us, more than for her) a symbol of the ordinary everyday pleasures in which she was being taught to participate.
>
> (O'Kelly, 1960: 9)

So close was Ó Laoghaire's technique to Soviet filmmaking practices that apparently the Soviet delegation at the Cork Film Festival of 1962 expressed an interest in showing his *Water Wisdom* (1962), aimed at encouraging rural communities to launch group water schemes, in the USSR.

Hickey specifically singles out Gerard Healy's contribution to the art of the educational film as heralding a significant filmmaking talent (although Healy died at an early age). Healy, who had a background in theatre, made films for the Department of Health under its controversial minister, Dr Noel Browne,[4] several of which contain extended dramatic sequences. In *Voyage to Recovery* (1952), for instance, a young husband discovers that he has T.B. (a disease Browne was committed to eradicating) and this allows for a pointed series of exchanges between his wife and family who have to be persuaded that this is not a matter of shame. As well as providing filmmakers with the opportunity to develop their skills, these short enactments introduced a generation of actors to the techniques of screen performance.

Not all documentaries of the 1940s, however, reflected the ideology of the State. In 1948 Liam O'Leary's *Our Country* proved that cinema screens were fertile ground for the dissemination of ideologically combative filmmaking. Made in advance of the 1948 general election for Seán McBride's radical Republican and social reform party, Clann na Poblachta, *Our Country* (1948) opens with a challenge to the viewer to consider what 'we' have achieved in 25 years. It proceeds to list the failures of that period, starting with emigration and moving on to rural deprivation and the low marriage rate. Shots of the Dublin slums are followed by a vision of consumer goods which, the voice-over points out, are unavailable to most. 'What is wrong with Ireland?' we are asked as scenes of this 'bleak, bare land' appear on screen.

The answer clearly was Fianna Fáil and, in due course, they briefly fell from power. *Our Country* enjoyed wide exposure to the public in advance of the election – cinema owners showed the film willingly as the current government was threatening to raise the tax on cinema-going (*Short Story – Irish Cinema*, 1986). The fact of its making alone was a recognition of the power of the screen image, as conversely was the response of Clann na Poblachta and O'Leary's opponents who accused the film of everything from communist sympathies to IRA funding (Rockett, 1987: 77–80). O'Leary himself made a number of safety films (*Mr. Careless Goes to Town* [1949], *Safe Cycling* [1949]) for the new government; if they lacked the confrontational approach of *Our Country*, they are distinguishable for their ironic sense of humour.

In 1944, a writer in *Sight and Sound* ventured the opinion that:

> It would appear that the documentary film – which necessitates a cold, reasoned survey of facts, a mind which will not be swayed one way or the other by emotionalism; and a firm grasp of the dialectical method – is not a type of film which comes naturally to Irish film makers. The Irish temperament is too volatile and does not take kindly to purely objective reasoning.[5]
>
> (Sherry, 1944: 72)

The body of documentary work that had amassed by the end of the 1950s suggested that, as Kieran Hickey puts it, 'Ireland was at last forming a cinematic image of itself' (*Short Story – Irish Cinema*, 1986) and that the filmmakers responsible for these short productions had a very specific engagement with Irish culture that was, indeed, neither cold nor reasoned. The films that emerge from this movement tend to be either fervently patriotic or gently humorous.

The popular success of what may be considered the crowning glory of the Irish documentary film movement in the post-war period, George Morrison's *Mise Éire* (*I Am Ireland*) (1959) and *Saoirse?* (*Freedom?*) (1961), indicates that the heroic-nationalistic idiom still carried substantial appeal. This was particularly the case in 1959, though the relative failure of the later *Saoirse?* suggests that by the early 1960s the moment was passing.

Gael-Linn, the body responsible for commissioning Morrison to make these films, had been established in 1953 to propagate Irish language speaking through the media. In 1956 they launched Ireland's first Irish-language newsreel *Amharc Éireann* (*A View of Ireland*) produced by Colm Ó Laoghaire. This was to become Ireland's longest-running newsreel service, only ending when television took over the role of news delivery (O'Flynn, 1996: 61–2). Both Morrison's films had the ostensible objective of promoting the use of Irish. In fact, as Harvey O'Brien has argued, their ideological trajectory seems to have been to create a celluloid monument to romantic nationalism (2000: 335–45). Morrison assembled his films from newsreels of the formative events of independence and juxtaposed these with stills taken from newspaper headlines; the images were accompanied by an explanatory disquisition in Irish and scored by the celebrated Irish composer, Seán Ó'Riada, in what was to become one of his best-known compositions. No English-language version was to be produced, nor were the films to be subtitled. *Mise Éire* commences with illustrations of evictions, locating the beginnings of revolution in peasant grievances. It proceeds to link, as did *Ireland A Nation*, the writer W.B. Yeats to nationalist history by including him in the flow of images that create their own narrative of progression. This proceeds through the events of 1916 (using much of the footage discussed in Chapter 2) to the final triumph of freedom (Sinn Féin's election victory of 1918) at which point the second film takes over. Even nature is drafted into the history lesson with *Mise Éire's* opening shots lingering on the incoming tide washing over footprints on the sand – 'erasing the stain of colonial occupation' (O'Brien, 2000: 337). The finished film was a triumph of vision and ideology even if it was not quite the innovatory piece of art its makers claimed it to be (ibid.: 339–40).

Mise Éire was shown at the 1959 Cork Film Festival and received its public premiere in the Gaeltacht (Irish-speaking) town of Gweedore in County Donegal. It proceeded to take the Irish press by storm, garnering ecstatic reviews, even in the anglophile *Irish Times*, whilst filling cinemas. The fact that a number of these press reviews describe the events of *Mise Éire* as the 'birth of the nation' suggests a confidence that, like D.W. Griffith's *Birth of a Nation,* this film would provide a template for the new cinematic nation as well as eulogising the construction of the current civil entity. It was:

> History at a glance, the story of Ireland's sorrows and heartbreaks, the story of the heroism and martyrdom of her sons. The story of the momentous years of her greatness in defeat, of her years following 1916 ... It is the most extensive pictorial history ever made in any part of the world.
>
> (*The Cork Examiner*, 1 October 1959: 12)

Morrison's achievement was to create a visual history of events that had been primarily the preserve of the oral and the literary. Whether *Mise Éire* succeeded in establishing the Irish language as the language of the revolution is another matter; the film's interspersal of newspaper headlines in English certainly militates against its coherence as a work of art in Irish whilst offering non-Irish speakers a tacit clue as to its content. This was, however, not enough for the members of the Belfast City Council who, on first viewing, decided to ban Morrison's film on the basis that they could not under-stand it. Conceding that Morrison's visuals were sympathetic to the history of unionism in so far as they included scenes of Carson and the Ulster volunteers and the Irish fighting on the side of the Allies in the First World War, the members were suspicious of what might be contained in the commentary. On being supplied with an English-language translation, the matter was put to the vote and the film was passed for viewing.

If *Mise Éire* was the apogee of the heroic-nationalist phase of documentary filmmaking, the movement continued to attract practitioners concerned with the construction of an indigenous cinematic view of Ireland. One of the most distinctive of these was Patrick Carey. Carey's background in fine arts led him to express a vision of Ireland that was deeply painterly and but also indebted to a visual tradition of pastoralism. Carey refined the poetic qualities of the documentary movement with his studies of Irish nature in films such as *Yeats' Country* (1965), *Oisin* (1970), and *Errigal* (1970), the first two being nominated for Academy Awards. His Ireland was one untouched by modernisation and infused with a sense of natural majesty that was itself credited as the wellspring of creativity. Although his work was appropriated for the burgeoning tourist industry, Carey's aesthetic was far removed from the bucolic version of Irish identity espoused by so many of the tourist films (O'Brien, 2002) and indebted to Ford's *The Quiet Man* (Gibbons, 2002: 91–7).

Whether as a prototype or a point of departure for counter representa-tions, John Ford's best-known Irish film has come to dominate cinematic depictions of Ireland. Ford was born Sean Aloysius O'Feeney on 1 February 1895 at Portland, Maine, USA. He was the youngest of six children to survive infancy and both his parents were immigrants from Galway. In his father's saloons, in his family home and on trips back to Ireland, he learned to speak Irish and became familiar with the myths, songs and history of romantic nationalism. These influences inform many of Ford's films, irrupt-ing into his narratives via his medley of Irish characters.

One of the greatest American film directors of his generation, Ford always embraced an image of himself as 'outsider'. In later life he spoke of his sense of relatedness to the various 'Indian' nations: 'Who better than an Irishman could understand the Indians, while still being stirred by the tales of the U.S. Cavalry? We were on both sides of the epic' (Gallagher, 1986: 341). This concept structures the first of the 'cavalry trilogy' films, *Fort Apache* (USA, 1948) where it is articulated through the fraught relationship between upright Easterner, Colonel Thursday (Henry Fonda), and Lt O'Rourke (John Agar) who has fallen in love with the colonel's daughter. The young officer is apparently a fully assimilated Irish-American and much is made of his having attended Westpoint. Yet for Thursday, O'Rourke is not good enough to marry Philadelphia (Shirley Temple).[6] In a telling scene, Thursday berates O'Rourke for taking his daughter riding whilst commend-ing him for a reconnaissance report that shows a particular (read Irish) understanding of the 'Indians'.

Throughout the cavalry trilogy, it is through the Irish characters that humour is expressed, often via the shambolic drunk Sgt Quincannon (Victor McLaglen). As the representative of an earlier generation of Irish-Americans, Quincannon incarnates the older ways that will be replaced by the younger generation's assimilated sensibilities. The bar-room brawl initiated by him in *She Wore A Yellow Ribbon* (John Ford, USA, 1949) prefigures *The Quiet Man* not only in content but in its shared musical motif. In Ford's world, Irishness betokens communality, the shared pleasures of a singsong or a virile punch-up; it is also the antidote to effete WASP mores. His Irish-set films foreground such characters, creating narratives around them that tend either towards the dark and the violent (such as *The Informer*) or the idyllic, of which *The Quiet Man* is the most artistically successful and the best known.

In 1952, Ford came to Ireland to make *The Quiet Man*, a pet project that had been long in the planning. Ford called it his first love story though it is more accurate to consider it the first film to foreground the love affair between two ostensibly incompatible personalities. In this case, they are the eponymous quiet man, Sean Thornton (John Wayne) and Mary-Kate Danaher (Maureen O'Hara). This coupling constitutes one of the first *mise en abîmes* of a film that is much discussed for its overt 'constructedness'. As McLoone phrases it, 'it is the one film in Ford's work that carries on a dialogue with his own narrative structures – a contrast between illusion and reality and a discourse on the illusion of illusion' (2000: 53). Wayne and O'Hara had starred as the estranged husband and wife of *Rio Grande* (John Ford, USA, 1950) who must overcome a traumatic event in the past (his burning of her Irish-American family estate) in order to be reunited at the film's end. In the earlier film, Wayne plays the classic outsider hero, 'a lonely man' as his wife puts it, 'a great soldier' according to his son. Ford reunited the two actors in a plot that would draw the Wayne character from the outside in, something that he can only achieve once he puts his scarred past behind him. Honour, sacrifice, regret, the violent rituals of masculinity and the redemptive love of a strong woman make one film the echo of the other. Again, song, in this case the ballad, *I'll take you home again, Kathleen*, and shared musical motifs link both works.

The Quiet Man has exercised Irish scholars considerably over the years. Anthony Slide remarks that Ford's vision of Ireland was 'that of a poet, but a decidedly second-rate poet, whose view was often patronizing and boorish' (1988: 79). A decade or so later, James MacKillop can confess that 'the film is not the piece of trash that I myself thought it was in the years I avoided seeing it out of expected embarrassment' (1999: 179). At one level, it is easy to dismiss it as sentimental farce and the opinion that it represents the worst excesses of an American fantasy of Ireland and the Irish remains current. Certainly, its Technicolor vision of a land of rosy-cheeked colleens, leprechaun-like intercessionaries and humane clergy united by song, drink and public brawling had little in common with the Ireland of the 1920s in which it is ostensibly set. On the other hand, the film lends itself readily to readings that affirm Ford's playful acknowledgement of his fictionalising. In *Cinema and Ireland*, Luke Gibbons cogently argued that the early sequence in which Sean Thornton pauses on a bridge to exclaim at his first view of White O'Morn, the cottage of his birth, is signalled as artifice through the use of a backdrop (1987: 225). Other such instances abound, the 'leprechaun' Michaeleen Óg's (Barry Fitzgerald) humming of a tune that has appeared on the soundtrack, the accordion player's performance of what had seemed to be diegetic music outside Cohan's pub, the villager posing within the picture frame as Mary-Kate's possessions are unloaded in front of her new home. We may go right back to the opening moments of the film where darkness falls over the outline of Ashford Castle and wonder if it is indeed all a dream. All these effects suggest that as much as Ford was constructing a 'mirage' (in Michaeleen Óg's words), he was also signalling to his viewers that this film should not be mistaken for reality. Manny Farber, in an otherwise mordant deconstruction of Ford's film, suggested that, 'a dense, gray atmosphere takes most of the hue and intensity out of the scene and makes for a curious picture that takes place in daylight yet has some of the sunless, remembered look of a surrealist painting' (1971: 109).

'Is that real? She couldn't be!', Thornton famously exclaims, glimpsing Mary-Kate Danaher (Maureen O'Hara) framed as a Dresden maiden herding her sheep through the fields, red locks flowing, her Irish colouring highlighted. She is another fantasy, the archetypal feisty colleen, lover and homemaker, the bearer of tradition. The film's exilic elision of mother, lover and land in this opening scene follows Sean's musings aloud with Michaeleen Óg over his own mother's life in White O'Morn, the idealised cottage in which he proceeds to install Mary-Kate. If further evidence is needed of Mary-Kate's rootedness in convention, it comes with the sequence inside her family home as she storms round the dinner table serving and scolding her brother, Red Will (Victor McLaglen) and the other men. Furthermore, Mary-Kate is visually associated with superstition and the irrational, specifically by way of the night-time scene in White O'Morn where she flits through the interior like an embodied spirit, shrieking when she catches sight of herself in the mirror. Yet, she is also, the film suggests, the emblem of a conventional society and so when she utters the ultimatum that marks the crux of her relationship with Thornton, that she will not share the marital bed with him until he has extracted her possessions and dowry from Red Will, she is simply demanding that he surrender himself to the conditions that guarantee the stability of the community which he so much wants to be part of.

Although this kind of characterisation, the suggestion that she is the shrew that convention demands must be tamed, is highly problematic, the film has come to be considered a triumph of feminine will over patriarchal authority. Janey Place reminds us that Thornton's failure is to respect her [Mary-Kate] as a person with a traditional past she needs just as he needs his. Without her furniture and dowry, she tells him, she will be a wife in name only, but really a servant as she has always been.

(1979: 199)

This is the economic base of the community and one that Thornton must heed if he is to realise his dream of joining it. Taking this one step further, Brandon French considers Mary-Kate's stance to be a progressive one in so far as she refuses to submit to her husband's demands. Emblematic in this sense is her gesture of tossing aside the stick 'to beat the lovely lady' which an older woman in the community hands Sean as he drags his recalcitrant wife off the train (French, 1978: 17–18).

The cathartic 'donnybrook' between Thornton and Red Will brings the inhabitants of Innisfree and the neighbouring villages out to watch and bet on the outcome. This is a quintessential Fordian expression of the pleasures of male physicality played as communal spectacle. As Luke Gibbons suggests, it allows Mary-Kate her honour and finally permits Sean Thornton to work through the moment he killed a man in the boxing ring, marking the film as a part of a cycle of 'therapeutic narratives' in which a visit to Ireland enables a troubled protagonist to put their past behind them (Gibbons, 2002: 97).

Figure 4.1 The Quiet Man (l-r): John Wayne (Sean Thornton), Barry Fitzgerald (Michaeleen Og Flynn), Maureen O'Hara (Kate Danaher) location shot. Courtesy of the Irish Film Institute of Ireland and The Connacht Tribune.

A number of critics (Lourdeaux, 1990; Giles, 1991) have detected in Ford's films, particularly in respect of their love of communality and their themes of sin and redemption, a strong indebtedness to the tenets and iconography of Catholicism. We may see these expressed most unambiguously in *The Informer* but they are also central to *The Quiet Man*. At the same time, part of the film's idealised vision of Ireland is created through its depiction of the homely figure of the Protestant Reverend Playfair (Arthur Shields) and his centrality to both the narrative and the lives of the Catholic villagers. It is he who explains Mary-Kate's principles to Thornton and he again is the only one to place the incomer as 'Trooper Thorn' with a past that he now wants to hide. In the closing sequences of the film, we witness the final deception as the villagers and their priest, Fr Lonegan (Ward Bond) pose as Protestants so that the visiting Bishop may leave with the impression of a thriving parish.

Luke Gibbons has drawn our attention to the manner in which the images from the film were incorporated into Irish tourist literature of the 1950s onwards and resurfaced in a number of minor films (2002: 91–9). Indeed *The Quiet Man* has evolved into a cinematic ur-text. It is quoted with some glee in the early sequences of *E.T.* (Steven Spielberg, 1982). Its premise is echoed and inverted in Jim Sheridan's *The Field* (GB, 1990) with the returning Yank (Tom Berenger) transformed into an unwanted harbinger of modernisation. In this version, the widow may wish to sell him her land but the community closes ranks against her. The priest no longer is the locus of moral authority and the violence of the overbearing patriarch leads only to murder. The feisty colleen is a landless tinker (Traveller), the cottage home to a family tainted by suicide, where husband and wife no longer speak to each other (Barton, 2002: 39–61). Sheridan has referred to Ford's Ireland as an 'incest culture' (ibid.: 151) and this is the way it has since been depicted in a series of films that rework this seminal imagery, notably Bob Quinn's *Poitín* (Ireland, 1978).

On its release, *The Quiet Man* received seven Academy Award nominations, winning in two categories – 'Best Director' and 'Best Colour Cinematography'. Reviewers from outside Ireland received it warmly with the main American trade paper affirming that it was 'an excellent money picture' (*Variety*, 14 May 1952: 6). Local critics were inclined to take a more rueful stance towards the film:

> Maybe Ford found a leprechaun sitting on the back of his director's chair when he went to work with John Wayne, Maureen O'Hara and Victor McLaglen in County Galway, and maybe it was the leprechaun that, with impish humour, blew all his thoughts of serious film-making out over Galway Bay.
>
> (*The Irish Independent*, 9 June 1952: 6)

Another writer noted that the film divided its audiences into 'those who have laughed heartily at a clever comedy, and those who came away aggrieved because it paints a grotesque picture of Irish rural life' (*Dublin Evening Mail*, 9 June 1952: 6)

Modernisation is generally assumed to have been initiated in Irish political discourse with the publication by the Department of Finance under its new secretary T.K. Whitaker of the economic study, *Economic Development*, in 1958. This advocated investment in industry with, if the need arose, foreign capital, an about-face in a country so long associated with cultural and economic isolationism. As our discussion of the documentaries has illustrated, in fact Ireland was gradually modernising in the late 1940s and through the 1950s.

Eventually, in 1957, the first signs emerged that Ireland was in a position to sustain if not an industry, at least a regular output of films. In that year, a new company entitled Ardmore Studios was formed in Dublin to make television films for British and American markets. The two main figures behind this project were Louis Elliman, one of the key figures in Irish exhibition, and Emmet Dalton who were also behind another recently formed company, Dublin Film and Television Productions Ltd. Their proposal was to make, in conjunction with RKO Teleradio Inc. of New York, a series of films with the Abbey Players based on successful Abbey Theatre productions. A site was earmarked for a proposed studio near Bray in County Wicklow, just outside Dublin. In addition to filling the new requirements of US television time, the films would have the added advantage of qualifying as quota films under the British regulations, ensuring them at least second billing in British cinemas. Shortly afterwards, another company was formed involving John Ford and Lord Killanin, Four Provinces Productions, that also targeted Abbey Theatre productions and the Abbey Players for future films.

Elliman and Dalton were largely instrumental in the construction of Ardmore Studios which were opened by the then Minister for Industry and Commerce, Sean Lemass, in 1958. As well as hosting the production of Elliman and Dalton's films, the studios became widely used by British and American filmmakers as a facility. Their location in highly scenic countryside was an added bonus for crews engaged in outdoor shooting whilst their proximity to Dublin reduced travel and overnight costs. Kevin Rockett has argued that the tendency of such outside production companies to use British union personnel meant that ultimately the studios functioned as little more than an outpost of the British film industry and little benefit accrued from them in terms of training and employing Irish crews. Despite government subvention, financial problems beset the venture and the studios lurched in and out of receivership over the next few decades (Rockett, 1987: 98–103). In its early days, Ardmore ran into trouble with the British Electrical Trades Union (ETU) when it was discovered that members of the Irish union were working on British productions and the dispute escalated to such a pitch that it was feared that the studios would have to close. The very existence of a facility located in Ireland was viewed with some suspicion within the British trade, which feared that Ardmore would lure indigenous productions away from the UK. That films made in Ardmore were eligible for the Quota, notwithstanding the fact that Ireland was not part of the Commonwealth, increased their anxieties. Initially, however, these problems were not apparent and soon after they were opened, Dalton's project was blessed with the arrival for studio and location shooting of the Anglo-American IRA thriller, *Shake Hands With the Devil.*

The first film produced by Dublin Film and Television Productions Ltd. was actually made in Britain, chiefly by British personnel, although featuring the Abbey Players and based on an Abbey stage play. *Professor Tim* (Henry Cass, Ireland, 1957) was a whimsical comedy very much in the stage-Irish tradition. This reliance on material that originated in stage performances is the most notable aspect of the rash of films made in the late 1950s and early 1960s. In fact, the Abbey Players had, as we have seen and for obvious reasons, been associated with the making of Irish films since the early days of silent cinema. This crossover between stage and screen acted as a guarantor of respectability in a business notoriously shy of its own somewhat downmarket image. Stage actors were also assumed to have the necessary expertise to appear on films and, furthermore, the Abbey was specifically associated with the formation of a separate Irish cultural national identity. Still, Dalton and Elliman played it safe by hiring non-Irish directors and a number of well-known British and American lead players for their films.

John Ford had always drawn on the Abbey Players for his films and many of them were introduced to Hollywood cinema as a consequence of taking part in films from *The Informer* onwards.[7] From the point of view of the Abbey management, cinema was a necessary evil that would go some way at least towards alleviating the massive financial problems it faced in the post-war period. The disadvantage to this alliance was that in the 1940s the Abbey was widely criticised for its unadventurous artistic policies and the 'Abbey Play' was regarded less as defining new artistic directions than the opposite, as being trapped in an outmoded concept of performance and relying on dated texts. The films reflect many of the drawbacks as well as the benefits of their association with the Abbey and in this we need to include Ford's own *The Rising of the Moon*[8] (Ireland, 1957) made by Four Provinces Productions.[9]

The Rising of the Moon is constructed around three unrelated stories, introduced and linked by Irish-American actor, Tyrone Power. The first, 'The Majesty of the Law' is based on a short story of the same name by Frank O'Connor; the second, 'A Minute's Wait' on a one-act comedy by Martin J. McHugh first performed in the Abbey; and the third, '1921' is a much bowdlerised version of Lady Gregory's play, *The Rising of the Moon.* The introduction makes explicit a trope inherent in Irish fictions since the early nineteenth century (Leerssen, 1996b: 33) of explaining 'ourselves' to 'others'. Addressing his assumed American audience, Power assures the viewer that this is just how life in Ireland is lived, rendering the country at once a fiction and a reality. The two first episodes derive their humour from their relentless parade of Irish stereotypes and situations. If 'A Minute's

Wait' visually recalls the opening sequences of *The Quiet Man* as a train draws into a station past a whitewashed cottage whilst a pony and trap veer off on another journey, it shows little of its predecessor's propensity for ironic deflation. The final story weaves the Abbey Players into the great nationalist adventure (as it so often occurs in Ford's cinema) by having them shelter and help escape an IRA prisoner on the run.

Following its release, Limerick County Council condemned *The Rising of the Moon* as a 'vile production and a travesty of the Irish people' and 'requested the Irish Justice Minister to contact all countries with which the Republic had diplomatic relations to demand that the film be withdrawn from circulation' (Slide, 1988: 83).[10] The reviewer in the *Evening Herald* considered that Ford and Killanin's film 'parades about every theatrical and cinematic cliché and absurdity – in both dialogue and action – that has ever been perpetuated against the country, omitting only the proverbial pig in the parlour' (*Evening Herald*, 1 June 1957: 4).

Faced with the ubiquity of a cultural stereotype that may have been irksome but that still enjoyed some potency outside the country (and even possibly within) and committed to an ailing theatrical tradition, Dalton and Elliman's task of establishing an indigenous Irish industry that would appeal to the crucial audiences of the United States and Great Britain was never going to be a straightforward one. In addition, they lacked the film-making expertise that Ford had at least been able to apply to *The Rising of the Moon*.

As a group, or at least those that can be viewed, the films tend towards static camerawork and a proliferation of interiors. They are dialogue-heavy and boast little in the way of dramatic action. Their settings tend to be modest, taking place in small villages and featuring stock characters such as the nefarious gombeen man (profiteer), the garrulous bar keeper, the fiery young colleen and the youth with ambitions to escape it all. In two, *The Big Birthday* (George Pollock, Ireland, 1959) and *This Other Eden* (Muriel Box, Ireland, 1959) modernity enters the village with the arrival of an English visitor, an event that throws the community into disarray in various ways. Both these films reverse the premise from which cultural nationalism drew much of its rhetorical energy, namely that such an intrusion would contaminate the lives of the simple-but-happy Irish, viewing in both cases the symbolic Englishman as a welcome harbinger of changes to come. This conciliatory, even warm attitude towards the English may be reflective of the initial audiences for the stage-plays, in essence the urban, Dublin middle-classes. This is also apparent in the manner that the films distance themselves from their working-class characters who tend to be objects rather than subjects of the dramas.

In their favour, two at least of the films did address issues of Irish identity with some considerable acuity. *Home is the Hero* (J. Fielder Cook, Ireland, 1959) was an adaptation of Walter Macken's play by the same name. Macken had already taken the lead role in the Abbey production and reprised it for the film. His performance came in for some considerable praise in local press reviews and it is this that gives the film its sense of self-willed tragedy whilst permitting it to end on the suggestion of a better future for its protagonists. Macken is Paddo, a man of fists who fights for the entertainment of the drinkers in his local bar. When he accidentally kills the somewhat pedantic Mr Green (Patrick Layde) he is jailed and his family rendered near destitute. On his return from prison, he finds himself hailed as a hero by his former drinkers whilst at home his son, Willie (Arthur Kennedy)[11] has overcome a disability incurred by his father's rough handling of him as a child and is providing for the family. Willy is planning to marry Green's daughter whilst his sister, Daylia (Eileen Crowe) is seeing a local figure of some disrepute, the bookie, Manchester Monaghan (Michael Hennessy). Paddo's wife has taken lodgers and started drinking. Paddo seeks to reimpose his authority on the household and reverse the events that have taken place since his incarceration but, at the end of the film, it seems that Willie's reason may outplay Paddo's bruised patriarchal sensibilities.

Home is the Hero carefully deconstructs the Fordian cinematic male as well as recalling a history of the stereotype of 'Paddy' the fighting Irishman. It locates Paddo's public displays of brawling and brute force within an archaic male drinking culture. Macken as Paddo appears a lost figure, bewildered by the changes that have taken place whilst he was in jail and, at some level, motivated by the belief that a reversion to the old order would be in the best interests of all those whom he loves. The community emerges with little glory, quick to ostracise Paddo's children and suspicious of its one representative who grasps the opportunities of the market economy, Monaghan, the bookie. That change is possible is suggested by Willy's intervention in his father's actions, though the manner in which he achieves this is dependent on an act of duplicity and the film leaves the future of its protagonists open.

The other interesting work to emerge out of the Ardmore productions is again valuable more for its source material than its manner of execution. *This Other Eden* is, on the surface, a conventional narrative of an Englishman who finds himself in a small Irish community that alternatively enchants and baffles him. There he falls in love with a young Irish woman who must be persuaded to reciprocate his affections.

If this plot device bears overtones of *The Quiet Man*, it is also a trope that has recurred throughout Irish and British fictions. The 'National Romance' has tended to be expressed according to historical circumstances as well as commercial expediency. From the Irish point of view, Anglo-Saxon aggression of the seventeenth century onwards was consistently allegorised in terms of the rape of a feminised Ireland by the male colonial aggressor. It is generally considered that this mode of representation came to a close in the wake of the Act of Union of 1800 when a new emphasis on compatibility emerged. Cullingford locates an early instance of this ideology of conciliation in Sydney Owenson's widely read novel *The Wild Irish Girl* (1806), in which the callow young Englishman Horatio is educated out of his anti-Irish prejudices by the beautiful Irishwoman Glorvina. Their eventual union signals a new contract between Ireland and England, which is to be guaranteed by mutual affection rather than brute force.

(2001: 28)

The nineteenth-century melodramas of Dion Boucicault popularised this trope further with, for instance, marriage in *The Shaughraun* (1874) between Englishman and Irishwoman representing a meeting of 'complementary equals not in colonial subordination' (Grene, 1999: 10). As both Cullingford and Grene argue, this altered perspective on the relationship between the two countries and their symbolic representatives was driven by commercial concerns as much as by political conditions. If these works were to attract English readers and audiences, they needed to offer a Utopian vision of historical enmities.

By the 1950s it was apparent that the Irish economy could be at least partially salvaged through tourism and, as we have seen, *The Quiet Man* played a strong part in influencing how Ireland was presented to the American market. British-Irish relations, already threatened by intermittent IRA bombing campaigns, had been badly damaged by Irish neutrality in the Second World War. As we have seen in the previous chapter, British cinema responded by emphasising the fundamental 'loyalty' of the Irish in films such as *Halfway House* and *Dangerous Moonlight*. In the post-war period, film-makers took a darker view of such a display of national treachery, producing a slew of films that suggested that the Irish were spying on behalf of the Germans: *Night Boat to Dublin* (Lawrence Huntington, GB, 1946), *I See A Dark Stranger* (Frank Launder, GB, 1948), *The Man Who Never Was* (Ronald Neame, GB, 1956). Increasingly the Irish countryside was represented as a dark, malevolent space whose depiction drew closely on the Gothic rather than the pastoral tradition of representation. Irish diabolism and irrationality reached their discursive apogee in Lance Comfort's *Daughter of Darkness* (GB, 1948). In this reversal of the conventions of the National Romance, the 'wild Irish girl', Emmy (Siobhan McKenna) comes to Yorkshire from Ireland as a servant with a violent past (she has already maimed one man). As the sons of the farm she works on fall in love with her, so she becomes correspondingly unhinged, her excessive and frustrated sexuality expressed in the increasingly Gothic scenes of her frantic organ-playing in the family chapel. It is here, amidst high winds, that she is faced down and finally sent onto the moors to be savaged by the dog whose master she attacked in Ireland (McFarlane, 1999: 83–8).

This Other Eden's insistence that English-Irish hostilities were a matter of a small misunderstanding and proposal that the symbolic Englishman might be the illegitimate son of an Irishwoman were based, therefore, on sound cultural and financial reasoning. Such a conciliatory plot would increase tourist potential (Farley, 2001: 17) and make it more likely that the film would succeed in the British quota market for which it was eligible.

There is much more to *This Other Eden* than this. Part of the film's satirical thrust is aimed at debunking the ideologies of cultural nationalism, which by the late 1950s were nearing the end of their hold on Irish society. Instead of seeing past injustices as legitimating present grievances, the film is evidently sympathetic to its Englishman's point of view that it is Ireland's duty to forget the past and England's to remember it. Dalton himself was the subject of Civil War whisperings, being reputedly either (according to which version you chose to believe) the man who was in the car when Michael Collins was shot or the man who shot Michael Collins. In either case, the jaundiced newspaper editor and former IRA man, Devereaux (Niall MacGinnis) may well be considered Dalton's fictional alter-ego.

This Other Eden's satire works on a number of levels. One of its targets is the lip service paid by officialdom to the promotion of the Irish language. In the film, only the Englishman and the politician speak the national tongue, the former badly, the latter strategically. The pieties of small town Ireland are sent up when the statue erected to their dead hero, Carberry, turns out to be a work of modern art that utterly disgusts them and in the course of events it is further revealed that one of the younger generation is Carberry's illegitimate son.[12] At the same time, the film treats its characters with some considerable warmth, inviting its viewers to laugh with them – not at them. In this, it is noteworthy for constructing an image of Irishness that emanated from within the national culture, rather than being imposed from without, as had happened with such consistency over the last few decades.

The establishment of Ardmore Studios and the release of its first films offered the occasion for some reflection as to what should constitute an Irish national film industry. Writing in *Scannán*, Riobard Breathnach was scathing about the international address of the Ardmore/Abbey films:

> The anomalous position of an Irish film industry making films mainly for an export market parallels the exploitation of the Irish scene by writers who are either moral or physical expatriates. Such films will possess a superficial gloss which will conceal their essential lack of substance. They will shirk serious themes and concentrate on humour, burlesque, satire and so on. If they touch serious subjects, the tendency will be to generalise them, and in making them more palatable for world audiences (Anglo-American in our case) to 'render' the reality down, so that all the exploration of the craggy Irish mind and its own intense drama will cease.
>
> (1959: 4)

Only *Mise Éire* met Breathnach's essentialist standards, it being, in his opinion, a true harbinger of a really indigenous industry (ibid.). It is remarkable how little the debate (semantics apart) evolved in the years to come with issues of address and funding dominating its agenda. The editorial of the same issue touched on another topic that was to echo through discussions of an 'ideal' national cinema. Should Irish films be 'tied to the apron-strings of the Abbey and "the Troubles"'? (Editorial, 1959: 3). Was Irish cinema to be a literary cinema, feeding off the other more established and illustrious medium, and was it to be dominated by the 'national question'?

The initiatives of Dalton and Elliman petered out in the early 1960s as Ardmore increasingly became a facility house for overseas productions, and for a number of years the only Irish themes to appear on film did so courtesy of a combination of foreign directors and Irish filmmakers working out of the British and American industries. Throughout the 1960s and 1970s and into the 1980s, it seemed as if the fears of *Scannán*'s contributors were thoroughly vindicated. A plethora of 'troubles' films and literary adaptations followed the Abbey Films, many of them made for television.

After tireless lobbying by a range of interested parties including members of the Film Society and John Huston (from 1962 an Irish citizen), a committee was established in 1968 to consider the requirements of local filmmakers. Its report recommended the establishment of a Film Board, but it was not until 1981 that a Board was eventually appointed. By this stage, a new generation of independent filmmakers had emerged, funded by a medley of sources and it is to this generation and its successors that the second part of this book is devoted.

Part II

ISSUES AND DEBATES IN CONTEMPORARY IRISH CINEMA

5

IRISH INDEPENDENTS

The emergence of a critical, independent cinema in the 1970s and 1980s

The small cluster of independent filmmakers who were responsible for the first wave of indigenous films in the 1970s and 1980s was marked by a desire to deconstruct received notions of Irish images and themes as they had appeared on screen up to this point and to confront the issues that were emerging within Irish society as modernisation took increasing hold. Variously, the works of directors such as Cathal Black, Joe Comerford, Pat Murphy, Thaddeus O'Sullivan and Bob Quinn addressed questions of social exclusion, emigration, religion, memory, nationalism and feminism. Collectively, they sought to establish a new Irish cinematic idiom, to break with the dominant and exogenous tradition of romanticism and to look at Ireland from the inside out, rather than vice versa. This they achieved by positioning themselves within an international movement of avant-garde, experimental and low-budget filmmaking practices.

As noted in the previous chapter, modernisation is usually seen to coincide with the start of the 'Lemass era' and the First Programme for Economic Expansion in 1958, although it might be more accurate to see the Republic as gradually modernising throughout the 1950s. This accelerated in the 1960s, due in some part to increasing media penetration, notably the establishment of Ireland's indigenous television station, Radio Telefís Éireann (RTÉ), on New Year's Eve, 1961 (Savage, 1996). Although the sexual revolution of the 1960s largely passed Ireland by, society did undergo a period of rapid change during this and the following decade. The most marked aspect of this was the country's shift from an agrarian to an urban society. The fiftieth anniversary of the 1916 Rising was the occasion for some national introspection, 1966 being, in Fergal Tobin's words, 'a year when the idealism of the past was constantly being recalled to mind' (1984: 152). The eruption of the Troubles in Northern Ireland in 1969, meanwhile, threw the 'national question' into the open again. This in turn fuelled the revisionism controversy (pp. 222–3) as the history and orthodoxies of nationalism were reassessed.

A documentary made in 1968 was to articulate the sense of confusion and division thrown up by the competing discourses that were circulating within Irish society. Peter Lennon's *Rocky Road to Dublin* (Ireland, 1968) used the form in a manner that recalls the earlier *Our Country*. A *cause célèbre* in its day, the opening voice-over (by the director) states its intentions: 'This is a personal attempt to reconstruct with a camera the plight of an island community which survived more than 700 years of English occupation and then nearly sank under the weight of its own heroes and clergy.' There then follows a relentless exhumation of Ireland's literary, cultural, religious and historical icons, none of which meets the disaffected authorial mark.

Lennon was at the time of the film's making a journalist working with *The Guardian* and *Rocky Road to Dublin* is an essay-film influenced by the experimental work of the French New Wave, in particular of Godard. Shot by Raoul Coutard, the film is edited to stress discontinuity or to question the inevitability of historical progress, Lennon's central theme. Scenes from the traditional Anglo-Irish social event of the year, the Dublin Horse Show, collide with revellers in a pub and a lengthy debate amongst a pompous grouping of Trinity students over current affairs. Lennon interviews those whose opinions he is sympathetic with, notably author Séan Ó'Faoláin and others, such as the representative of the GAA, whose ideas are self-evidently regressive. As well as critiquing the educational system, the film is deeply sceptical of the Church, expressed in a sequence where Fr Michael Cleary (a priest since accused by his 'housekeeper' of being the father of her child) demonstrates his 'trendy' touch, drinking, smoking and jollying along hospital patients. In the final sequence a young woman recalls how she approached the priest for advice over the use of contraception when she felt that she did not want to have any more children and was told to sleep in a separate room from her husband. Her isolation is highlighted and ironically counterpointed with shots of lonely beaches, the symbol of that traditional Ireland in which she is trapped.

Lennon's film was greeted with some considerable hostility amongst the press whilst (unfounded) suggestions that it was funded by communist money did not help its cause. Despite a successful screening at the Cannes Film Festival, it received only a limited release in Dublin and has not, to date, been shown on Irish television.

The sense that politics was a corrupt affair, peopled by self-serving members of the bourgeoisie, accumulated to public life from the 1980s although the extent of this dishonesty only became fully evident in the wake of the various tribunals of the early 2000s. Both at the time and retrospectively, the figure who attracted most suspicion of sinister goings-on in high places was politician and sometime Taoiseach, Charles J. Haughey, whose exclamation that a mysterious murder case associated with the Attorney General in 1982 was 'grotesque, unbelievable, bizarre and unprecedented' led to his time in office being nicknamed the GUBU years.

Referenda over abortion and divorce, in 1983 and 1986 respectively, culminated in victory for the conservative majority but not before bitter divisions in the body politic had forced themselves into the public eye. Indeed the latter half of the twentieth century was remarkable for mobilising public debate around gender politics. These, in turn, inform the films of the period and are dealt with in greater detail in Chapter 7.

State borrowing to fund economic expansion combined with a downturn in the international economy to culminate in massive inflation in the 1970s followed by severe cuts in public spending in the 1980s. Immigration returned to bleed Irish life of its youth, notably young university graduates and professionals. Such was the sense of crisis by the mid-1980s that it seemed that the official commitment to modernisation was little better than earlier policies of economic isolation. This disenchantment seeped through into all modes of artistic expression. Another documentary, by emerging filmmaker Alan Gilsenan, gave expression to this mood. Forming an unofficially triumvirate with *Our Country* and *The Rocky Road to Dublin*, Gilsenan's *The Road to God Knows Where* (Channel 4, 1988) reflects Lennon's film not only in its choice of title but in its sense of help-lessness. Unlike Lennon, Gilsenan focuses on 'ordinary people', intersper-sing shots of a bleak, depopulated landscape with interviews where individuals reflect on the past, or discuss their experiences of emigration, and a focus on young children apparently running wild on a housing estate. One of these reads aloud the Proclamation of Independence of 1916, invit-ing the viewer to question the direction that the 'socialist' State has taken. A reference to the Pope's triumphant visit to Ireland in 1979 is counterpointed with a flashcard that in turn references the dissenting lyrics of punk band, the Boomtown Rats, 'it's a rat trap, and you've been caught'.

As Lennon did two decades earlier, and O'Leary before him, Gilsenan expresses a sense of angered disappointment, bordering on disgust, with the failure of the State to live up to the ideals of independence and the consequences of this, particularly for the children of the dispossessed work-ing classes (Gilsenan followed up this documentary with *Road II* [RTÉ 2001] though to considerably less effect).

Before proceeding further to discuss the films of the period, we need to differentiate between the independent cycle of films made from the mid 1970s through to the late 1980s (which we might conveniently bookend at each side with the release of Bob Quinn's 1975 film *Caoineadh Airt Uí Laoire* [The Lament for Art O'Leary] and Jim Sheridan's *My Left Foot* [GB, 1989]) and the later films of the Second Film Board years. The first group-ing of works has come retrospectively to be regarded as something of a golden age of Irish filmmaking, distinguished by a level of formal experi-mentation as much as by its political engagement.

Although the principal object of address of the films discussed here is an Irish audience, their productions belong within a wider movement of avant-garde and critically deconstructive filmmaking. Unlike the avant-garde movements of New York and London, however, which were based around filmmakers' co-operatives (founded in 1962 and 1966 respectively), the Irish filmmakers were not part of any official grouping, nor did they have control over distribution or exhibition of their work. Moreover, they were inevitably in competition with each other for the very limited sources of Irish finance (the Arts Council Film Script Award, launched in 1977 and, from 1981, the Irish Film Board). As a result, many of them sought British finance, primarily from the British Film Institute (BFI) Production Board, which actively supported avant-garde works, and later Channel 4 Television with its remit for minority programming. On the other hand, most of those engaged in filmmaking during these years worked on each other's films, arguably contributing to a similarity in aesthetics and style. This commitment to experimentation was not unique to Irish cinema but is also associated with other indigenous modes of contemporary artistic expression, notably theatre (Murray, 1997: 231–8). They too were being blown by the prevailing winds of historicity and the vibrancy of the theoretical movements of the 1970s – of, *inter alia*, structuralism, semiotics, Marxism and feminism.

As this moment passed, so we can detect a gradual abandonment of formal innovation (and the aesthetics of 'unpleasure') in favour of an emphasis on narrative coherence. The later films of the 1980s are more conventional in terms of filmmaking practices although they still display a higher level of stylisation than mainstream cinema in general.

Many of the films discussed here are indebted to the aesthetics of modernism, where:

> the intentionality of the artist, the supposed creator of a specific 'message', is brought into question; and the material character of the medium in use, instead of being treated as 'invisible', is given an absolutely primary value, often through the suppression of 'content' as such.
>
> (Rayns, 1977: 100)

To what extent the avant-garde ought to reflect and advocate the political concerns of the period was a question that informed much debate about these productions and, in an Irish context, is equally applied to films about the Troubles. Rayns argues that the avant-garde works which the BFI Production Board was (partly) funding were both political and aesthetic and 'There is no consensus on whether a political position should (or even can) be overt in the work' (ibid.). Peter Wollen, however, distinguished between the North American avant-garde (centred on New York) and the European avant-garde (associated primarily with Godard but also including Oshima, Straub-Huillet and others) suggesting that the former was linked to modernism and its concern with formal experimentation – 'The frontier reached by this avant-garde has been an ever-narrowing preoccupation with pure film, with film "about" film, a dissolution of signification into objecthood or tautology'(1982: 97) – whereas the latter, with its indebtedness to the cinema of Eisenstein and Brechtian theatre, was more overtly political. Crucial here was the issue of 'unpleasure', itself viewed as the desired consequence of breaking with the conventions of dominant cinema.

An example of a work that comes close to functioning as 'pure film' is *Coilin & Platonida* (GB/Germany, 1976). Made by James Scott (son of the painter William Scott) with the Berwick Street Collective, *Coilin & Platonida* is a fragmented, elliptical piece of filmmaking with little or no narrative thrust. Shot on Super-8 and blown up to 16 mm, the film is almost completely silent save for brief interludes of ballad singing (*Una Bhán*) and any narrative information that is supplied is done so with the use of intertitles. The film is an adaptation of a short story by the nineteenth-century Russian writer, L.S. Leskov, which is in turn drawn from older versions which had circulated for several centuries in Russia, but, as the *Monthly Film Bulletin* reviewer conceded, 'the [filmic] story itself has become virtually illegible, and one must consult Leskov's original in order to spell out much of the implied action' (Rosenbaum, 1976: 248). The plot, such as it is, follows the story of Coilin (Coilin O'Finneadha) who as a child was dressed as a girl and brought up in a convent where his mother was working for the nuns. After being expelled from school for 'backwardness', Coilin meets up with a 'master of all knowledge' to whom he becomes an apprentice. When his cousin, Platonida's (Frankie Allen) husband dies, she lives with her father-in-law whom she tries to kill after she finds him outside her bedroom window. Coilin is arrested and Platonida too goes to the nuns. By the end of the film she is glimpsed as a blind nun and we are told that her son has become a 'great warrior'.

The opening titles tell us that this happened 50 years ago, in a period of turmoil, therefore, in Irish society. How important this is to the working through of the film is difficult to know. Certainly the opening framed shot of a glowing red house intimates destruction; a zoom then brings us into it as if into history, or alternatively into the womb. These twin themes, of destruction and rebirth echo through the film, creating a temporal conjunction between the end of the Russian Empire and the last throes of colonial Ireland. The suggestion of a peasant society at the mercy of a more powerful merchant class is a further common link. The appropriation of the conventions of primitive filmmaking – overexposed images, no dialogue, the creation of a split-screen effect by juxtaposing and then re-shooting the original Super-8 footage on a white screen – enhances the sense of the historical at a visual level.[1] The camerawork tends to be static and although colour is employed, the palette is largely limited to reds, greens and browns. The casting of the various characters from members of the local Connemara community appears to be based on the practice of 'typage' advocated by Eisenstein as a way of escaping the inauthenticity of the professional actor in favour of non-actors who would look like the characters they were portraying. Scott makes frequent use of facial close-ups and interpolates very few scenery or even establishing shots. The elusive quality of the work as a whole – just as some kind of narrative thread seems to be discernible, it vanishes – destabilises received interpretations of the past, suggesting that we can only recollect what has gone before as an accumulation of flickering memories borrowed perhaps from other narratives and narrative forms. In common with avant-garde practices, we are denied any process of audience identification either at the level of the narrative or the image.

Coilin & Platonida recalls the work of Chris Marker, in particular his 1962 film, *La Jetée* (France), which deals with similar themes of time and memory, although in a more accessible manner than does Scott. The involvement of Irish independent filmmakers in this film (Bob Quinn plays a dinner guest, Joe Comerford was part of the production unit) reflects the exchange of interests within the avant-garde movement of the 1970s. It is convenient and probably more accurate to consider *Coilin & Platonida* as representing the British rather than the Irish avant-garde; the latter did not tend towards works of 'pure film' but instead employed the disruptive processes of avant-garde filmmaking to produce a politicised, historically engaged cinema.

If divisions existed within the international avant-garde over questions of pure cinema, a further theoretical debate arose over whether realist practices were compatible with political engagement. The central issue was whether a realist cinema could be political or whether realism closed off conflicting interpretations and thus reduced the level of active audience participation in the meaning-making process. As Wollen notes:

> the supporters of Godard and Straub-Huillet, by distinguishing their films from those of Karmitz or Pontecorvo, are constantly forced to assert that being 'political' is not in itself enough, that there must be a break with bourgeois norms of diegesis, subversion and deconstruction of codes.
>
> (1982: 101)

These issues did concern Irish filmmaking practices as the debate over Joe Comerford's *Down the Corner* (Ireland/GB, 1977) illustrates. Whilst employing the techniques of 'poor cinema', *Down The Corner* is a realist work and an early forerunner of the shift towards greater realism that came to characterise independent Irish cinema. The film's narrative concerns a group of boys who hang around the working-class Ballyfermot area of Dublin, one of whom eventually ends up in casualty after an accident robbing an orchard. Comerford highlights the poverty of the area and the sense of aimlessness which characterises the children's and adults' lives. The film's construction denies the conventions of Hollywood filmmaking, refusing either to fetishise poverty or to suggest that the central characters will triumph over their environment. Identification is minimal and there is little sense of narrative drive. *Down the Corner* was made as a Ballyfermot Community Arts Workshop project and the 'actors' were drawn from local children and adults. Its documentary 'look' led to some criticism of its failure on the one hand to abandon fully the tenets of realism (Rockett, 1978) and on the other, through its emphasis on the hopelessness of the characters' existences, to provide a 'realistic' portrait of working-class life (Kelly, 1978: 15). This emphasis on issues of class and environment, combined with its mode of construction, places Comerford's film at a tangent to the greater thrust of the early Irish independent filmmakers who largely favoured the

Godardian over the Pontecorvian school of filmmaking. On the other hand, it could not be argued that the film offers the same level of 'pleasure' as, say, the films of Pontecorvo or Costas Gavras or that it was designed to appeal to a wider audience. It is also more specific in its concern with a particular segment of Irish society than the other early independent films that are more interested in wider issues of history, representation and national identity.

Self-confessed maverick (Quinn, 2001), Bob Quinn is one of the most interesting and innovative filmmakers to emerge out of the new Irish cinema of the 1970s. In 1969 he left RTÉ and moved to Connemara where he formed his own company, Cinegael. His films have consistently questioned the basis on which the status quo rests, whether it is the idea of the Irish as a pure Celtic race (in his television series *Atlantean* [1984]), the romanticisation of the West of Ireland (in *Poitín*) and the Catholic Church (in *Budawanny* [Ireland, 1987] and *The Bishop's Story* [Ireland, 1994]) and the concept of family, the short film, *The Family* (Ireland, 1978). Quinn makes his films in the Irish language which itself is a political act, reflecting at once the suppression of Irish under colonialism and its marginalised status in contemporary Ireland.

Caoineadh Airt Uí Laoire was funded by the Marxist-oriented Sinn Féin, The Workers' Party, and is based on a popular oral lament, ostensibly composed by Eileen Dubh O'Connell. Although its authorship is disputed, and may be ascribed to two writers, the story of Art O'Leary of Raleigh in Macroom, Co. Cork, who refused to sell his horse to the magistrate, Abraham Morris, as required under the penal law and was later shot by Morris' henchmen, carried enormous political and emotional resonances in the period up to and after Catholic Emancipation.[2] The fact that O'Leary's widow was aunt to Daniel O'Connell (the Liberator) also contributed to the poem's fame. Even in translation, this is a rich, emotive piece of writing in which the widow bewails the loss of her fine husband and grieves that she wasn't with him when he was killed. Her voice is alternated with that of Art O'Leary's sister, although the lack of any shift in register between the two is an indication of how little the written version may correspond to the original oral rendition.

Caoineadh Airt Uí Laoire is an experimental work with a somewhat complex narrative structure. The film centres on a group of actors who have already performed in a film of the lament and who are now being directed by an English director (John Arden) in a mixed media performance that blends the film footage with live performance. While the actors watch the replaying of the film, the man who plays Art O'Leary (Séan Bán Breathnach), tries to disrupt the group, attempting on a number of occasions to undermine the director's authority. As the film develops, the distinction between the replayed film and the rehearsals becomes increasingly blurred. A further complication, that Morris is also played by the director, leads to a standoff between him and Art which mirrors the standoff on film.

The film opens with a quote from James Connolly: 'Fortunately the Irish character has proven too difficult to press into respectable foreign moulds'. This lays out the film's concerns: the resistance to foreign authority expressed by Art O'Leary in the eighteenth century and mirrored by the actor's resistance to the director; the different natures of the British and Irish and the subversive delight in impropriety associated with the Irish.

The central *topos* of the film is the effects of colonisation both in the past and the present. It returns over and over again to a commentary on the injustices of the British system; for instance, the narrator of the film within the film lists the exports of grain and livestock from Ireland in 1767 and then adds that, 'in the same year ... half of the people of Ireland were starving'. On a couple of occasions, a voice-over reads out the penal laws over the action. Towards the end of the film, the director enjoins the cast to choose between ending the story as tragedy or farce and reminds them that, 'We all know the terrible results of romanticising history. You know as well as I do that if Irish history had been taught properly the North would never have happened'. Yet as much as Quinn critiques the romanticisation of Irish history, he does not fully jettison its romantic elements. As the above examples demonstrate, he further subscribes to a nationalist approach by blaming the British (seen in the film within the film as being upper-class caricatures) unreservedly for starving and oppressing the Irish. Whether this should be taken as justification of the pursuit of an anti-imperialist policy in Northern Ireland remains, however, unresolved. Indeed Quinn's tone, in this as in his other films, is primarily that of ironic deconstruction.

In terms of its structure, *Caoineadh Airt Uí Laoire* can be clearly located within the avant-garde tradition and bears many similarities to *On A Paving Stone Mounted* (Thaddeus O'Sullivan, GB, 1978; discussed below). It destabilises the notion of character and draws attention to the ideological composition of plot, specifically historical narrative. It most closely approximates to the model of an anti-colonial cinema proposed by the advocates of Third Cinema practices in both address and by virtue of its formal construction. Martin McLoone has argued that the concept of Third Cinema, defined as operating outside of the dominant entertainment-based practices of Hollywood and an auteur-driven, largely European model that remains bound up with the ideology and politics of the establishment, offers a template for a politically engaged Irish cinema and this will 'promote a socialist consciousness, both stimulating debate and finding a space within and without dominant culture where this can take place' (2000: 123). Paul Willemen writes that one of the defining characteristics of Third Cinema is 'the aim of rendering a particular social situation intelligible to those engaged in a struggle to change it in a socialist direction' (1989: 20). In fact, it is debatable whether such a model remains practicable in a world that has relegated avant-garde practices and concerns to the spaces of the art gallery and socialist aspirations to history. As we will see in our look at those works that attempt to describe and analyse the Troubles in Northern Ireland, any filmmaker with ambitions to reach a wider audience must engage with that audience from within the discourse of popular cinema. Although the production of the occasional avant-garde film such as *I Could Read the Sky* (Nichola Bruce, GB/Ireland/France, 1999) suggests that there is a space for such filmmaking albeit for a minority audience, even Bruce's film lacks any polemical political engagement. Alternatively, we might consider that the filmmaking practices discussed in this chapter correspond to what Colin McArthur urges regions such as this adopt, namely a 'poor Celtic cinema'. McArthur offers practitioners the advice that, 'the more your films are consciously aimed at an international market, the more their conditions of intelligibility will be bound up with regressive discourses about your own culture' (1994: 119–20). Bigger budget films, he considers, are inevitably compromised and salvation lies in a practice that originates not only in the work of certain Third World filmmakers but equally in low budget European cinemas, from the Italian neo-realists onwards. Such films should be cinematic and not literary and need not be made to the standards of the avant-garde or deliver 'unpleasure'. They should be rooted in a sense of history and society.

Behind such pronouncements lies a faith in achieving an authentic representation of the native culture. Luke Gibbons follows this continuum when he writes on memory. There are, he stresses, different registers of memory, 'one that is contained and legitimised within the confines of the monument and the museum, and the other having to do with endangered traces of collective memory, as transmitted by popular culture, folklore, ballads, and so on' (1996: 172). This group of independent films is notable for its sense of history and society and the manner in which historical memory is perpetuated. Whilst a frequent motif in Irish films about the past is the schoolroom history class (invariably viewed with a high degree of cynicism), in fact the films discussed in this chapter are less concerned with countering institutional modes of relaying historical discourses than questioning the 'unofficial' dissemination of the same, of foregrounding and problematising the narration of the past.

Three films – *Down the Corner, On A Paving Stone Mounted* and *Maeve* (Pat Murphy/John Davies, GB, 1981) – contain scenes that reflect on the recreation of the past, through memory and media images as well as in the schoolroom. In *Down the Corner*, one of the boys' grandmother tells them about the time when her boyfriend shot a British soldier (a comparable scene occurs in the short film *Our Boys* [Cathal Black, Ireland, 1981] where we hear a recollection of resistance to the British being recounted on the radio). The sequence is shot in grainy, somewhat unfocused, black and white which, in combination with its theme of heroism and action, establishes a contrast with the bleakness and tedium of the boys' lives, suggesting perhaps that 'the heroic memories of 1916–22 are far removed from the stark economic reality of the contemporary working-class environment' (Rockett, 1987: 137). These memories may be remote but they are also enabling. It is the children who request the story and it could be argued that there is something comforting about the process of repetition (they have clearly heard this story many times before) associated with oral transmission of history.

Thaddeus O'Sullivan's film for the BFI Production Board, *On A Paving Stone Mounted*, similarly focuses on memory, in this case in the context of immigration to Britain. Presented as a collage of images shot in black and white, the film moves between dreams of an English way of life, to documentary footage of Ireland, to a series of encounters in England. The film's style is deliberately amateurish, shot with lurching camera movements and making use of over-exposed stock. Figures frequently appear between the camera and its subject and voices overlap and crowd each other out. Both fantasies of England and memories of the past are seen to be media creations – the English protagonists move within a comfortable middle-class environment which resembles a television sitcom (O'Sullivan has said that the imagined life in England is drawn from 'newspapers and the "B" feature movies which dominate the Irish cinema circuits' [Cowie, 1978: 37]) – the Irish memories include footage of de Valera's funeral cortege. The point is that the past is inaccessible save through mediation. In another sequence, an unseen group is shown around Kilmainham Jail, their understanding of the past filtered through the explanatory words of the tour guide and in a sequence again very similar to one in *Our Boys*, a schoolmaster gives a class on Irish history – 'We're going back to the past to celebrate the days of the chieftains and the old castles'. The film opens with a disquisition on the art of storytelling, apparently as a way of introducing a storyteller (possibly to a group of tourists) but the story is not told until the end. England as it is imagined, picture postcards and Regency terraces, becomes on arrival the England of immigrant pubs and boarding houses, whilst Ireland is remembered through shots of pilgrims climbing Croagh Patrick and the Puck Fair, celebrations, memories, that is, of an old-fashioned country stuck in rituals of religion and drink. The film is ambiguous as to whether it considers these to be enabling memories but suggests again that these stories and memories are not just comforting but need to be preserved in the face of other competing and hostile narratives. *On A Paving Stone Mounted* expresses what Louis A. Montrose calls the 'textuality of history', the idea that:

> we can have no access to a full and authentic past, a lived material existence, unmediated by the surviving textual traces of the society in question – traces whose survival we cannot assume to be merely contingent but must rather presume to be at least partially consequent upon complex and subtle social processes of preservation and effacement; and secondly, that those textual traces are themselves subject to subsequent textual mediations when they are construed as the 'documents' upon which historians ground their own texts, called 'histories'.
>
> (1989: 20)

Surprisingly few of the early independent filmmakers were concerned with critiquing gender representations or the gendering of history/history of gender; indeed a criticism that could be justly levelled at *Caoineadh Airt*

Uí Laoire is that the women are sidelined in the 'present-day' sequences as much as in the film of the original story, an irony given that the genesis of the film is in a strong, defiant woman's voice.

Only Pat Murphy, whose work we will be considering further in Chapter 7, has consistently addressed gender issues in her films although her difficulties in attracting film financing reflect the problems that this type of filmmaking faces. In her first feature film, *Maeve* (co-directed with John Davies), the dissemination of historical narratives through folk tales and memory is scrutinised for its gender implications. In common with later works of the 1980s, this film, whilst formally indebted to the avant-garde, is more interested in questioning nationalist rather than colonial constructions of history. Pat Murphy's work is evidently influenced by the feminist agenda, pioneered by historians such as Sheila Rowbotham and Aileen Kraditor, of (re)constructing a 'women's history'. In Rowbotham's *Hidden From History* (1973), she demonstrated the theory that women had been largely marginalised from history's narrative and at best considered appendages to the Great Men who were responsible for creating those narratives. Through retrieving the history of past female militants, she sought to endow the new generation of activists with a sense of continuity that had hitherto been repressed.

Later historians and theorists, whilst indebted to the writings of Rowbotham, Rosen and Haskell were to move away from an examination of the text, be it the narrative of history or the narrative of cinema, to a questioning of how those narratives had been constructed and were being perpetuated. Thus it became important to look at the construction of women's roles, in history or cinema, in order to learn from that process.

Of the films by Murphy discussed in this book, *Maeve* is the most avant-garde. The narrative concerns the return home to Belfast from London of a young woman, Maeve (Mary Jackson), her relationship with her boyfriend Liam (John Keegan) and her family. In the background to the film, the Troubles continue; interwoven into the film's structure are flashbacks to Maeve's childhood and her teenage years. The central concern in the film is to explore the relationship between republicanism and feminism and to highlight the narrative of nationalism as a male construct. Thus, in a key sequence in a ringed fort (an icon of Celticism), Maeve's father, Martin (Mark Mulholland), embarks on one of his rambling tales of the past and, as he speaks, the young Maeve (Nuala McCann) walks in the other direction, leaving his voice to fade away (Johnston, 1981; Willemen, 1994; Gibbons, 1996). As the film progresses, Martin is listened too less and less by the women of his family until finally he is left alone to tell his stories directly to the camera.

The central character in *Maeve* is articulate and informed and has access to the language of political discourse; more than that, the position she takes denies the conventional concept of woman as the link with the past and as the repository of memory (discussed later in Chapter 8). The following exchange illustrates the conflict between Liam's republican view of the relationship between the past and the present and Maeve's desire to inscribe a feminist position into republicanism:

> Liam: The work is to take hold of the myth and move forward, to appropriate it and not be used by it like our fathers were.
>
> Maeve: You're wrong. The past has its own power. It feeds off people believing in it. The more you focus on it, the more reality it gains.
>
> Liam: What are you saying? That people should live in some kind of vacuum without memory? That our whole history be cast aside just because you happen to find it irrelevant?
>
> Maeve: ... You're talking about a false memory ... the way you want to remember excludes me. I get remembered out of existence.

Their conversation takes place on Cave Hill, a location historically associated with the United Irishmen. If Liam and Maeve cannot agree on an ideal way forward, Murphy is careful to establish that Maeve's radical politics are not a reflection of the wider female community. For young women such as her sister, Roisin (Brid Brennan), the immediate problems of dealing with sexually marauding British soldiers or the pleasures of a night out in the pub take precedence over any wider, ideological engagement.

Just as Maeve refuses to succumb to a linear concept of history as a master (literally) narrative, so the film jettisons conventional cinematic signifiers of time passing in favour of more discreet cues (the central character's haircut most commonly signals to the viewer that the film is going backwards or forwards in time). Overall, *Maeve* offers little potential for character identification or conventional narrative engagement.

Where Murphy's film is, like those works discussed above, influenced by the formal conventions of the political avant-garde, other filmmakers sought to deconstruct aspects of Irish life under cover of a more realist cinematic style. A key strategy in this respect has been to provide a counter-narrative of the family (as nation). The pre-eminent position enjoyed by the family unit in the ideology of nationalism had been confirmed by the wording of the 1937 Constitution which recognised 'the Family as the natural primary and fundamental unit of Society ...', 'the necessary basis of social order and as indispensable to the welfare of the Nation and the State' (Bunreacht na hÉireann [Constitution of Ireland], 1937: 138)

The discursive trope of denying the notional happy family and of refictionalising it as an oppressive, verging on dysfunctional, institution is indebted to an Althusserian analysis of society that conceptualises the family unit as one of the 'Ideological State Apparatuses' through which the State exercises indirect control over its subjects (Althusser, 1971: 145). It thus refutes the ideal of the Irish as 'one happy family' and legitimises social alternatives to the biological family. Added to this was, of course, the enduring influence of Catholic teaching which also insisted on the primacy of the (Holy) family. To deny the myth of the happy Irish family or the Irish as one happy family was in this context a radical trope though its ubiquity has since rendered it virtually a cliché. Whilst the central focus of these films is that of the divided and unhappy family as a metaphor for the submerged rifts within Irish society, there is also a tentative exploration of the potential for the 'surrogate' family, usually a coming together of a group of marginalised contemporaries.

A relentless deconstruction of family life takes place in *Poitín*, the story of two poteen agents who attempt to double-cross their boss Michil (Cyril Cusack). The film is set in a bleak West of Ireland, a landscape of barren fields and cold, inhospitable interiors; Michil's cottage overlooks an estuary, cut off from the wider vistas of the ocean; he lives alone with his daughter, her mother's absence unexplained. The daughter, Maire (Mairead Ni Conghaile)'s life is a round of stoking the fire and hanging the washing out on the line; she and her father barely speak. The two poteen agents (played by Niall Toibin and Donal McCann) are clearly rogue 'boys', eternal bachelors, functioning in an environment that is alien to the domestic. They drink too much, they do not appear to have a home life of their own, they are evicted from community of the pub and, in the final scenes, they destroy Maire and Michil's home.

The two 'boys' clearly begrudge Michil his ownership of property; they describe themselves ironically as 'servants' and through their actions place themselves outside of the domestic whilst still yearning for it. Emotionally and sexually immature, one breaks into Maire's bedroom where her laughter at him suggests that he suffers from impotence. The agents' violent assault on the living quarters of the cottage, culminating in the shattering of the statue of the Virgin Mary (with a potato!) is an assault on the system that oppresses them and Maire. The organisation of rural domestic life renders them all powerless and all subject to the 'man of the house' – Michil. State authority (in the figures of the gardaí [police]) has little place in the system of things, it is land and kinship that empower. Standing behind this system is the Church, with its idealisation of the Virgin Mary (the statue is in a dominant position) and its insistence on devotion, humility and obedience to the patriarchal figure. It is up to the patriarch, not the State, to dispense justice – by sending his agents to their death in a leaking boat. What we are left with is no solution, but a strong impression that domesticity is as undesirable as is exclusion from it. To be inside the home is to be as psychologically stunted as to be outside of it.

The first words spoken in Cathal Black's *Pigs* (Ireland, 1984) are 'Home, Sweet Home' as Jimmy (Jimmy Brennan) enters the decaying Georgian house that is to be his squat and the locus for the construction of an 'alternative' family. The interior of the squat is filled with symbols of disintegration – broken cisterns, dirt encrusted cookers, pinups of nude women. Outside, small children sniff glue, teenagers roam the streets and bonfires burn. This is an excremental society where the borders between order and disorder are only barely retained. In the words of the young guard, the squatters live like pigs, yet from their perspective he is the pig.

The inhabitants of the squat represent the marginalised of society. The prostitute, the black musician, the paranoid case, the drug dealer, the older man who dons his pin-striped suit and pretends to go to work, and Jimmy who is homosexual, are excluded from the dominant order. Instead, the disparate group of squatters forms its own family. Jimmy in his skirt/towel is 'mother', putting up curtains, raising the dough, arbitrating disputes; George (George Shane) is 'father', ostensibly going to work every day. 'Nice and quiet and respectable, that's the way to keep it', he remarks to Jimmy in a parody of bourgeois concerns. The other members of the squat are their unruly children, given to squabbling amongst themselves and, occasionally, defying their 'parents'.

The climax of this metaphor of family life is reached at the dinner table scene. Jimmy is cooking pizza and chiding Tom (Maurice O'Donoghue), the difficult child, for refusing vegetables. George plays a practical joke on the 'family', producing a trick set of false teeth that Jimmy uses to flute the edge of the pizza. Jimmy as pseudo-mother is doubly threatened by patriarchy – in the belligerent form of the police who are pursuing him for social welfare fraud and by the queer bashers who attack him. The film ends with the dissolution of the 'family', the abandonment of the squat and the triumph of law and order.

No less pessimistic, Joe Comerford's *Reefer and the Model* (Ireland, 1988) follows the meeting of Reefer (Ian McElhinny) and a young pregnant woman, the Model (Carol Scanlan). He is an ex-IRA man and along with his two associates/friends, Badger (Ray McBride) and Spider (Sean Lawlor) runs a nebulous smuggling business from their trawler. The film is set in 1981 and newspaper headlines provide a commentary on the progress of the hunger strikes. *Reefer and the Model* is shot in a disjointed, Godardian fashion and, in that spirit, a relationship is struck up between Reefer and the Model. The group decide to stage one last bank heist, to 'protect the family', but they are caught by the guards. In the final scene, the Model is left alone at the helm of the trawler and, as Reefer tries to board the boat, she goes into labour, losing control of the tiller. It is left to us to speculate whether or not she and Reefer survive.

One of the incidental characters in the film is the seaside photographer (Birdy Sweeney) who takes instant 'snapshots' of holidaymakers. The false air of happiness of these images, themselves the quintessential armoury of family life, is articulated by the island woman (Maire Chinsealach): 'I don't trust them pictures. I have one from my honeymoon. I look happy in it but I wasn't happy at all. It's faded now.' In a subsequent scene, the group poses on the fore deck of the trawler. 'Look, we're like a family in this!' the Model exclaims, but the older woman looks away, denying the fantasy. Like the grouping in *Pigs*, Reefer's crew and companions are indeed a ship of fools; Spider is on the run from the North and Badger has a disruptive, subversive sensibility – in one scene he is bound up in toilet roll and lowered onto the quay where, like a mummy, he playfully menaces the children. This device of the masquerade is the key to the film, as each of its members adopts and

Figure 5.1 Reefer and the Model (l-r): Ray McBride (Badger), Ian McElhinney (Reefer) and Sean Lawlor (Spider). Courtesy of the Irish Film Archive of the Film Institute of Ireland and Joe Comerford.

abandons multiple personae, Reefer is at once a member of the Anglo-Irish Ascendancy and a cowboy hero; the Model is Mary Magdalene, she says, only to deny it in the same breath.

As one reviewer of the film proposed in response to the quotation above:

> There are many pictures of Ireland which should not be trusted – we look happy in them. Joe Comerford's first feature is a welcome corrective to such images, whether emanating from tourist boards or from filmmakers enchanted by our landscape, our charm, our 'Irishness'.
>
> (Hannigan, 1989: 30)

Like the other two films that deconstruct the trope of the happy family, Comerford in this feature dismantles the visual and narrative conventions of depicting Ireland that have accrued through the history of Irish cinematic images as well as through complementary discourses, notably tourism. Each of these key filmmakers from this period is notable for their vigorous plundering and dissembling of Ireland's imagery, Quinn through *Poitín*'s constrictive shooting style, his refusal to romanticise the West of Ireland setting of his film, Black through his preoccupation with interiors and their perverse domesticity, Murphy through her gendering of space, and Comerford and O'Sullivan by refusing to adhere to any one visual register. Although *Reefer and the Model* contains moments of intense lyricism, expressed in particular through shots of the trawler heading out to sea with Dolores Keane singing the ballad, 'After the Dream' on the soundtrack, it also changes swiftly to become a generic road movie, complete with failed heist, and a Western with Reefer as its omnipotent hero.

This referencing of American cinema is complemented by the centrality of 'The American Bar' to the island community. It is here (in a pub that may have been financed by American earnings or may just be expressing an embrace of the Americanisation of culture) that Badger can 'come out' sexually and dance with the soldier in uniform at the céilidh. This, one of the few developed gays scenes in Irish cinema of the period (and even now) has been debated at length by Martin McLoone (2000: 136–7) and Lance Pettitt (1997: 261). Pettitt argues that:

> Their participation in the céilidh defies 'mainland' codes, and their kiss is a moment of remarkable tenderness between two men that provides for a poignant screen moment: showing a northern Presbyterian man coupling with a soldier from the Irish Republic suggests a vision of sexual and political daring.
>
> (ibid.: 261)

McLoone argues that the location of this sequence risks affirming gay sexuality as a marginalised sexuality. The same might be said about the depiction of homosexuality in *Pigs* where it is part of 'deviant' culture and in this respect Pettitt also concludes that, 'The film could be said to reflect the popular consensus in Ireland about homosexuality at the time: at worst, an evil, sub-human or pathologically criminal condition; at best, an unfortunate failing deserving sympathy and compassion' (ibid.: 257).

These responses to the independent films illustrate the difficulty of producing a counter-cinema – in the process of breaking down the dominant signifiers you risk simultaneously affirming them. Quinn and Comerford's vision of the West of Ireland as a lawless culture with a propensity to violence confirms its geographical and cultural peripherality. The centre, in these films, is a repressive space that exerts its control through its agents, the police. In another of Quinn's films, *Budawanny*, the centre claims dominance over the periphery in an equally summary fashion when the Church intervenes in the love affair between the island priest (Donal McCann) and his pregnant girlfriend (Maggie Fegan). Even the disruption of formal conventions is no guarantee of representational revolution.

A further ontological strand within the independent films discussed in this chapter is the critique of hegemonic Catholicism. This is the core of *Budawanny* and also Cathal Black's *Our Boys*, a film that so shocked one of its financiers, RTÉ, when it was completed in 1980 that it was shelved for a further ten years before it was considerably suitable for transmission. *Our Boys*, shot in luminous black and white, intersperses footage of the Eucharistic Congress of 1932 with staged scenes of a dwindling religious community of Christian Brothers preparing to move out of education, with interviews with old boys who had been physically abused by the Brothers. Two other works, *The Kinkisha* (Tommy McArdle, Ireland, 1977) and Robert Wynne-Simmons' *The Outcasts* (Ireland, 1982) emphasise the primacy of a pagan, superstitious way of life over one characterised by Christian devotion.

The latter film tells the story of three daughters, Breda (Brenda Scallon), Maura (Mary Ryan) and Janey (Bairbre ní Chaoimh) and their father Hugh O'Donnell (Don Foley). The family lives in a remote cottage set in muddy fields and surrounded by bare rocky mountains and wind-stunted trees. When the pregnant Janey marries local farmer Eamon (Mairtin Ó Flathearta), Maura, who is regarded as being backward, is whisked off by Scarf Michael (Mick Lally). He is an outcast from the community who lives in the world of the supernatural and Maura watches him cast spells on the revellers. When she begs him to take her away, he refuses and after this a series of misfortunes is visited on the country people, including the failure of the potato crop. The villagers drag Maura down to the water to drown her but Scarf Michael appears and rescues her. This time he agrees to take her away but when she begs him to teach her his magic, he demurs, suspecting that her magic is even greater than his. When she comes back to the village she is chased away and the film closes with her tapping in vain on the window of her father's cottage as she watches the family carry on their old lives.

The success of *The Outcasts* lies in its fusing of the natural and supernatural with no concessions to whimsy. It constructs an Ireland which makes little distinction between religion and superstition and whose inhabitants are intolerant of difference. As the negotiations over Janey and Eamon's marriage indicate, they are also able to swallow their principles when land is offered in exchange for the pregnant bride-to-be. In a common trope of Irish rural dramas (the heritage films excepted), the villagers and country people, women as much as men, are represented as a barely civilised mob who at the least provocation will turn violent.[3] Nor does the film romanticise the lives of the outcasts, Scarf Michael and Maura. Placed between the two is the priest (Paul Bennett), himself, his accent indicates, an outsider, whose advice is ignored by locals and Maura alike. Threaded through the film are multiple references to Irish legends; the country people retell them around the fireside and the bonfire, and Maura tells them to herself, murmuring as she stands apart from the others, 'It's your lover, Dermot, returning from across the sea'. In her imagination, Scarf Michael thus becomes recast as Dermot, Grania's lover with whom she fled, according to myth, from marriage with Finn McCool. The name Hugh O'Donnell is also a resonant reminder of early Irish history, but the character of Maura's father is less tribal chief than bullying patriarch who beats Maura, is easily persuaded to trade Janey, and is felled with a stone when he tries to rescue Maura from her death. Robert Wynne-Simmons has said of the film that 'it's in the style of a folk-tale but it isn't actually a folk-tale. Rather it's redolent of a lot of folk-tales, a subconscious putting together of a lot of mythic things to which I

Figure 5.2 The Outcasts. Mary Ryan (Maura O'Donnell). Courtesy of the Irish Film Archive of the Film Institute of Ireland and Robert Wynne-Simmons.

could relate' (Dwyer: 1981, 11). The composition of the film, its treatment of time and narrative suggest the influence of storytelling practices, a feature it has in common with Third Cinema filmmaking. As Teshome H. Gabriel writes:

> All cinema manipulates 'time' and 'space'. Where Western films manipulate 'time' more than 'space', Third World films seem to emphasise 'space' over 'time'. Third World films grow from folk tradition where communication is a slow-paced phenomenon and time is not rushed but has its own pace.
>
> (1989: 44)

This reflects Luke Gibbons' interest in collective, folk memory and can be seen to constitute a distinct current in Irish filmmaking of this period.

In conclusion, the independent films have in common a relentlessly counter-hegemonic drive, their overturning of the tropes of Irish cinema and cultural life achieved at times through formal disruption and at others at a narrative level. In the end, it seems to me that they belong most accurately to a 'poor Celtic cinema' rather than in 'Third Cinema' model, in so far as they embrace both Third and Second cinema practices to often similar ends. Where we may distinguish them from the films that were to follow is in the sense of the 'real' that they retain. By deconstructing Ireland, they suggest that they will expose some kind of truth or truths about Irish life in the present, reveal some kind of authenticity. Since then, as Colin Graham has written, the 'reality' of Ireland has receded ever further into the representational distance (2001: 2). Acknowledging that cinema's signification processes can only produce fiction and not fact, and in deference to the proliferation of such signifying practices, the image-making process has become ever more playful and removed from a sense of any kind of rapprochement with the 'real'.

6

THE SECOND FILM BOARD
YEARS

The re-establishment of the Irish Film Board
and its policies, 1993 to the present

Many of the films discussed in the previous chapter were financially aided by the Irish Film Board between the years of its establishment in 1981 and its dissolution by Charles J. Haughey in 1987 on the basis of inadequate returns. During that period it part financed ten feature projects and a number of documentaries on what was theoretically a 'loan' basis. Its policy was to spread its financing but to focus on feature films capable of theatrical release.

The Board saw its remit as the fostering of a diverse film culture that would embrace the idiosyncratic views of Bob Quinn as expressed in *Atlantean*, feminist filmmaking practices (Pat Murphy), creative documentary (Patrick Carey) as well as the work of directors from Northern Ireland (John T. Davis, Bill Miskelly). Despite the small sums of money at its disposal, the Board's achievement was considerable, particularly given that this was the first sustained attempt to create an indigenous film culture since the inception of the State.

The Board enjoyed little financial return (8.5%) from the £IR1.247m it invested in feature films and it was on this pretext that its activities were suspended (Rockett, 1994: 128–9). This money provided part funding for the productions with the remainder, in most cases, coming from outside sources, chiefly Channel 4 Television but also the BFI Production Fund, RTÉ and a combination of British film companies and private sources. The Board's controversial decision to award half of its annual budget to Neil Jordan's debut production, *Angel* (Ireland/GB, 1982) cast its decision-making procedures under some suspicion. Jordan was a protégé of John Boorman who was a member of the Board and executive producer of the film. The latter also appeared to be at loggerheads with many independent filmmakers and after the *Angel* controversy was quoted as saying: 'I have to constantly remind myself that they [the independent producers] are a group of malcontents and mad dogs. They are in love with martyrdom. After years of self-imposed martyrdom, they are in a position to make films. Instead they complain' (Dwyer, 1997: 27). Independent producers were also critical of government subsidies of Ardmore Studios, which had been purchased by the State in 1973 after a series of disastrous financial investments (Rockett,

1987: 98–103). In the long term even this investment failed to render Ardmore financially viable and in 1982 the then Minister for Industry and Energy, Albert Reynolds, announced that the studios would be closed. Since then, they have regularly changed hands and remain reliant on overseas' productions to sustain profitability.

In the years after the Board's suspension, filmmakers continued to campaign for its re-establishment. The success of *My Left Foot* in 1989 and later of *The Crying Game* (Neil Jordan, GB, 1992), both films principally funded by British television and outside sources, fuelled the lobby for the support of a national film industry. It was argued that this would not only be culturally important but that it would boost the economy, then in the doldrums, and create considerable knock-on investment in jobs and services.

In 1993 the Irish Film Board was re-established, relocated to Galway and awarded an annual budget of £IR1m. In 2003 it had a budget of approximately €9.153m (www.filmboard.ie; accessed 5 February 2003). As well as offering filmmakers financial assistance through development and production loans, the Board acts as the co-ordinating body for the publicly funded infrastructure of the Irish industry. As such, it plays a part in supporting training, distribution and publicity. The Board supports the financing of feature films, short films and animation and, until 2003, some television production. Outside of the organisational criteria for submitting proposals to the Film Board, there is also a somewhat nebulous cultural element involved in funding decisions. The official publications of the Board suggest that Irish film should represent:

> a very wide diversity of styles and subjects: the rural and urban, the contemporary and the ancient, the high brow and the low brow ... We should see films from the traditional communities of agrarian Ireland to the Cork or Belfast working class, the different generations, cultures and classes that make up this island, including Irish language films which indicate the continuing vibrancy of Irish and its place in contemporary culture.
>
> (*Irish Film Board Review*, 1993: 3)

Most but not all of the films made in Ireland since 1993 have been supported by the Film Board and thus they could be best considered to constitute an 'official' Irish film culture. These years have seen an extraordinary growth in film production; ten years after its inception, the Board was able to lay claim to having supported the making of nearly a hundred feature films as well as several hundred short films and documentaries, this in a country that produced 18 feature films during the 1980s. In common with many other European countries, Irish State aid is issued in the form of development and production loans allocated by the Irish Film Board rather than straight subsidy. The latter is generally seen as deterring filmmakers from considering the commercial viability of productions; however, the fact that little return is expected from the loans, which in the Irish case can be up to 25 per cent of the total budget or, in exceptional cases, greater, means that they operate in a manner not dissimilar from a subsidy. The Film Board's recoupment in the period to 2000 has averaged 13 per cent (*Brief prepared for the Minister for Arts, Heritage, Gaeltacht and the Islands in advance of the Irish Film Board (Amendment) Bill, 2000* [unpaginated]).

Another source of State funding is the Irish Arts Council which partially subsidises spaces for film viewing such as the Irish Film Centre, Dublin, filmmaking organisations and resource centres in Cork, Dublin and Galway, film festivals and the magazine, *Film Ireland*. The Arts Council is consistently criticised by film organisations for its low level of support for film (3.1 per cent of its annual budget in 2000 [Sheehy, 2002: 36]), and we may assume that this is a consequence of its ambiguous status as an artform.

Crucial to the success of the evolution of an Irish film industry since 1993 has been the system of tax relief for film investment, initially known as Section 35 and latterly as Section 481. The scheme was established in 1987 and allowed, under Section 35 of the Finance Act, companies to claim tax relief on sums of up to £IR100,000 invested in qualifying films. The sums involved were increased in 1989 and comprehensively overhauled in 1993. A number of amendments have since been made. These incentives have been aimed at encouraging foreign productions to shoot in Ireland (with knock-on benefits in terms of training and services) and local filmmakers to raise investment money. The immediate success of Section 35/481 was obvious with production rising rapidly: 'From a norm of 2/3 films produced per annum, the number increased dramatically and by 1994, eighteen feature and eleven TV productions were commenced or completed' (*INDECON Report*, 1995: 18). The value of this investment varied on an annual basis and tended to be skewed by the shooting of overseas blockbusters such as *Braveheart* (Mel Gibson, USA, 1995), *Saving Private Ryan* (Steven Spielberg, USA, 1998), and *Reign of Fire* (Rob Bowman, GB/Ireland/USA, 2002). The policy of attracting such productions was based on anticipated secondary investment in jobs, tourism and other services. More importantly, in terms of creating a body of films that addressed Irish culture and concerns, the tax incentives scheme allowed local producers access to funding that was subject to no external artistic control. The investors in Section 481, likewise, have little say in the final product (given the nature of such investors, few have any knowledge of filmmaking), and their representatives are looking at best for pre-sales (to overseas distributors) and a completion guarantee; most of these investors simply need the film to be completed and for the production company to stay in business for three years (the length of time of their investment). So, essentially, this has been no-strings attached money.

Obtaining accurate figures for Section 481 funding is enormously difficult and shrouded in claims about confidentiality. Figures supplied by the Inland Revenue for feature film financing during this period are shown in Table 1 (it should be noted that this covers non-indigenous as well as indigenous films).

Table 1 Feature Film Financing

Year	Amount raised	Tax cost
1993–1994	£IR43,611,623	£IR19,967,979
1994–1995	£IR82,877,123	£IR38,329,891
1995–1996	£IR42,903,135	£IR19,125,511
1996–1997	£IR30,337,608	£IR11,263,642
1998–1999	£IR73,323,025	£IR26,952,073
1999–2000	£IR58,659,880	£IR21,576,037

Source: Figures courtesy of the Office of the Revenue Commissioners.

The other potentially significant source for feature film funding in Ireland is the national broadcaster, RTÉ. As a consequence of the 1993 Broadcasting Authority (Amendment) Act and the establishment of the Independent Production Unit (IPU), RTÉ has been obliged to outsource a percentage of its overall production. The Act stipulated that this should be £IR5m in 1994, £IR6.5m in 1995 increasing to £IR12.5m or 20 per cent of TV programme expenditure in the preceding financial year (whichever was greater) by 1999. In the end, RTÉ committed a total of £IR16m in 1999 and this amount increased to £IR17.8m in 2000 (*The Economic Impact of Film Production in Ireland, 1993* [IBEC Report]: 20). Although these sums sound large, in fact very little of this money has been allocated to feature film funding.

RTÉ commits funds to indigenous feature filmmaking through equity investment or the purchase of transmission rights. RTÉ has come under sustained criticism from the filmmaking community for its lack of commitment to Irish feature production. In its defence, it has claimed that the cost per hour of feature films is often considerably higher than that of a top-of-the-range TV drama series, yet TV drama series gain higher ratings than one-off TV films (*INPRODUCTION*, 1998, 3: 13). It has, however, screened nearly all the recent Irish-made films (although it tends to pay a much lower than average figure for acquisitions [McWilliams, 1999: 22]).

The granting of an increased licence fee to the national broadcaster (effective from January 2003) was accompanied by a somewhat nebulous requirement that 5 per cent of the net proceeds from the new fee was to be put aside for a special broadcasting fund for new, additional, innovative content, from which all free-to-air broadcasters could draw. This ought to amount to approximately €8 million annually but its dispersal is as yet unclear.

As the figures in the Appendix indicate, it is clear that few Irish films have made any significant impression at the Irish box office. Those that have, have been larger budget films made under what might be described as conventional commercial conditions – *Angela's Ashes* (Alan Parker, GB/USA, 1999), *Michael Collins* (Neil Jordan, USA, 1996), *In the Name of the Father* (Jim Sheridan, Ireland/GB/USA, 1993), *The Butcher Boy* (USA, 1997), *Circle of Friends* (Pat O'Connor, USA/Ireland, 1995), *The Boxer*

(Jim Sheridan, Ireland/GB/US, 1997), *Some Mother's Son* (Terry George, Ireland/USA, 1996), *The General* (John Boorman, Ireland/GB, 1998). That this is not a guarantee of success is reflected in the poor theatrical performance of *Ordinary Decent Criminal* (Thaddeus O'Sullivan, Ireland/ Germany/USA/GB, 1999) an upbeat Dublin gangster movie starring Kevin Spacey and Linda Fiorentino. Of the low-budget, indigenous product, the most obvious success story was the gangsters-on-the-run comedy, *I Went Down* (Paddy Breathnach, Ireland/GB/Spain, 1997). However, this success was not repeated overseas, presumably because of the film's quirky style and, possibly, because of its lack of recognisable stars (the film took just $500,000 on a release of 80 prints in the USA [Power, 2000: 5]). The same goes for *About Adam* (Gerard Stembridge, Ireland/GB/ USA/, 2000) and *When Brendan Met Trudy* (Kieron J. Walsh, Ireland/ GB, 2000), both local successes that took just $159,668 and $133,376 in the USA respectively (INPRODUCTION, 2002, 5, 4: 13). A surprise success was *A Love Divided* (Syd McCartney, GB/Ireland, 1999). The strong performance of *The Magdalene Sisters* (Peter Mullan, GB/Ireland, 2002), which took €975,441 in its first four weeks (*INPRODUCTION*, 2002, 5, 6: 17), confirmed a public appetite for dramas highlighting the corrosive effects of Church hegemony in the past when filtered through individual hardship narratives. A proportion of the Film Board films have to date received no theatrical release, other than a showcase screening at the Irish Film Centre, and a number of these have gone straight to television. In most cases, the films have attracted substantially greater audiences on television; though this percentage decreases in inverse proportion to the film's theatrical figures. To put these figures into perspective, *Waking Ned*[1] (Kirk Jones, GB/France/USA, 1998), a British/Manx/ French co-production, shot on the Isle of Man by an English director, took £IR2.2m in its first ten days sending it straight into the number one slot (*INPRODUCTION*, 1999, 2:2, 18). Another Irish-interest release, *Titanic* achieved £IR7.5m at the box office (*Film Ireland*, 2000, 75: 10). A top box office film could expect to take between €4m and €7m in Ireland in 2002. Local Irish films tend to be tagged with the 'arthouse' label and so, in a country dominated by multiplex cinemas committed to Hollywood fare (Ireland has three arthouse cinemas, in Dublin, Cork and Belfast), audiences often do not have an opportunity to see these films other than on television.[2] Analysis of individual films has been intermittent at the level of the national press and the demise of the magazine *Film West* in 2001 further decreased the space available to develop a critical film culture. Only *Film Ireland* (published by the resource centre, Filmbase) remains as a journal of record and debate and even this was threatened throughout 2002 with closure until its rescue by an increased Arts Council grant and as a consequence of internal cost-cutting.

The relatively poor performance of Irish films at the local box office has been the subject of some discussion, with critics suggesting that their content has failed to engage with the national audience. For many academics in particular, the commercial exigencies of international funding have resulted in a cinema of compromise. These extend from plot choices to casting and location decisions, to a bastardisation of dialogue. Thus, for instance, Martin McLoone has argued that:

> the danger is that, to attract financial support, such films [co-productions] propose a view of Ireland that is already familiar to international funders and which funders in turn believe audiences are likely to recognise and identify with. Ultimately, they offer conservative images of Ireland that do not challenge existing cinematic traditions.
>
> (2000: 114–15).

In similar vein, Kevin Rockett remarks that, 'many films inevitably responded in the first instance to the demands of the international marketplace. In this regard, such films often reinforce rather than challenge the inherited stereotypes of the Irish in the cinema' (1999: 24). It is, of course, impossible to quantify the extent to which funding sources have influenced the content of individual films; not surprisingly, producers will reject the suggestion that their films' content has been dictated in any sense by their sources of finance.

The increase in European and international incentives for overseas film-making lowered Ireland's competitiveness and in recent years the relative weakness of the Irish pound, now euro, against sterling and the US dollar was largely responsible for maintaining the inflow of overseas productions. At the same time, numerous copycat investment schemes in countries with lower wage structures and a less unionised industry have diverted foreign productions away from Ireland; internally, the attractiveness of the scheme was also lessened by the fall in Irish interest rates. This coincided with a period of fiscal retrenchment as the so-called Celtic Tiger economy of the mid to late 1990s faltered. This economic boom mirrored the filmmaking boom and both were constructed on similar premises – that inward investment by multinational corporations would enable the country to develop an economy and infrastructure that it could not otherwise secure from internal resources. In the short term, both were blindingly successful, creating a consumer culture and a production basis that were the envy of many other older economies and filmmaking cultures. Critical voices soon emerged, however, to critique the new 'cappuccino' society as a vacuous replica of American consumerism, and one equally insouciant about its less privileged members (Allen, 2000; Kirby 2002). Similarly, as we have seen, Irish films of this period were deemed to have sold out to corporate pressure.

It is in fact reductive to dismiss these films so easily or indeed to subscribe to the kind of puritanical academicism that automatically critiques anything that smacks of the frivolous. As I will be arguing below, the Celtic Tiger economy and society may have glossed over many pressing social issues but it also allowed filmmakers to escape from the old obsessions, notably of nationalism and the State; moreover, as we shall see in the final chapter of this book, a number of recent films have indeed addressed and continue to explore issues of marginalisation and dispossession.

In this respect it is interesting to note the new 'Low Budget Feature Initiative' and the 'Micro Budget/Digital development Initiative' announced by the Film Board in 2002. This argued that:

> There has been a polarization in the market place with €10m and higher budget films at one end and low budget films at the other. The heretofore mid-range €3m to €5m film has become very difficult to finance and Bord Scannán na hÉireann/the Irish Film Board intends to encourage indigenous filmmaking at lower budget levels.
>
> (www.filmboard.ie; accessed 5 February 2003)

The focus is, therefore, to be on digital filmmaking which, in the case of the 'micro budget' initiative is also to reflect 'creative bravery and originality/innovation in style and content' (ibid.) The first two films funded by that scheme were the kinetic *Dead Bodies* (Robert Quinn, Ireland, 2003), a particularly misogynistic murder/caper, clearly influenced by *Shallow Grave* (Danny Boyle, GB, 1994) and *Goldfish Memory* (Elizabeth Gill, Ireland, 2002; discussed in Chapter 7). In 2003, the Film Board further announced that it would focus on its core activities and no longer fund television mini-series (ibid.). This suggests a new sense that greater control will be available at micro-budget level and that this is now considered to be the way forward in developing a national cinema.

In the Budget of 2002, the Minister for Finance, Charlie McCreevy, announced the termination of the Section 481 tax incentive from 2004; however, following concerted opposition from the filmmaking community, Mr McCreevy backed down, and the incentive has been extended to 2008.

The remaining chapters of this book are devoted to discussing the films of the second Film Board years (although reference is made to earlier works). As we shall see, Irish film culture has shown a marked shift away from an interrogation of the legacy of nationalism to a new fascination with issues of individualism and the self, most markedly expressed through gender representations. Simultaneously and hesitatingly, a new filmmaking practice has emerged in Northern Ireland that has sought to leaven political issues with black humour and, equally, to move towards a greater exploration of issues of individuality and cultural redefinition.

For many of the new generation of Irish filmmakers, it has become crucial that their work circulate as part of an international cinema defined by its engagement with multiple cultures, specifically with youth culture, rather than the national culture. Thematically the new generation of Irish filmmakers has shown itself keen to escape from the old concerns of the post-1970s filmmakers. As one of their most successful representatives, low-budget independent filmmaker John Carney expresses it, '90% of stories should be able to be told anywhere, unless specifically historical or something. What's bad about a lot of stories, especially Irish films, is that they're overly stuck on three or four preoccupations and everything else is avoided like the plague for some reason' (Shields, 2001: 12).

It is possible to detect in works such as *Accelerator* (Vinny Murphy, Ireland, 2000), *Disco Pigs* (Kirsten Sheridan, GB/Ireland, 2000) and *On the Edge* (John Carney, USA/Ireland, 2001) a sustained critique of Celtic Tiger Ireland with particular and, given the youthfulness of the films' makers, unsurprising focus on issues of youth and exclusion. The sense of a new a-political generation, divested of social concerns and corrupted by their positioning within the global economy is not wholly substantiated by their output. Many of them in turn have rejected the concerns of earlier cultural practitioners and have deliberately sought to create a space for themselves in the new economic order.

These preoccupations are spelt out in Frank Stapleton's subversive skit on Irish creative life, *The Fifth Province* (Frank Stapleton, GB/Germany/Ireland, 1997), when its gormless protagonist hero attends a workshop for aspiring scriptwriters: 'What we don't want,' he is told, is 'any more stories about … Irish mothers, priests, sexual repressions and the miseries of the rural life. We want stories that are upbeat, that are urban, that have pace and verve and are going somewhere' (McLoone, 2000: 169).

The relative success at the Irish box office of two such films, *About Adam* and *When Brendan Met Trudy* suggests that this is exactly what Irish audiences wanted as well. In itself, the decision to make two films that did not deal with 'state of the nation' themes, that were set in the present, in a hip glossy Dublin, that, in the case of *When Brendan* … consciously references the icons of international cinema is in itself a political statement, a rejection of the old shibboleths of Irish cinema of any period. Both films, and the later *Goldfish Memory*, are romantic comedies that consciously foreground their urban setting.

Stembridge has argued that his film is notable for portraying a middle-class Dublin at ease with its identity (Tierney, 2001: 16) and the very positive local reviews of the film vindicate his assertion, many of their writers welcoming *About Adam* exactly for that reason. This and its attitude to sex render it, according to its director, a political film whose politics are specific to its local context:

> One of the things that interests me is that it would have an entirely different emphasis in Ireland than elsewhere; here it has more to say about issues like guilt, the secular society and the liberal agenda. Rather than depicting a Government view of society I would sooner bring it to the Labour Party Conference and say, 'Here is the liberal agenda on film. Here are people who are no longer priest-ridden, here are people who have no guilt.'
>
> (ibid.)

The response of the *Sight and Sound* film critic to Stembridge's film is thus interesting: 'There's a sense that the film-makers were so keen to appeal to an international audience they have strained out everything that might have made *About Adam* distinctive ... this is a film without a clear sense of local identity' (Macnab, 2001: 38).

Here is a production that responds to a culturally specific desire not to be culturally specific. The only nod to older Irish cinematic conventions is in the characterisation of Peggy (Rosaleen Linehan) who departs little from the (benign) stage Irish mother. Given the type of filmmaking that digital equipment lends itself to and the Film Board's espousal of such practices, it is likely that the future will see a good deal more of the kind of filmmaking practices represented by *When Brendan Met Trudy, About Adam, Dead Bodies* and *Goldfish Memory.*

7

THE DEFLOWERING OF IRISH CINEMA

Gender in contemporary Irish cinema

'Is that real? She couldn't be!' Sean Thornton's response to his first view of Mary Kate Danaher in John Ford's *The Quiet Man*, might summarise the history of gender representation in Irish cinema. Thornton is seen here as the archetypal Irish-American, yearning to put his battling past behind him, return to the Ireland of his dreams and rediscover his mother/lover, a fresh if feisty Irish colleen. The other side of the coin is represented by the sullen, dangerous freedom fighters beloved of British films about Ireland, a lineage which stretches directly from *Odd Man Out* to *The Crying Game* (Neil Jordan, GB, 1992). If Mary Kate Danaher is the projection of an emigrant fantasy of return, Kathleen in *Odd Man Out* is the antithesis of the quintessential bourgeois heroine of British cinema, a reminder to British audiences of what happens to a country that lacks a class with a civilising mission. Similarly, Irish men are violent (a trait that is endearing in the American films, and self-destructive in the British productions) and prone to alcoholic excess. Many of the films made about Ireland centre around an outsider (usually male) who is drawn in to the local community in search of some kind of redemption. This may end happily (*The Quiet Man*) or, as the next chapter discusses, in tragedy (*Ryan's Daughter* [David Lean, GB, 1970]).

The embodiment of Ireland as young and feminine and an object of pure love, or alternatively as an old woman sheltering her sons in times of adversity, has a long representational history and is the subject of much academic commentary (Cairns and Richards, 1991; Innes, 1993; Meaney, 1998; Nash, 1997). Indeed, the gendering of nation has most commonly been portrayed as a dynamic of opposites, John Bull and fair Rosaleen, masculine England versus feminine Ireland (Leerssen, 1996a). The 'queering' of the nation disrupts this representational binary, allowing writers and playwrights in particular to modulate and play with this history of association, liberating signifier from signified (Cullingford, 2001). Although less attention has been paid to the emasculation of the fictional Irishman, this has been no less the case and is explored lucidly by Declan Kiberd as the consequence of a tradition of failed revolutions (1996: 380–94). Weak fathers beget rebel sons but the dynamics of patriarchy render them politically impotent and hence driven to excesses of performative masculinity.

The disadvantage of having access to such a highly defined set of emblematic relationships is that the creators of contemporary artworks have often struggled to free their characters from that history of representation. Too often, women and men in Irish films seem burdened by symbolism and lack any organic relationship to the lived experience of their real life prototypes in and outside of Ireland, historically and in the present. A related tradition that also overshadows cultural production is the obsessively oedipal nature of Irish representation. The centrality of the family unit as a metaphor for colonial, national and historic relations has already been mentioned. The clash of generations opposes past and present and, invariably, father and son. The mother figure is alternately and simultaneously, Mother Ireland and the Virgin Mary, devoted and a-sexual, her own desires subsumed into the maternal. At the same time, she dominates the domestic space, often dislodging the emasculated male as head of the family. This has been ascribed to a post-Famine tradition of Church domination whereby the priest won control of the household through his alliance with the mother (Inglis, 1998) and, equally, to a history of failed revolutions. Thus, 'the Irish father was often a defeated man, whose wife frequently won the bread and usurped his domestic power, while the priest usurped his spiritual authority' (Kiberd, 1996: 380). The daughter may align herself with her suffering mother or adopt the revolutionary aspirations of her brothers and male suitor. 'When is this trouble going to end, this killing and more killing?' Frankie's sister declaims in *The Informer*. 'It's hard on you women, I know', is the resigned response from IRA leader, Dan Gallagher.

Critical approaches to gender representations in Irish fiction have been dominated by questions of nationalism. These are succinctly summarised by Colin Graham as revolving around the definition of the subaltern and new readings of nationalism. Women,[1] as a consequence of their disempowerment by the State, may be defined as constituting a subaltern. On the other hand, if nationalism is to be rescued from its now discredited position as a recidivist orthodoxy and reclaimed as revolutionary, then it cannot also be the case that women are oppressed by nationalist discourse (Graham, 2001: 102–31). The relationship between feminism and nationalism, and feminism and unionism, has been widely debated (Longley,1994: 173–95; Meaney, 1993) without any position of agreement being reached as to whether nationalism/unionism can accommodate feminist ambitions.

Certainly, many films overtly make connections between gender representation and the legacy of nationalism. The solution for some is the discovery of personal identity politics outside the orbit of political and religious orthodoxies. The danger for others is the descent into essentialism that always threatens to overwhelm the retrieval of the subaltern for radical politics. There are also larger issues of how to treat the middle classes within such a configuration since it seems unlikely that the critics whom Graham discusses, notably David Lloyd, are particularly concerned about their place within the nationalist-subaltern axis. Ironically, it could be claimed that fictions about the bourgeoisie offer a radical opportunity to leave behind the symbolic figures of nationalist representation.

The desire to interrogate the relationship between feminism and nationalism coincided with a period of extreme trauma in the Republic when a series of occurrences threw into relief the oppressive history of State interference in what otherwise might be considered personal behaviour. To summarise these events briefly, in 1984 the body of a baby stabbed to death was found on a beach in County Kerry. A police investigation revealed the alleged culprit, a young woman named Joanne Hayes. In fact it was to turn out that she had given birth to a different baby who had been buried in her garden. The manner in which the investigation was carried out led to extreme criticism of the police methods, particularly from a number of leading feminists. In the event, it was impossible to get to the bottom of what had really occurred. Earlier that year, a pregnant schoolgirl, Ann Lovett, died whilst giving birth at the foot of a statue of the Virgin Mary. In 1992, another pregnant teenager, raped by a friend of the family, was banned by the State from travelling to Britain for an abortion. The 'X' case, as this came to be called, mobilised the two opposing forces of liberal and conservative Ireland and eventually the Supreme Court allowed the victim to travel to England on the grounds that she was suicidal and that in effect her life was in danger. Abortion was then and is now banned in Ireland and the constitutional ramifications of that decision are still being pursued. Later on in 1992, the Kilkenny Incest Case focused the country's attention on the plight of a young woman, living on a remote farm, who had been subjected for over a decade to persistent and violent rape by her father and had a son by him. The Bishop Casey revelations, in which it emerged that a much respected Irish Bishop had fathered a child and 'borrowed' from church funds to support (financially though not emotionally) his son in America began to look tame as the nineties and 2000s threw up instance after instance of religious paedophilia. Even nuns were not exempt as the Magdalene laundries scandal and similar cases brought to the public attention the systematic abuse of single mothers, much of it uncomfortably recently. At the same time as these narratives were entering the public domain, a secondary and linked anxiety was being aired: that the family unit was under threat and that teenage pregnancy and single motherhood, particularly attributed to the urban working class, were the cause. On a political level, the repression of sexuality which so strongly characterised both rural and urban Irish society from the turn of the century onwards and which was endorsed by the profoundly conservative post-Independence regime resulted in a traumatic release which was just beginning to make itself clear in the early 1980s and has continued to erupt into Irish cultural discourse.

It was with Pat Murphy's two feminist works, *Maeve* (1980) and *Anne Devlin* (1984) that the notion of a woman's cinema entered Irish filmmaking. With the latter film, we can see Murphy begin a move away from her origins in the avant-garde towards a more realist-based mode of production. This trajectory was completed with the release of *Nora* (Ireland/GB/

Germany/Italy, 1999), based on Brenda Maddox's eponymous biography of Nora Barnacle (published 1988). *Anne Devlin* is dedicated 'to the women forgotten by history. The women who worked for freedom and are imprisoned for their beliefs' and draws on the diaries[2] of Devlin who in standard historical accounts went to prison for the love of the man for whom she acted as housekeeper (Robert Emmet was the leader of the 1803 uprising of the United Irishmen whose failure directly led to the Act of Union). *Nora*, too, is motivated by the ambition to rescue James Joyce's lover and, later, wife from the lesser status to which she has been relegated by literary history.

Both films are marked by a stylised, painterly shooting style, particularly evident in their rich evocation of interiors and their use of lighting. *Anne Devlin* is shot partly as an historical epic and partly as a series of still tableaux. The opening scenes are set in the aftermath of the 1798 Rising as the women collect their dead. It moves on to 1803 when Anne (Brid Brennan) volunteers to pose as housekeeper to Emmet (Bosco Hogan) so that the conspiracy can take place under cover of normalcy.

Despite Emmet's assurances, she is as much servant as political go-between since many of the men still expect her to keep house for them. In the aftermath of the failure of the Rising, Anne is taken to prison, tortured and kept in solitary confinement but refuses to inform. In 1806, with the change of government in Britain, she is released and in voice-over recounts how she passed a group of Emmet's men in the street who did not acknowledge her and whom she did not ask for help although she was destitute.

Any reading of *Anne Devlin* needs to take into account the various earlier cinematic representations of Irish women, since the film, like Murphy's previous *Maeve*, is clearly designed as an intervention in this process. We can see it as a response to a number of factors: the denial of women's roles in history; prevailing cinematic images of women; the failure of the early filmmakers in the first years of independent production to create positive images of women and the idealisation of a nurturing, passive concept of motherhood fostered by the post-Independence authorities. A secondary challenge was to make a period film that did not accede to the voyeuristic pleasures of the conventional costume drama. Most importantly, in both *Anne Devlin* and *Nora*, Murphy has had to negotiate the danger of idealising the subaltern. The key, in both films, was the creation of a distinctive visual and spatial register that avoids the conventional signifiers of nostalgia for a peasant simplicity.

Thus, in an early sequence in *Anne Devlin*, we watch Anne moving silently from one room to another in the house that forms the headquarters of the conspiracy. She passes from darkness into a cold blue light, glancing at the books and writings on Emmet's desk, touching his papers, smelling the contents of a bowl. As she is standing against the wall in the light thrown by the shutter, Emmet enters the room and begins to speak to her, closing the shutter and obscuring her, literally and metaphorically. In this sequence, the accompanying classical score associated with Anne Devlin's movement through the film militates against intimations of 'peasant intuition'. In *Nora*, a similar moment occurs in the latter part of the film after Joyce (Ewan McGregor) has embarked on his masochistic fantasy that Prezioso (Roberto Citran) is having an affair with Nora. The scene opens with the men ranged against the wall watching as her portrait is sketched out, Nora poised against a plush blue cloth background. It cuts to Nora and Joyce making love, he accusing her of infidelity, and back to a shot that includes the artist's hand sketching her and of Nora herself modelling. Joyce enters the room and claims that he knows nothing about painting, coming as he does from an 'oral tradition'. Joyce then announces that he has sent the children on holiday, thus setting Nora up with Prezioso. Impatiently, Nora moves away from her position as model and confronts Joyce. Shortly afterwards, she watches, half hidden behind a door as Prezioso looks at the sketches, the current one located to one side of the frame. These moments suggest her struggle to retain a subject position in face of her constant objectification – by Joyce and his companions, and later by history.

Previously, Nora has told Joyce the story of Michael's death after an afternoon at the cinema has brought back memories of him that come to her as images but which Joyce transforms into words. Images and words repeatedly clash: Joyce's ironic claim to an oral tradition is traduced by his interest in cinema as a business venture but also as the locus for his own sexual fantasies – here he masturbates to letters (words) from Nora. Each lays claim to image-making, expressing themselves through words, in turn inspired by

Figure 7.1 Nora. Susan Lynch (Nora Barnacle).

images. To be subject not object, both understand, is to be victor; yet the camera suggests that Nora's struggle to de-objectify herself, to escape entrapment is only a partially won battle.

Nora's bedroom, to which she retires after receiving the series of letters from Joyce, accusing her of sexual promiscuity, is a clear, bright space, quite different from the heavy, blue-hued interior of the living area where the painting takes place. As Murphy has explained it:

> The room that she has, you never see Joyce in that space because he has gone to Ireland and it's like *her* mind. When she's devastated by the letter and goes in and closes the door, that space is her space. And the later apartment that they're in, I feel it's like his mind, that she moves round in his space, and that she is quite trapped in it.
>
> (Barton, 2000b: 13)

If Nora is associated with an uninhibited sexuality and caustic tongue, in the earlier film Anne Devlin's silence is a token of resistance to patriarchy. It is in her passivity that her strength lies and it is this that establishes her difference and superiority to the men who cannot resist action. As Pat Murphy has said, *Anne Devlin* has a three-act structure but, unlike conventional historical epics or romances, there is no one climactic act, such as Emmet's death, Anne Devlin's death or even her release (which we do not see). Instead:

> The climax of the film is the whole third act, because this is where her energy, which has been gathering over two previous acts, is released. It's released very slowly, and the music plays an important role here. I'm very interested in the strength that Anne Devlin had – it wasn't explosive like the rebellion, it was released very slowly and that was what defeated her opponents.
>
> (Petley, 1986: 4)

Murphy has remained the most stylised and formally inventive of the Irish generation of women filmmakers actively engaged in constructing a 'women's cinema'. This project was augmented by the work of the short-lived Derry Film and Video Workshop, which owed its brief existence to Channel 4's regional funding scheme, notably the productions of Margo Harkin and Anne Crilly. Harkin's *Hush-a-Bye-Baby* (Ireland, 1989) was inspired by the Abortion Referendum of 1983 in the Republic as well as by the Ann Lovett and the Kerry babies' stories. At the same time, it actively engages with the intersection of women's issues and nationalism. Much of the cast was non-professional and the film also features singer Sinéad O'Connor in an early cameo role. In the story, a teenager from a nationalist background in Derry becomes pregnant; by the time she recognises this, her boyfriend is being detained under suspicion of terrorism. She manages to conceal her pregnancy, only confiding in her best friend (Cathy Casey). The film ends with her going into labour, which (the visuals leave it unclear) may be dangerously premature. In a series of images, the film links the pregnant teenager, Goretti's (Emer McCourt)[3] fears of revealing her pregnancy three-fold: with the cult of the Virgin Mary, with the traditional values of Catholic Ireland and with the then current arguments employed by the Pro-Life movement in the debate surrounding the abortion referendum. Unlike *Maeve* or *Anne Devlin*, *Hush-a-Bye-Baby* offers many of the aesthetic pleasures of mainstream, small screen entertainment conventionally associated with British 'quality' television. The young women go to discos and play tricks on their teachers and the film carefully portrays a society run by a strong female network. On the other hand, its symbolism is overt and unmistakeable, particularly its nightmarish vision of the various statues of the Virgin Mary the teenagers encounter.

Hush-a-Bye-Baby has been widely analysed for its exploration of the intersection between nationalism and feminism. Thus, Luke Gibbons writes that films such as this and others (*December Bride* [Thaddeus O'Sullivan, GB, 1990] and *The Playboys* [Gillies MacKinnon, GB, 1992]), 'operate politically, as alternative national narratives to the official discourses of faith and fatherland' (1993: 13). Richard Kirkland views the film 'as a daring and experimental work with an explicit educational function and yet simultaneously a text caught in those very traps of identitarian politics it seeks to evade: a dilemma signalled by its ambiguous, almost weary, closure' (1999: 110). Meanwhile, Elizabeth Cullingford has focused on the moment in the film where Goretti is faced in class with Seamus Heaney's poem, 'Limbo' about a mother drowning her infant child. Harkin, she argues, inflects Heaney's own ambiguous nationalism with a feminist reading, appropriating his art for cultural politics (2001: 234–57).

The urgency with which *Hush-a-Bye-Baby* addresses its concerns has left it susceptible to the passage of time, locating it within a specific moment in Irish cultural history. Its achievement was to create sympathetic young female characters and depict a contemporary world – of discos, school locker room gossip and furtive teenage sex – that had not previously been seen on Irish screens. Overlaid with a swingeing critique of a culture embedded in a regressive, male-dominated nationalism, it suggested that it was possible to combine the political and the personal and to centre them around a set of female concerns. As it happens, it remains a rarity, a testimony to how Irish cinema could have developed.

Orla Walsh's short film *The Visit* (Ireland, 1992) was one of the few successors to *Hush-a-Bye-Baby* and again raises the issue of the place of women in communities defined by their allegiance to nationalism. In this case, the central character, Sheila (Magael MacLaughlin) is left alone shortly after her marriage when her husband is imprisoned in Long Kesh (the Maze). After an affair, she finds herself pregnant but decides to abandon her lover and, in the final sequence of the film, we presume that during the course of her visit, she is going to inform her husband of her pregnancy. Walsh has said that her film, 'was taking the intellectual ideas of

Maeve but placing them in the context of ordinary people' (Sullivan, 1997: 37). This claim is somewhat contradicted by having Sheila reach a point of self-discovery which makes her assert that by keeping the baby, she is, for once, doing something for herself: 'It's not really a feminist tract but an independence tract' (ibid.: 38). If Harkin can see no viable way out for her teenage protagonist in *Hush-a-Bye-Baby* and so refuses closure, Walsh's liberal, humanist optimism suggests that Sheila has realised her individualism in the face of an alarmingly (for her to have any realistic chance of happiness) recalcitrant community, hell bent on punishing dissident members.[4]

The radical ambitions of Harkin's and Walsh's films may be usefully contrasted with the adaptation of Roddy Doyles' securely paternalistic and patriarchal novel of the same name *The Snapper* (Stephen Frears, GB, 1993). Set in a lower middle-class estate, Frears' film does not deal with issues of nationalism but rather contemporary social anxieties over teenage pregnancy. When Sharon (Tina Kellegher) announces that she is pregnant, the family rallies round, loudly abusing those neighbours who dare to pass judgement on their offspring. In the absence of a father for the child, Mr Curley (Colm Meaney) steps in and the bad father (a hapless local middle-aged husband played by Pat Laffan) is thrown out and replaced by a good father. This process is made particularly clear in the scenes where Mr Curley begins to show an interest in the pregnancy, furtively scurrying around the public library to hunt out manuals on the female body, through to his whole-hearted involvement in the event. In effect, the pregnancy becomes his and the threat of the single mother bringing up her child in a non-paternalistic family unit is dispelled.

The feminist/activist agenda coincided somewhat bizarrely with popular cultural attitudes in their combined assault on the venerable figure of Mother Ireland. On the one hand, the other production from the Derry Film and Video Collective, Anne Crilly's 1988 documentary, *Mother Ireland*, elicited in interview the responses of a cross-section of Irish women to the tradition of representing Ireland as a mother and as an old woman.[5] For many, this representational history was either ridiculous or oppressive, but others saw in it a recognition of the centrality of motherhood, both to them and to the national self-image. This deconstructive and eminently fair-handed approach contrasts with the eruption of an ontological backlash that elided the figure of the Irish mother with that of Norman Bates' parent in *Psycho* (Alfred Hitchcock, USA, 1960). Thus, one such example, the short film, *A Mother's Love's A Blessing* (Ireland, 1994) written by Pat McCabe and directed by Charlie McCarthy, plays out an obsessive rural mother–son relationship as dark comedy. 'Mammy' (Joan O'Hara) has brought up her only son, Pat (Pat Kinevane) on a diet of guilt, smothering love and 'hang' (ham) sandwiches. Increasingly bitter, he dresses himself up as the neighbour, Mrs Tubridy, only to reveal his disguise by forgetting to change his shoes. On this occasion, Mammy foils his attempt to stab her but a final shot of a gravestone in the back garden suggests that matters have been resolved to his satisfaction. The same material is plundered for similar effect in *Driftwood* (Ronan O'Leary, Ireland/GB, 1996), *The Fifth Province* and comic contrast in the television film, also directed and this time written by Charlie McCarthy, *Home for Christmas* (Ireland, 2002).

In terms of gender representations, one of the most provocative of the early independent directors was Kieran Hickey. At first glance, his works seem conventional, and unlike say Bob Quinn or Joe Comerford, he was content to restrict himself to an unobtrusive though elegant shooting style. It is the subject matter of his films that Hickey was remarkable for. In works such as *Exposure* (Ireland, 1978) and *Criminal Conversation* (Ireland, 1980), he systematically stripped away the bravado and smugness of the male pose assumed by the professional classes who had emerged out of the transformed Irish economy of the 1960s. In *Criminal Conversation* these are Frank (Emmet Bergin), an estate agent and Charlie (Peter Caffrey), an advertising executive. The men are best friends and Frank is Charlie's client. Their wives display the classic symptoms of female middle class alienation – their perfect homes run themselves and they have no income (and therefore no status). Both marriages are 'barren' – Frank and Margaret (Deirdre Donnelly) have adopted a child in an attempt to retrieve their relationship and Charlie and Bernadette (Leslie Lalor) have decided against children, because in Charlie's words, 'it's great with no children'. The film makes it clear that she would like to have a family but that that would conflict with his aspirational lifestyle. The thin papering over of the cracks falls apart when Margaret reveals that she has had an affair with Charlie, Frank confesses that, despite appearances, he is not actually unfaithful, and Bernadette concedes that she knows Charlie is unfaithful.

Underneath the brittle veneer of success lies a tale of frustrated ambition (Charlie would have really liked to have been an artist), wasted lives and sexual inadequacy (nothing they do compares with the robust sexuality of the teenage baby-sitter and her boyfriend). Frank's machismo is meaningless and even the friendship of men turns out to be built on sand. Despite all this, the film retains a certain sympathy for its protagonists (more than in *Exposure*, certainly), presenting them as the victims of class rather than nationalist history.

The 1990s have been marked by an increased interest in exploring masculinities, often in the context of the relationship between nationalism and the male performance of violence. In Gerry Stembridge's *Guiltrip* (Ireland, 1995) in particular but also in the short films of Kevin Liddy, *Horse* (Ireland, 1993) and *A Soldier's Song* (Ireland, 1997), aggressive male roles are seen to emerge out of a history of socially sanctioned violence. *Guiltrip* is the chronicle of a cycle of domestic conflict. Working as a series of flashbacks, it follows one day in the life of a young couple, Tina (Jasmine Russell) and her soldier husband, Liam (Andrew Connolly). She fantasises about shopping and a hi-fi salesman while he alternately abuses her and remembers his encounter with the salesman's wife, whom he eventually murders. The neighbours cannot and will not help; small town Ireland is seen less as a community than as the locus of alienation and estrangement. Neither male nor female friendships work and the two marriages around which the film revolves are failures. Central to the film's success is the performance of Andrew Connolly who previously played the romantic lead in *Joyriders* (Aisling Walsh, GB, 1988). As Liam he is both a monster, forcing his wife to keep a 'Standing Orders Book' into which she must write his house rules and account for what she has done during the day, and a failure, cold-shouldered by his military colleagues and, in his encounter with Michele (Michelle Houlden) sexually impotent. Kevin Liddy's short film *Horse* focuses on the relationship between a child, Michael (Ruairi Conroy) and his father, Patrick (Mick Lally) who is dying of tuberculosis. Although a bare 30 minutes in length, this is a visually stunning film that reconstructs rural life with a cold, detailed eye. Ireland of the 1960s is a brutal and lonely place, dominated, the camera suggests, by its religious and historical legacy, where people barely communicate except through acts of aggression. In one of these, Michael's neighbour just stops short of drowning him when he catches him raiding the chickens. In another scene we see his father start a fight with a neighbour, 'you must never turn the other cheek', he tells his son as he is beaten to pulp. In the final scene, Michael in turn beats the neighbour's dog to death. In a key sequence, Michael circles the Cú Chulainn statue in the General Post Office, the centre of the 1916 Easter Rising. The statue, executed by Oliver Sheppard in 1914, depicts the legendary hero dying for Ireland after having lashed himself to a stone pillar in order to fight his enemies to the last (the overtones of blood sacrifice and Christian martyrdom particularly commended the statue to Patrick Pearse despite the incongruity of an essentially Ulster hero being appropriated by Nationalist ideology). As Michael tries to read the words (of the Proclamation of Independence) on the base of the statue, passers-by move between him and it, obliterating his vision. What remains is the image of combat without the contextualising written explanation. Michael is surrounded with the triumphant celebration of male aggression and he too must become part of that cycle. Liddy was to reprise many of these themes in his feature, *Country* (Ireland, 2000); however, by the time this narrative of abusive and domineering patriarchs was released, the cinematic exploration of masculinity had pushed towards a new desire to depict a more sensitive male hero and Liddy's feature seemed to belong to an earlier era.

This 'new man' made his appearance across a range of productions including David Keating's *The Last of the High Kings* (Ireland/GB/Denmark, 1995), *I Went Down, The Last Bus Home* (Johnny Gogan, Ireland, 1997), *About Adam, When Brendan Met Trudy* and *On the Edge* (John Carney, USA/Ireland, 2001). These films have in common a desire to address a new, modern Ireland and to free themselves from the conventional signifiers of a traumatised national identity. Thus, in *The Last of the High Kings*, cultural nationalism's appellation of a past of heroic failure is mocked and parodied in its central character, Frankie Griffin's (Jared Leto), refusal to behave as if he were indeed the last in line of the high kings of Ireland. This lineage is foisted on him by his mother who is marked out as a demented eccentric from the film's opening sequences. Frankie identifies himself, as do his friends, through a global youth culture that revolves around devotion to Elvis Presley and the availability of teenage sex. Modelling themselves primarily on the 'coming of age film' with its fixation on masculine identities and promiscuity, these works variously position their youthful male central characters as victims of their parents' outmoded preoccupations with history and politics and of their own cultural inheritance. As we saw in the previous chapter, they deliberately espouse global filmmaking practices as a liberating strategy.

I Went Down achieves this through transposing the postmodern, post-Tarantino gangster/road movie to an Irish setting. Here, two amateur criminals, Bunny (Brendan Gleeson) and Git (Peter McDonald) embark on a surreal journey across Ireland at the behest of a master criminal towards a final rendezvous where their collective past catches up with them. Widely acclaimed by the local press, the film enjoyed substantial box office takings in Ireland though failed to transfer with any conspicuous success to overseas territories. Part of the film's trajectory as a road movie is to force Bunny to face up to an event that occurred when he was in prison, namely a homosexual encounter which he confesses to Git was not entirely unwelcome. Problematically, the film is unable to commit itself to rendering Bunny's sexual orientation any more explicit than this and there is a sense that access to a queer identity is little more than a signifier of some kind of unexplored

Figure 7.2 I Went Down. Brendan Gleeson (Bunny Kelly).

but protean masculinity. In this, it is at least able to counter the associations between homosexuality and perversion established by an earlier foray into the gangster genre, *The Courier* (Joe Lee, Frank Deasy, Ireland, 1987). The fact that homosexuality was decriminalised in the Republic of Ireland only in 1993 is indicative of the slow acceptance of non-normative sexualities in Irish culture. As Lance Pettit has discussed, the fusion of sexual politics with identity politics may already have become questionable in 'mainstream' culture but in the relatively arriviste model of Irish modernisation, this has remained a feasible strategy (Pettitt, 1999).

We need to remain wary, however, of establishing a gay/straight binary that conveniently serves to distinguish contemporary from traditional Ireland (as for discussing representations of lesbian sexuality, the viewer was, until the release of *Goldfish Memory*, left with naughty Scandinavians) – *Snakes and Ladders* [Trish McAdam, Ireland/GB/Germany, 1996] and perverted housewives, *Crush Proof* (Paul Tickell, GB/Netherlands/Ireland/ Germany, 1998]). It is, for instance, tempting to read the apparent suicide of Petie (John Cronin), the gay punk band member in *The Last Bus Home* as consequent upon his parents' narrow-minded, 'old Ireland' disgust at his disclosure of his queer sexuality, and the film seems to encourage such an analysis. The difficulty lies in this traumatising of homosexuality and its discussion as marginal to dominant Irish culture. The same trajectory affects the depiction of Dublin bus conductor, Alfie Byrne (Albert Finney) in *A Man of No Importance* (Suri Krishnamma, GB/Ireland, 1994). Loosely paralleling Oscar Wilde's life, Byrne is assaulted after cruising a gay bar and

Figure 7.3 The Last Bus Home (l-r): John Cronin (Petie), Annie Ryan (Reena) and Brian F. O'Byrne (Jessop).

attempts suicide. These sequences are distinctly at odds with the otherwise whimsical tone of the film and enforce the 'shock' that its otherwise mild exploration of gay identity entails. In this instance, some hope of social integration appears on the horizon, although, given the reaction of most of the central characters to Byrne's 'outing', this is less than probable. Homosexuality as trauma marks the discourse of many of the short films that have enjoyed greater freedom to depict gay identities on screen, notably Orla Walsh's *Bent Out of Shape* (Ireland, 1995) which, like so many of the films discussed in this and Chapter 5, culminates in a queer bashing sequence.

In *2by4* (Jimmy Smallhorne, USA, 1997), issues of gay and bisexual identity are relocated to the Irish-American diaspora. Somewhat problematic in its apparent linking of paedophilia and homosexuality (Pettitt, 1999: 63), it opens a space for a more fluid definition of desire and sexual orientation. Here, the central character, Johnny (Smallhorne) exhibits moments of severe trauma linked to memories he cannot recover. His uncle, Trump (Chris O'Neill), on whose site he works as foreman, embezzles the wages to gratify his need for masochistic sex with the black male prostitutes he despises. Jimmy himself finds a measure of redemption through an affair with an Australian rent boy that ends his relationship with an Irish girlfriend. Ultimately, in a moment shot as a kind of rebirthing scene, he identifies the cause of his recurrent nightmare, Trump's abuse of him as a child in Ireland. Smallhorne's film plays with many of the conventional signifiers of Irish-American ethnic identity, notably the idealisation of the 'mother' country, in this case reconfigured as an abusive fatherland (McLoone, 2000: 198). New York is represented through Declan Quinn's edgy digital camerawork as a kind of Scorsesean hell into which the Irish easily fit. Smallhorne still manages to find moments of lyricism in this social detritus, notably in the sequence where the labourer, Joe (Joe Holyoake) reads out his poetry of immigration and in the final moments when a rearranged version of the ballad *Danny Boy* is performed as a gay anthem.

The sense that gay identities can only be confronted when relocated from the 'native soil' is echoed in one of the few short films to explore lesbian desire. *Black and White* (Ireland, 1994), written by Kathy Gilfillan and directed by Alan Robinson, makes explicit connections between national and sexual identities. Here, a recently arrived young Irishwoman, Carol (Julie Hale) delivers a framed photograph to a young American woman, Marie-Louise (Elizabeth McGovern), in her minimalist, designer London apartment. Carol is somewhat gauche but confesses to a fascination with Marie-Louise who is positioned as sexually knowing and sophisticated. Home, for the Dublin woman, is both a place of nostalgic recollection and atavistic trends, notably associated in her mind with Irish men and drink. However, when she discovers that Marie-Louise operates as an up-market prostitute, Carol is appalled and swiftly backs off the budding relationship, exclaiming, 'Call me Irish or call me old-fashioned!' That dual inheritance is, the film suggests and Marie-Louise articulates, her 'hang up'. Again, lesbianism, or bisexuality, is positioned as (national) trauma rather than as unexceptionable sexual behaviour.

Arguably, Gerry Stembridge's quintessential Celtic Tiger film, *About Adam* moves in the direction of naturalising gay and bi-sexual desire in its depiction of its central character, Adam (Stuart Townsend).[6] Stembridge has said that he wanted the film to be 'a joke about the new man, the sensitive man, the caring man, the man who listens' (*Director and Cast Interviews*, DVD [region 2]). A reworking of the premise of *Theorem* (Pier Paolo Pasolini, Italy, 1968), Stembridge's film centres around a middle-class Dublin family of mother, three daughters and their brother. Unbeknownst to each other, all four children have or desire to have a brief sexual encounter with Adam, and one, Lucy (Kate Hudson) announces that she is marrying him, a plan that he amiably goes along with. Shot in a chic, upbeat Dublin of designer interiors and lifestyle shopping, the film emphasises Adam's willing accession to the role of commodity, obliging those whom he encounters with real and fantasised sex. Whilst, however, sex is always a promise in terms of his heterosexual dalliances with the sisters, his night out with David (Alan Maher) is another matter. Despite Adam's apparent willingness, the two men do not have sex since it is a barrier that David is unable to cross. Only with *Goldfish Memory* did gay and lesbian sexuality enter Irish cinematic discourse in a positive and celebratory fashion. Made under the new, low-budget digital programme initiated by the Film Board, Gill's setting has much in common with the chic, metropolitan

Figure 7.4 About Adam. Stuart Townsend (Adam) and Frances O'Connor (Laura).

Dublin familiar to viewers of the RTÉ series, *Bachelor's Walk*. *Goldfish Memory*'s characters agonise over their multiple relationships in brightly lit café-bars and remove themselves to loft-style apartments for a variety of same sex and opposite sex encounters. Marriage is presented as a worst case scenario, whilst the central lesbian couple's desire for babies is viewed with warmth. *Goldfish Memory* displays many of the difficulties inherent in bridging the divide between a mainstream and niche gay/lesbian audience, sliding frequently into stereotype, yet it is also an important landmark in the depiction of non-normative sexual attraction in an Irish context.

If the 1980s were associated with a brief moment when women asserted their right to dominate cinematic space (in those films discussed above and also in other productions such as *The Country Girls, The Girl With Green Eyes, The Lonely Passion of Judith Hearne*), it seems that questions of masculinity have returned as the pre-eminent discourse of Celtic Tiger and post-Celtic Tiger Ireland. Despite the work of women filmmakers such as Geraldine Creed, Trish McAdam, Maedbh McGuckian, and Kirsten Sheridan, the dominance of oedipal configurations in Irish cinema might be ascribed to the overwhelming number of male directors operating in the arena. Of these, Neil Jordan and Jim Sheridan most consistently return to themes of father/son relationships and the metaphorical elision of family and nation (Barton, 2002). Jordan is also responsible for the film that most notoriously muddied the waters of gender representation and national identities, *The Crying Game*. A reworking of *Guests of the Nation* and Brendan Behan's *The Hostage* (*An Giall*, 1958) that is moulded along the lines of Jordan's repeated trope of the rescue fantasy, the film has been much

Figure 7.5 Goldfish Memory (l-r): Fiona Glascott (Isolde), Sean Campion (Tom), Fiona O'Shaughnessy (Clara). Courtesy of Liz Gill; photography by Pat Redmond.

discussed for its depiction of the relationship between reluctant IRA gunman Fergus (Stephen Rea), black British soldier, Jody (Forest Whitaker) and black, transvestite London hairdresser, Dil (Jaye Davidson). Like so much of Jordan's elliptical oeuvre, *The Crying Game* is an opaque text that defies any single reading. Thus, bell hooks has critiqued its conventional representation of black femininity as nurturing and submissive (hooks, 1994: 53–62). David Lloyd discovers in Jordan's film the potential to disrupt the borders of modernity and of racial and gender identities, arguing that the film's ending, however, returns its subjects to their previously fixed positions under patriarchy (1999: 63–76). Slavoj Zizek reads Jordan's film as 'the ultimate variation of courtly love' (1993: 105) and acclaims it as running counter to the conventional separation of private sexuality and political power-play – 'In short, the subtitle of *The Crying Game* could have been "Irishmen, yet another effort, if you want to become republicans!"' (ibid.: 107). As a radical text, *The Crying Game* is undermined by its regressive depiction of women, specifically the terrorist Jude (Miranda Richardson) who is represented as a classic castrating avenger (Edge, 1995), though Elizabeth Cullingford describes the relationship between Jody and Fergus 'as the nexus of nationality and desire [that] is the culmination of one strand of Irish theatre history', namely the symbolic love affair between Englishman and Irish colleen (2001: 62).

Ultimately, the film is best read as reflecting the continuing assertion of the validity of identity politics over State politics. Jordan himself has said of the film:

> To me it had a lot do with the IRA at the time, to see if they could change. Could people's narrow identifications of themselves change? This country has been blighted with a sense of exclusive identification of people who see themselves as Catholic, Protestant, Unionist or Nationalist. It was an exploration of self. That's what I wanted to do with it. If you strip away all the masks these human beings wear, is anything left underneath? Is anything left for Fergus when all this stuff is stripped away from him? In, fact, there is, and he turns out to be a human being.
>
> (Falsetto: 1999: 172–3)

The politics of self and a humanist agenda, in other words, replace old orthodoxies and liberate the individual from the claims of nationalisms, just as they did in *The Visit*. Yet, Jordan's own interpretation sits uncomfortably with his central parable, of the Scorpion and the Frog, which asserts a determinist world view – people cannot change and must do what their nature dictates. Fergus is the classic existential hero who can only retrieve his true identity after surmounting a series of personal, psychological obstacles. His political and sexual encounters offer him the opportunity to discover aspects of his own self, a process that is forestalled, as Lloyd suggests, by the forceful and, perhaps fortuitous, intervention of the State. Whether he would have gone the distance with Dil had he not found himself behind bars remains unanswerable. Like so many of his cinematic predecessors, he may only experiment with heterodox sexual identities by leaving nationalist Ireland behind and entering the fluid, polymorphous environment of the postmodern metropolis. Contrary to Zizek's benevolent interpretation, Fergus must abandon his political aspirations, here associated with regressive gender and racial attitudes, if he wants to participate in this new multicultural, multi-gendered space, one that is only gradually opening up in Ireland.

8

ANOTHER COUNTRY

The representation of history and the past

As we have seen so far, Irish cinema, both locally produced and otherwise, is notable for its apparently obsessive desire to reproduce narratives of history on screen. From the earliest silent films through to a number of key recent productions, cinema-goers have been exposed to a variety of interpretations of Ireland's past that may well tell us as more about the era in which they were made than the incidents and periods they ostensibly portray.

Where the films of the Kalem Company and the Film Company of Ireland reflected the urgency of legitimising revolutionary aspirations via a history of justifiable insurrection, the productions associated with the early years of the Free State were focused on heroising the events of independence. Until the late 1950s few films (*Guests of the Nation* is an exception) sought to critique the legacy of 1916 and still fewer to explore the contested history of the Civil War of 1922–23.

The outbreak of the Troubles in 1969, their continuation until the 1990s and the fragility of the Peace Process have provided filmmakers with what has become a genre in itself – 'Troubles Cinema' – and this is considered in greater detail in Chapter 10.

The discourses surrounding the contested theories of revisionism have further complicated depictions of armed Republicanism in contemporary cinema. Although revisionism may be dated back to the 1930s, it emerged as a hotly debated subject in the wake of the outbreak of the Troubles. To simplify the issues considerably, they have accrued over the question of the 'proper' way to treat republican history in the present. Revisionists argue that the mythologising processes of nationalism, its celebration of armed resistance and blood sacrifice, have acted as a regressive force in Irish society whilst alienating Unionist sensibilities and lending legitimacy to the activities of republican paramilitaries. Against this, anti-revisionists have posited that Republicanism enabled the birth of the post-colonial State and was in its day a modernising influence. It deserves to be celebrated for this and as a guarantor of national identity (Brady, 1994).

In the 1980s and 1990s it became apparent that there was a new popular interest in the more recent history of the post-Independence State directed in particular at an exhumation of what came to be perceived as the 'dark days' of the 1950s, a period characterised by a 'fairly widespread sense of cultural and social despair' (Brown, 1981: 212). Films such as *Korea* (Cathal

Black, Ireland, 1995) and *Broken Harvest* (Maurice O'Callaghan, Ireland, 1994) revisited this period, finding in it a narrow-minded, Church-ridden society still nurturing the festering sores of the Civil War. The role of the Church itself in retarding social growth has slowly begun to be recognised in Irish cinematic fictions, although until recently this has been largely the preserve of television. The notoriety that has accrued to the Church and the institutions it was responsible for – education, orphanages, industrial schools, the Magdalene laundries for 'wayward' women – have been revealed in a series of high-profile television documentaries and docu-dramas such as Louis Lenten's *Dear Daughter* (RTÉ, 1996) on the Goldenbridge orphanage, the three-part RTÉ exposé of institutional child abuse, *States of Fear* (1999) and the BBC investigative programme, *Suing the Pope* (2002) on child sex abuse in a parish in Wexford. Only in 2002 did a film appear, *The Magdalene Sisters*, that drew on these television documentaries to provide a brutal portrait of the treatment of girls deemed by the hierarchy to be too sinful to circulate within Irish society. Mullan's film was directly indebted to the chilling Channel 4 documentary, *Sex in a Cold Climate* (1997 produced by Steve Humphries – director not credited). This consisted of interviews with survivors of the laundries who recounted their stories – of sexual abuse by the priests, brutality by the nuns, and of unpaid, Victorian working conditions. These stories were then partially fictionalised by Mullan with the additional dramatic device of having all four young women meet in the same laundry (whereas in reality they were in separate institutions).

Thomas Elsaesser, in his comments on the prevalence of Vietnam fictions in American cinema, has noted that:

> the United States has been fortunate to have a public art (the cinema) that may be said to have done 'mourning work' on behalf of the nation, thus allowing the Vietnam war to enter 'history' and not just the history books.
>
> (1996: 146)

We may argue that *The Magdalene Sisters* and the films discussed in this chapter perform a public function of enabling their viewers to work through the legacy of Irish history in its more traumatic formulations. At the same time, such works satisfy expectations that Ireland is a country absorbed by its past and many of them rehearse the signifiers of Irishness that outside audiences expect from Irish fictions.

It is the rural past that has dominated representations of history. As a metonym for the 'real' Ireland, the Irish countryside, particularly the remote vistas of the west, bears the visual signifiers of history whilst also being represented as a living past. Ruined castles, abandoned famine cottages, empty fields testify to the ravages of history, even as winding roads, rituals of haymaking and babbling brooks allow for a visual indulgence in a type of pastoralism that collapses past and present. Dublin, on the other hand, and the principal Irish cities exist as architectural tributes to mer-cantilism and colonialism. The great Georgian buildings of Dublin, Limerick and Cork suggest a history of triumph rather than dispossession, and the general intermingling of Norman with Anglo-Saxon reflects a bastardised heritage that is less easily identifiable with the notion of a pure, Celtic Ireland.

Most recently, and in the wake of the 'new' Ireland of the Celtic Tiger economy and its aftermath, there has been a movement away from what has seemed to outsiders as a national obsession with history towards a more postmodern rejection of all grand narratives of which history is just one (and Catholicism another). Such a cinema lives firmly in the present and touches on the past only to parody it (*The Last of the High Kings*, *The Fifth Province*). The commercial success of reminders of the traumas of the Irish past, *Angela's Ashes*, *The Magdalene Sisters*, and the continued release of films set in that past – *Love and Rage* (Cathal Black, Germany/Ireland, 1998), *How Harry Became A Tree* (Goran Paskaljevic, GB/France/Italy/Ireland, 2001) – suggest that the subject still has resonances within Irish culture and, in the case of the first two films, outside of it.

By looking at some of these films in more detail, we can see how certain themes have come to dominate the subject. By far the most enduring of these is the concept of Irish history as personal and thus, in allegorical terms, national trauma. Starting with works that allegorise the consequences of the colonial encounter, we will trace a movement away from 'closure' – the happy ending – associated with the films discussed in Part I of this book, towards a sense of chaos and irreparable disruption, returning in the present to a tentative conclusiveness.

Focusing on the contrasting experiences of Rudyard Kipling and George Orwell, Ashis Nandy has argued that the former represents, 'the pathetic self-hatred and ego constriction which went with colonialism and the latter the relative sense of freedom and critical morality which were the true antith-esis of colonialism and which one could acquire only by working through the colonial consciousness' (1983: 35–6). Nandy's argument, that colonialism was as debilitating a discourse for the coloniser as the colonised, is reflected in a series of films made from the 1970s onwards that revisit the history of Anglo-Irish relations from this perspective.

One of cinema's greatest chroniclers of the end of Empire in the last century was the director David Lean, whose themes moved between the madness of the British military tradition (*The Bridge on the River Kwai* [GB 1957], *Lawrence of Arabia* [GB, 1962]), the end of the Russian Empire (*Doctor Zhivago* [GB, 1965]) and the fall of India, *A Passage to India* (GB, 1984). In 1970 Lean released his Irish folly, *Ryan's Daughter* (GB, 1970), the film that all but sank his reputation.

Ryan's Daughter reproduces many of the conventions of British-Irish fic-tions, including the love-across-the-boundaries theme. The plot, a rework-ing of the *Madame Bovary* story, centres on the failure of the central character, Rosie Ryan (Sarah Miles), to find the answer to her romantic aspirations in marriage to the somewhat older local schoolteacher, Charles Shaughnessy (Robert Mitchum). A sub-plot follows the efforts of the IRA leader, Tim O'Leary (Barry Foster), to land armaments from the Germans in a scheme that is foiled by the publican, Rosie's father, who is also the British garrison's informer. When a shell-shocked young soldier, Major Doryan (Christopher Jones), arrives in the village, Rosie and he embark on an ill-hidden love affair. In the finale of the film, Major Doryan shoots Tim O'Leary and the villagers take their revenge on Rosie's assumed treachery by cropping her hair. The Major commits suicide and Rosie leaves for Dublin with Charles.

Anyone hoping to learn more about Irish history from a native perspective will certainly be disappointed if they are to rely on *Ryan's Daughter*. This is a film about the encounter between a victim of colonialism and a victim of a narrow, prudish society, the latter a repeated motif in Lean's cinema. The sole characterised representative of the British colonial regime in Ireland is the shell-shocked, delicate Major Doryan. Played by the least significant member of the cast, in his confusion, bordering on insanity, he could be seen to represent the most extreme outcome of the experiences undergone by the principal characters of *The Bridge on the River Kwai*. What he finds in Ireland is not the restoration of his masculine identity through feats of heroism but instead a deadly process of psychic healing through his affair with Rosie.

The inverted mirror into which Doryan must look in order to establish his difference as a colonial master is pictured as the figure of the village idiot, Michael. To emphasise the connection between the two, Lean has Michael played by one of the great names of the British theatrical tradition and a fellow Englishman, John Mills. Michael shadows Doryan and Rosie, acting as both informant and intermediary. Ultimately, it is he who inadvertently alerts the villagers to Rosie's adultery and he who brings Doryan to realise that he cannot survive in this hostile environment and that only madness and death lie ahead.

Michael's mocking strut behind Doryan visually links the two men. If Doryan's limp and his mental fragility are the consequences of the great imperial war – the First World War – so Michael's body is a reminder of the history of Irish 'inferiority' as it has been pictured in the imperial imagination: 'Michael's twisted body and grotesque features deliberately recall the simian Paddy of post-Fenian, post-Darwinian Victorian cartoons' (Cullingford, 2001: 52–3). In his final walk along the sand dunes, Michael follows Doryan at a short distance, the fairground music adding a carnivalesque aura to the moment that the idiot apes the officer. As an acknowledgement of his gift of a cigarette, Michael then reveals the hiding place of the guns to Doryan, opening up the containers in front of the Englishman. Inside each box Doryan finds not just explosives but a mirror. He may look in this mirror to confirm his own identity but he does not choose to, instead keeping his gaze on his alter ego, Michael. In the end, out of shot, he takes Michael's gift of a grenade and kills himself.

Despite being made during the outbreak of the Troubles, *Ryan's Daughter* does not present itself as an analogy to the contemporary political situation, and the reviews of the time do not suggest that it was seen to be one. In common with many earlier British films about Ireland, it is not interested in trying to understand the causes and consequences of the trajectory of Irish historical events but reproduces them as signifiers of incomprehensible otherness. The fact that it is the Irish themselves who cause their own downfall, through the efforts of the informer, and the British role in the political denouement is relegated to a few hysterical shots, suggests the viewpoint that the British have no part to play in Irish matters. The Irish natives are depicted as an ignorant rabble that exercised a malevolent and uncontrollable energy. They even lack the exotic promise of other natives in other colonies, as Major Doryan is told on arrival: 'There's no local crumpet. It's married or virgin here.' This mob is the detritus of history and will reappear as such in a later reworking of Lean's failed Irish epic, another 'flawed masterpiece', Jim Sheridan's *The Field* (GB, 1990), as the roaming villagers who cheer on the drama's doomed protagonists. This film, as I have argued in greater detail elsewhere (Barton, 2002), offers a particularly traumatic re-working both of Irish cinematic history and nationalist history, and we have already seen how it directly comments on the romantic vision of *The Quiet Man*. If the great, Lear-like Bull McCabe (Richard Harris) is the mouthpiece for romantic nationalism, he is also cast as tragic hero, brought down by his own grand delusions.

If the thrust of *Ryan's Daughter* was to project onto an Irish narrative the anxieties of end of Empire, a cycle of films made from within Irish filmmaking culture, the Protestant and Big House films re-worked these themes from the perspective of the remnants of the colonial order, the Anglo-Irish. Most but not all of these films are adaptations of or inspired by the Big House novel and most draw on the visual and literary tradition of the Irish gothic.

These novels were often written by women, many the inhabitants of the houses themselves (Maria Edgeworth, Elizabeth Bowen, Somerville and Ross, Molly Keane), although there also exists a substantial body of recent work which recreates the period as self-conscious historical text (for instance, *Langrishe Go Down* [Aidan Higgins, 1966], *Troubles* [J.G. Farrell, 1970], and novels by Jennifer Johnston, William Trevor and John Banville). Not only has cinema been attracted to these works but they have also enjoyed successful runs as television adaptations, most notably the series *The Irish R.M.* (Channel 4, 1983–85).

The Irish gothic has been principally associated with Anglo-Irish, Protestant literature, often with a Big House setting. It is generally considered to have arisen out of a sense of rootlessness; belonging neither to the culture from which they originated nor the culture in which they now lived, the Protestant Ascendancy led a schizophrenic existence. It was also generally centred on women who exhibited a high degree of hysteria occasioned by feelings of guilt and helplessness in the wake of their specific historical inheritance. Gerry Smyth puts it thus:

> In the gothic vision, any hope of social change in the present is belied by the persistence of the sins of the past. The message is that we are all victims of history, only most have not recognised it yet. Gothic thus becomes a way of indicting the present, allowing the novelist to offer a perspective on the immediate in terms of the metaphysical and the universal, but without having to invest in any consoling vision or compensatory myth, precisely because there is nothing to be done.
>
> (1997: 52)

John Hill notes that the Big House films are generally regarded as unexceptional additions to the British heritage tradition but that in fact:

> Ireland in the 1920s, especially during the War of Independence, is much less readily available as an object of nostalgia than the comparable period in England (and even India). The past, in this respect, is so obviously characterized by violence and social tension that it is clearly difficult to project it as any kind of 'golden age'.
>
> (1999: 118)

The British heritage films, costume dramas such as *Chariots of Fire* [Hugh Hudson, GB, 1981], *A Room With a View* [James Ivory, GB, 1985], *Maurice* [James Ivory, GB, 1987], *Carrington* [Christopher Hampton, GB, 1995]) and colonial fantasies typified by *A Passage to India*, have come under substantial critical scrutiny within British film studies. For many such writers, they are exercises in nostalgia that privilege spectacle over historical inquiry and fetishise period detail (Higson, 1996). Others have argued that in their display of costume and foregrounding of relationships, such films offer a space for female pleasure (Monk, 1995). That multiple positions can be accommodated in one film is acknowledged by Hill who proposes that *Chariots of Fire* offers itself simultaneously as social critique and nostalgic recreation (1999: 20–8). One of the most striking differences between the British and Irish of the Big House/period dramas is their representation of history and historical events. In the British films, most of them set in England, history functions as little more than background information and is seldom if ever problematised. The Irish films are about history and its legacy. The bearers of this legacy as well as its victims are the genre's central, often hysterical female characters.

The foregrounding of Irish historical events and the desire to understand rather than simply depict the divisions caused by Independence may be read against a heightened awareness of the Northern troubles in a manner which is much more pronounced in the Big House cycle than in *Ryan's Daughter*. The overt connections between past and present that characterise the Irish cycle further distinguish these films from their English (the word is used deliberately) counterparts. In keeping with their theme of hybrid origins, the Irish Big House films – *Ascendancy* (Edward Bennett, GB, 1982), *The Dawning* (Robert Knights, GB, 1988), *Fools of Fortune* (Pat O'Connor, GB, 1990) and *The Last September* (Deborah Warner, GB/Ireland, 1999) – are themselves formally hybridised. They borrow their generic formulae from the British period films but then re-work these to concentrate on local, Irish concerns.

Linking all of these films is the concrete embodiment of colonial rule in Ireland, the Big House itself. The stately homes of the English films and the society that inhabits them are structured on a naturalised hierarchical system that encompasses both the aristocracy and their servants, a system of control that is articulated through costume, ritual and other visual motifs such as the formal garden. If the films do express any critique of the system (*Angels and Insects* [Philip Haas, GB/US, 1995] for example), the solution is posited not as the abolition of that hierarchy but escape from it. In the Irish films, on the other hand, the Big House is both alien to the landscape and under constant threat, of decay and attack. The houses themselves have been described as 'rather poor in architecture but impressive enough to be in sharp contrast with the natives' cottages' (Fehlman, 1991: 15) and this has been maintained in the films. Whilst they are substantial, they are never visually fetishised in the manner of the English country homes. They are the embodiment of their ownership, decaying, isolated and vulnerable (to attack – *Ascendancy, Fools of Fortune, The Last September,* to commercial interests, *The Dawning*[1]). Similarly, their grounds are never laid out in the kind of formal gardens that one associates with the English films but in fact are frequently represented as a kind of hostile nature waiting to reclaim its dominance. Thus, *Fools of Fortune* features a repeated motif of a character climbing though the undergrowth which constantly threatens to entangle them and the house is seen after its burning as enmeshed with weeds and creepers. Tennis can never be satisfactorily played in *The Last September* due to the condition of the courts and an invasion of ants threatens the inhabitants of the house. This motif of a hostile nature further distinguishes the Irish end of Empire films from what I will be defining later as the Irish heritage cycle of the 1980s and 1990s.

It is in their depictions of women that we can most clearly distinguish the contradictions embodied in the cycle. To this extent, the films conform to a general anxiety suggested by end of Empire narratives that it was women who were to blame for the dissolution of the colonial structure. Richard Dyer has argued that this could take the form of sexual longing for the (more potent) native, undue identification with the (feminised) native or simple irrationality (1997: 184–206). This contrasts with the traditional role of women in the cinema of Empire, where Richards notes, 'the Imperial lady was required to devote herself to her husband and efface herself . . . The memorable Imperial ladies are the elderly ones, those spirited, no-nonsense, umbrella-wielding memsahibs, whose Imperial days are done

but who retain that strength of character which saw them through them'
(1973: 93).

Margot Backus has argued that many of the Big House narratives speak
the 'unspeakability' of Anglo-Irish colonial history by constantly referring to
the family's origins: 'In particular, these recurring narrative conventions
testify to the continuing cost that is being exacted from children born within
a settler colonial order that prioritizes loyalty to an abstract national identity
above local cooperation and identification' (Backus, 1999: 19). This problem of unresolved national allegiances recurs throughout the Big House
films, bearing down with most force, as Backus suggests, on the younger
generations. In *Ascendancy*, Connie's (Julie Covington) father implores her
to return to England. The young officer (Ian Charleson) tries to rescue
Connie and take her 'home' but she refuses to leave. 'We didn't create
this chaos, we inherited it', he responds in vain. Three generations of
Quinton family wives in *Fools of Fortune* are English and the suggestion is
that it is their failure to understand the country they have come to live in that
is responsible for their tragedy. Each in some way betrays the family: Willie's
great-grandmother begs to be allowed to help the famine victims; it is
Willie's mother's undisguised sympathy for the IRA leader which eventually
leads to the burning of the house and Marianne drives her own child into
insanity through her stories of the past (Hill, 1999: 121–2). In *The Last
September*, the major source of disruption within the film is the arrival of a
family friend, Miss Norton (Fiona Shaw), from England and it is to England
that Lois finally escapes.

The cycle of films creates a wider set of associations between Englishness
and betrayal, and reverses the historical equation of Englishness with masculinity and rationality, of John Bull versus Dark Rosaleen/Mother Ireland.
These women are perverse Britannia figures who, by coming to live in the
country, re-enact the original moment of settlement. The suggestion of
perversion is carried to its limit in *Ascendancy* where it is implied that
Connie's relationship with her brother was an incestuous one; she is also
physically deformed (she has a crippled hand) which is revealed to be a
psychosomatic symptom. At the same time, the women insist on their
Irishness and reject the notion that England is home, yet they lack true
understanding of the native Irish temperament and must always be divided
from them by their positions (as gentry) and their locations (the Big House).

Women, the films suggest, are the bearers and conduits for historical
memory. As Connie says: 'I remember everything. I keep it safe inside
me.' The child's inheritance of historical guilt emerges specifically in *Fools
of Fortune* as a central theme. The film follows William Trevor's source novel
in suggesting that the narrative of history is passed from mother to child and
that by the time it is retold to the youngest of the female characters, the
Englishwoman's daughter, Imelda (Catherine McFadden), it bears so much
force that she is driven hysterical and then mute, no longer able to continue
the oral transmission of the family tragedy. The moment where she is
brought literally face to face with this history is depicted with full gothic

relish. Walking through the woods she is accompanied by the ghosts of family members whom she appears to take for granted or ignore. She then approaches the unburnt wing of the Big House where her mother, Marianne (Mary Elizabeth Mastrantonio), now lives and overhears an argument between Marianne and Father Kilgarriff. He advises Marianne to return to England, to forget the events of the past and accuses her of neglecting Imelda. The child turns and the film is suddenly flooded with images of the burning of the house and the murder of its inhabitants as the sound track fills with the sound of screaming, this in turn dissolves to reveal Imelda curled up in foetal position screaming on the floor of the schoolroom and being comforted by the nuns. It is from this point that she is rendered mute.

The notion that the history which these women embody is too traumatic ever to be spoken of and thus rendered 'safe' is one of the devices that links the films' historical past with the present of the Troubles. Both *Ascendancy* and *Fools of Fortune* invite analogous interpretations of their narratives; in the former, this is further achieved through a series of visual clues: the omnipresence of the Orange Order, the street riots into which Connie wanders to witness snipers, patrolling soldiers and women beating dustbin lids. In *Fools of Fortune*, scenes from the past are intercut with scenes from the present in a manner that proposes a parallel reading. None of the films, however, offers a satisfactory solution to the dilemmas they explore, suggesting that the present Troubles emerge from those of the past and that closure is impossible.

'Memory ...,' according to Anthony Smith:

> is bound to place, a special place, a homeland. It is also crucial to identity. In fact, one might say: no memory, no identity; no identity, no nation. That is why nationalists must rediscover and appropriate shared memories of the past. Identification with a past is the key to creating the nation, because only by 'remembering the past' can a collective identity come into being.
>
> (1996: 383–4)

These films suggest that personal memory, in this instance, female memory, has been voided from the official version of Irish history, and when it does re-enter this discourse, its consequences are too disruptive to be tolerated. By filtering their reconstructions of the past through characters that are both Protestant and female, these films accede to their own marginality. History is viewed by its victims, yet as Protestants they too must bear some of the blame for the processes of colonisation that have culminated in the events portrayed.

Such filmmaking practices (excepting *The Last September*) arose out of a period, the 1980s, in which Irish society appeared to be unable to escape from the past. Nationalist aspirations to a collective identity had been founded on the denial of conflicting identities, whether defined by religion – Protestant, Unionist – or sexuality. In the immediate post-Independence period, as we have seen, mainstream cinema largely colluded with this fabricated consensus. The eruption of the Troubles in the North, however, exposed the instability of that self-image as did the challenges to the social order that emerged from the private sphere. The 1990s, by contrast, were characterised by a growing confidence that the Troubles might be resolved and that modernisation was indeed both practicable and desirable in the Republic of Ireland. Their central theme is the relationship between male subjectivity and the legacy of militant nationalism. Returning repeatedly to the 1950s, these films display an increasing confidence that the past can be overcome.

Set in 1952, *Korea* is based on a short story by John McGahern. Living with his widowed father in a dark cottage hung with photographs of the Civil War, young Eamonn Doyle (Andrew Scott) is hemmed in by the past. His father, Doyle Senior (Donal Donnelly) plans to send him to America, but, knowing that he will have to enlist for the war in Korea, Eamonn refuses to leave. His rebellion is heightened by his love for the daughter of his father's old Civil War enemy, Moran (Vass Anderson), who has just lost his son in the war. The film is ambiguous over Doyle's intentions: does he hope for compensation money too or is he simply set against the love affair that reminds him of his own loss, the early death of his wife, Eamonn's mother? In the original text, the issues are clearer – locked into young Doyle's consciousness, we understand that his father has been reminded of his Civil War past because he is thinking of sending his own son to America. As the boy sees it, this is so that his father too will benefit financially from his military wages (since he will be conscripted), and then from his death. For these reasons, he refuses to leave.

The film is permeated with a sense of loss and death and structured by the intermittent voice-over of young Doyle. 'We were the last to fish the freshwater for a living', Eamonn remembers, his voice entering into the narrative from some undefined point in the present. It is also the last summer he will spend with his father. Eamonn's recollections of the past are dictated more by *Schadenfreude* than nostalgia; his father's on the other hand, particularly his flashback to the death of the young volunteer in the Civil War, punctuate the narrative as moments of trauma. Consolation is only available via the overvalued and sentimentalised revisiting of his courtship of Eamonn's mother on a picture perfect Howth Head. Even then, as the gorse seeds pop in the sunlight so images of the volunteer's buttons bursting as he is being led to his execution ruin his day and both images compete in later life with each other in his memories. That Doyle's reminiscences of his happiness with his wife are unreliable is suggested by Moran who insinuates that it is as a result of Doyle's neglect that she died.

Symbolically, the sense of a community blighted by its civil war divisions and trapped in the past is reinforced by the repeated visual motif of the eels in the underwater cage. The Doyles are ineffectual, victims as much of their own stasis as of the despondency of post-war Ireland. Even electrification (the conventional signifier of modernisation) is meaningless, as Doyle says,

'There's lots of things the coming of the electric can't change'. Similarly the 'old Free Stater', Ben Moran and his daughter, Una (Fiona Moloney), whilst being the ostensible beneficiaries of the new order (they can pay for electricity with the compensation money from America) are in thrall to death.

Korea remains one of the few Irish films to engage with the issue of Civil War guilt. Exacerbating this historic divide is another little discussed facet of Irish life – financial envy. Where Doyle has to face the loss of his source of income (eel fishing) to tourism, Moran has benefited financially from his son's death. Indeed, as much as Doyle and Moran are estranged by historical enmities, they are equally separated by financial differences. Moran is the wealthier of the two and has positioned himself to benefit from the greater affluence that modernisation will bring him and his family. Being on the 'winning side' in the Civil War has left Doyle no better off and he repeatedly bemoans what he sees as the betrayal of the ideals for which he fought, in particular the economic necessity of emigration to America, associated here not with freedom and opportunity but with money and death. Unlike in the heritage films, discussed in the next chapter, there is no sense that this was a better or more desirable Ireland. The elegiac score that lends the film much of its mood of regret enhances its overall sense of loss, less in this case, of happier times, than of opportunity.

The narrative tension lies with the issue of whether Eamonn will submit to his father's will or insist on staying in Ireland and thus committing himself to the 'love-across-the-divide' relationship with Una (an addition to the original story). The denouement suggests that not only will Eamonn succeed in doing this, he will also have aided his father in 'working through' and thus overcoming his traumatic memories. As he faces down his father in the boat and they lay aside the old pistol that, like a Chekhovian portent, has been hanging over them, so they can put to rest a violent personal and national past.

This kind of heavily oedipal conflict is central to the films of the 1990s. In another Civil War narrative, *Broken Harvest* and the later *This is My Father* (Paul Quinn, Canada/Ireland, 1998), the story of a son's return from America to find out the truth about his father's death, the sons must relive events of the 1950s from the perspective of the 1990s in order to gain control over them. In these films, actions associated with Independence and the Civil War are seen to have been responsible for the brutality and repressiveness of the 1950s. Further, Ireland of the past is imagined as a stunted society marked by veniality and a strong class hierarchy. The challenge of confronting twentieth-century Irish history on screen structures two of the most ambitious of Neil Jordan's Irish films, *Michael Collins* and *The Butcher Boy*. Jordan's work is in many ways typical of his generation of Irish artists and writers in its desire to confront the shibboleths of nationalist discourse. At the same time, in *Michael Collins*, he created the first modern, indigenous epic of Irish history and in doing so laid himself open to accusations of romanticising militant nationalism. In the later *The Butcher Boy*, he countered an incipient nostalgia for the past with a tale of a demented child adrift in a small town populated by nightmarish women in curlers, abusive priests, drunken fathers and overshadowed by the threat of nuclear annihilation.

Formally, *Michael Collins* constitutes an exception to Jordan's general filmmaking practices. His Irish works in particular have tended to focus on small intimate narratives. By the time of *Michael Collins'* making, even the idea of epic filmmaking was anachronistic. The great historical epics of the mid-century were a celebration of the visceral pleasures of Hollywood cinema and the attraction of films like *Gone With the Wind* (Victor Fleming, US, 1939) and *Quo Vadis?* (Mervyn LeRoy, US, 1951) was largely that of scale and spectacle. This is particularly evident in the films of the 1950s whose:

> moments of diegetic exhibitionism ... are part of an overall process in which cinema displays itself and its powers through the re-creation of a past so distant that much of its impact derives simply from the evidence of the scale of the re-creation involved (from details of costume and decor to the construction of whole cities) and through the telling of a story felt to match that scale, such as the story of Christ, the fall of the Roman Empire, and so on.
>
> (Neale, 1987: 35)

The classic epics were in large part Hollywood's response to television, an attempt to lure people away from the constrictions of the small black and white screen in their living rooms and back into the cinemas.

The decision to make an epic version of the events of Independence and its aftermath might well be seen in a similar light, as a statement that Irish cinema was not just a production facility for small-scale home movies but that it might, to adapt Robert Emmet's challenge, take its place among the filmmaking nations of the world. In the tradition of the historical epic, *Michael Collins* was made with much fanfare, notably surrounding its use of thousands of voluntary extras who turned up to a casting call, an event widely reported in the nation's press. We may further situate Jordan's film within a minor revival of the epic congruent to the film's making. In the 1990s a new didacticism in historical filmmaking emerged as a consequence of the pedagogical zest of auteur-directors such as Steven Spielberg and Oliver Stone. Films such as *JFK* (Oliver Stone, USA, 1991) *Schindler's List*, (Steven Spielberg, USA 1993) and *Saving Private Ryan* (Steven Spielberg, USA, 1998) sought to engage audiences with the recent past whilst offering personal/political and didactic readings of that past.

In an era where the idea of history itself has come under rigid academic scrutiny, these exercises in historical reconstruction are highly problematic. Certainly, they feed a popular interest in history evidenced by the proliferation of historical documentaries on public-access television and specialised channels. On the other hand, such films open up little space for alternative versions of the events they describe, presenting themselves as 'truth'. This approach is especially difficult given that most historiographers agree that history can no longer be considered a 'master narrative'. The notion that history unfolded of its own accord and that the vision of the past embedded in the textbooks of Western culture with their good kings, their righteous battles and their Utopian vision of a better future informed by the mistakes of the past is now unacceptable not just to academics but to those representatives of history's marginalised and excluded. Instead, history is now most commonly reviewed for its 'constructedness', its omissions as widely interpreted as its inclusions.

In its favour, it could be argued that the controversy surrounding the reception of films such as *Amistad* (Steven Spielberg, USA, 1997) and *Michael Collins* establishes a secondary discourse which has the effect of opening the films up to an engaged and critical set of arguments that in turn destabilise any acceptance of the text as containing a 'closed' meaning. The reception of *Michael Collins*, in Ireland especially, demonstrated an almost hysterical jostling for knowledge/power in the Foucauldian (Foucault, 1980) sense as individual historians, media commentators and the general run of newspaper letter writers competed with each other to establish their interpretation of the events surrounding Michael Collins' life and death as the 'correct' one. Reading through the various letters and newspaper articles, the overall impression one gains is of a concerted policy of wiping out the alternative position and capturing the flag (of 'truth'). Ultimately, *Michael Collins* the film was to become only one of a number of competing interventions in a contest to establish a dominant narrative of Irish history.

Jordan's hurried publication of his diary of the film's making (Jordan, 1996) may be seen as an early shot in a battle to gain control of the meaning of *Michael Collins*. In it he represents his project as one of honest endeavour thwarted by studio intervention and misinterpreted by mealy-mouthed historians. By this stage, revisionist anxiety that nationalist history might be used as a justification for violence in Northern Ireland had already been applied to Jordan's film in the making by historian Paul Bew writing in *The Sunday Times*. Dismissing the film's politics, Bew argued that the Easter Rising was targeted 'not so much [at] the British Empire, but that large slice of Catholic nationalist Ireland – politicians, lawyers, officials and policemen who had come to an understanding with London' (1996: 6). It was suggested that Britain would have ceded Ireland under any circumstances and that therefore Collins' military campaign represented an unnecessary waste of life.

Unfortunately for Jordan, the film's release coincided with the breakdown of the IRA ceasefire in 1996, signalled by the Canary Wharf bombing, and certain elements within the film, notably the gleeful blowing up of an RUC van, were seized upon as endorsing acts of terrorism. The director continued to appear on television and to contribute articles to the papers defending himself against anticipated attacks. Much time was spent debating the merits and message of *Michael Collins* in the Irish media whilst the negative reception of the film in much of the British press was reported with some satisfaction as an example of outdated imperialist thinking. In the end, it is difficult to gauge to what extent media interventions in a film's reception actually affect audiences' responses to it. If as box office takings and reviews testified, American and British audiences largely failed to see the point of Jordan's epic, at home the film was greeted as a national event; as one writer expressed it, 'For good or ill, the Neil Jordan film is going to constitute our first shared story of the foundation of this state' (O'Faolain: 1996, 14).

To what extent does *Michael Collins* function as didactic message? Like the films of Spielberg and Stone, Jordan's film is a 'closed' discourse. History is presented as 'knowable' and recoupable. It further endorses the 'great man' interpretation of the past, allocating a considerable measure of agency to its two chief protagonists, Michael Collins (Liam Neeson) and Eamon de Valera (Alan Rickman). This reinstatement of Michael Collins as *the* hero of Independence is the most effective feature of the film. Collins' character is deliberately presented to us in a way that will engage our sympathies. In terms of casting, he is played by an Irish actor who has gained an international reputation. Most particularly, he would at that point have been associated with the role of Oscar Schindler in Spielberg's *Schindler's List*, a part that was again one of a flawed hero who stood up against authority (the Nazis) to defend the underdog (his Jewish workers). Physically, he resembled Collins closely enough to give a reasonable impression of veracity; Aidan Quinn in the role of Harry Boland would also have been familiar to Irish audiences through a series of performances as sympathetic characters in films such as *The Playboys* and *Hear My Song* (Peter Chelsom, GB, 1991). On the other hand, de Valera is played by an English actor who had no previous association with Ireland and whose prior roles numbered Hans Gruber, the sadistic, smooth-talking villain of *Die Hard* (John McTiernan, US, 1988) and the Sheriff of Nottingham in *Robin Hood: Prince of Thieves* (Kevin Reynolds, US, 1991). Nor was there any great public enthusiasm for Julia Roberts in the role of Kitty, a part that was, in any case, underwritten and did little justice to the real-life counterpart.

Throughout the film, Collins is distinguished by his singularity; physically dominant he is also presented as slightly apart. He makes his decisions alone and in settings such as the meetings of the cabinet, he is positioned outside of the group. Most commonly, de Valera will be framed at a distance from him, amongst the other cabinet members. Both Collins' intimate friendships, with Harry Boland and Kitty (Julia Roberts), are characterised by a dominant-subordinate relationship. De Valera, in comparison, is, from the outset, established as Collins' nemesis. Not only that, he is not even a worthy nemesis. Collins is brave, spontaneous, romantic with a devoted male friend and a pretty fiancée. De Valera is not allowed a private existence, although in fact, the reality of the historical figure's private life is the stuff of classic Hollywood fiction. The filmic creation is cautious, bookish, misguided in his foreign policy and a poor military leader. Whilst the evidence is open to debate, the film strongly suggests that de Valera sent Collins to the Treaty negotiations with an accurate idea of how they would evolve so that Collins would take the blame for their outcome.

In terms of camerawork, the audience's line of vision is guided towards a fetishistic admiration of Collins' physique. However, we are seldom invited to share his point of view and the central historical moments are viewed from the POV of the absent 'narrator', the eye of God. Thus, in the sequence where his men assassinate 12 members of the British Secret Service, Collins is absent, this time in a hotel bedroom with Kitty. The intercutting of the assassinations with Kitty's realisation that each bullet is a 'love-letter' and Collins' agonising over the morality of the action he has initiated (which remarkably he never sees in religious terms) distance him from the event whilst establishing his absolute control. Neither is he seen in military action during the assault on the Customs House, and his participation in the Civil War skirmishes is minimised.

The moment of Collins' assassination is drawn out through alternating it with scenes of Kitty trying on her wedding dress to the sound of Sinéad O'Connor singing the ballad, *She Moved Through the Fair*. Whilst this technique of intercutting mirrors the 'Twelve Apostles' scene (the murder of the agents) and might be read as a just response to Collins' own ruthlessness, this is offset by the presence of Kitty in both instances so that the force of the tragedy of Collins' life and death is emphasised through the repeated motif of her suffering (we never see anyone mourn the assassinated British).

The effect of this adherence to both the format of the historical epic and the classic realist text is to locate the events of the film firmly in the past, as over and complete. This is reinforced by the closing sequence of newsreel footage of Collins' funeral (a reminder of the film's claims to veracity). Not only is he indisputably dead but so is Harry Boland. De Valera has been reduced to a cowering figure in a haystack and the new generation, symbolised by the insolent young assassin (Jonathan Rhys-Myers), has taken over.

Where the film fails is in its project of bridging the past and the present, of effectively suggesting that the situation in Northern Ireland should be resolved through negotiation rather than paramilitary tactics. It may end with the admonition that Collins died as he was trying 'to take the gun out of Irish politics' but, given that it has so effectively celebrated its hero as a strategist and as the father of guerrilla warfare, there is little sense that progress may be made through a new policy of negotiation and conciliation. On the contrary, although it may wish to endorse constitutional nationalism, this is countermanded by its extreme nostalgia for Collins as a gung-ho hero and man of action.

In his second Irish historical film of the 1990s, Jordan returned to the intimate personal dramas that have been at the heart of his filmmaking practice. Based on the novel by Pat McCabe, *The Butcher Boy* is set in Ireland, according to the opening narration, 'twenty or thirty or forty years ago' and describes the childhood of Francie Brady (Eamonn Owens) whose father (Stephen Rea) is an alcoholic musician and whose mother

(Aisling O'Sulllivan) suffers from mental illness. In an increasingly surreal manner, the film follows the disintegration of Francie's friendship with Joe (Alan Boyle) and Francie's obsession with another child's mother, Mrs Nugent (Fiona Shaw). Sent to reform school, Francie is faced with the sexual attentions of one of the priests, Father Sullivan (Milo O'Shea), and has visions of the Virgin Mary (Sinéad O'Connor). When he returns home, his father dies and Francie lives alone with the dead body (his mother has already committed suicide) and works in an abattoir. When he is discovered with his father's body, he is sent to a mental institution. He escapes from there, goes to visit the guest house in which his parents honeymooned, and breaks in to Joe's boarding school. After returning home he kills Mrs Nugent and sets fire to his house. He is again sent to a mental institution. At the end of the film, he is released, apparently cured, and has another vision of the Virgin Mary.

The film's visual construction, in particular, but also the performances and the casting choices, undermine to the point of, literally, exploding received images of rural and small town Ireland (McLoone, 2000: 214–15). At the same time, its themes are in many ways similar to those explored in the previous works and reflect the ubiquity in contemporary narratives of the 'miserable Irish childhood', the dysfunctional family and a sense of the past as trauma. *The Butcher Boy* also rehearses many of Jordan's recurrent motifs, notably an intense but doomed homosocial friendship, a troubled father-son relationship and the fusing of memory and trauma, all played out against a background that is at once threatening and informed by a nostalgia that is embedded in image and soundtrack. The refusal to distinguish between 'reality' and fantasy and the surreal register of much of the drama are also features of Jordan's work as a whole. As the storyline indicates, the film had all the potential to become another lugubrious tale of unhappy lives in rural Ireland. Instead, it becomes almost a celebration of Francie's anarchic energy whilst never losing sight of its tragedy. Issues of individuality, religious domination, and class are all questioned primarily through a parodic narrative voice. Thus Francie is seen to be different from those around him and to be constrained by the limitations of small town Irish life; the Church fails him and even abuses him; he is ostracised by the community.

In common with many of the films of this period, *The Butcher Boy* is deeply critical of the legacy of cultural nationalism. In particular, it satirises the 'Mother Ireland' image both through its storyline and the casting of Sinéad O'Connor as the Virgin Mary. Mother figures recur throughout the narrative: it is the desire to return to his mother which brings him home after running away to Dublin and he brings her back a characteristically kitschy souvenir/gift of an Irish cottage bearing the words 'A Mother's Love's A Blessing' and featuring a woman in traditional dress sitting weaving outside the cottage. This in itself references the earlier short film scripted by Pat McCabe, *A Mother's Love's A Blessing* discussed in the previous chapter. Later, the mother figure becomes the other icon of Irish womanhood, the Virgin Mary, Sinéad O'Connor visualised as a cheap figurine. The link between Francie's mother and the Virgin Mary is cemented when the cera-mic figure outside the cottage 'comes alive' and is again played by Sinéad O'Connor. The casting choice of O'Connor who has consistently spoken out against the family unit and particularly her own parents, publicised hav-ing an abortion and chosen firstly to exclude the father of her second child, journalist John Waters, from her life before giving him custody of the child, is one of the film's more seditious acts. On the other hand, its depiction of Mrs Nugent as the conventional repressive/castrating Irish mother is some-what less than challenging. Ultimately, this is a film about the failure of all forms of authority to be either controlling or compassionate; it does not lay the blame with any one source but spreads it equally. What characterises the community is its blanket inertia, one that will ultimately suffocate the only source of energy – Francie's.

Alongside the play on the motifs of Irish fiction and the subversion of nationalist iconography, lies a further discourse, on cultural influences. The film's opening credits play over screen-sized comic book illustrations, the last of which materialises to become the figures talking to Francie in his hospital bed after he has set fire to the house. Television screens play Westerns and issue nuclear warnings. Francie refers to himself as Algernon Carruthers and speaks in the idiom of the comic book. In one of the film's set pieces, his town is blown up in a nuclear holocaust, the 'ladies' (the small town women) becoming frozen pigs, and the alien leader riding through debris like one of the Four Horsemen of the Apocalypse is an insect/human mutant. In a highly sympathetic essay, Martin McLoone has discussed these scenes as 'the most subversive representations of Ireland that the cinema has yet produced' (2000: 214). Thus, Francie stands for rural Ireland 'caught in the cusp between two types of tradition and conflicting notions of moder-nity – between the formative, yet stifling aspects of *rootedness* and the liber-ating, yet empty cosmopolitanism of *transcendence*' (ibid.: 222). The women in the shops, a farmer Francie meets in the countryside all constantly refer to the threat of nuclear annihilation; equally we could argue that eventually the complacency of small town Ireland will be blown apart not by the atom bomb but by the revelations of institutional abuse such as Francie experi-ences during the course of the narrative. For Francie, fictional characters are both a liberation and a barrier between him and reality. They enable his moments of most intense pleasure yet when he attacks Philip Nugent (Andrew Fullerton) in the shed, the scene is shot in flickering, almost chiar-oscuro light as if Francie has entered the world of an old television set.

Clearly, this is not a nostalgia film, yet like *Michael Collins* it also incor-porates moments of nostalgia in its evocation of brand names and its recrea-tion of styles of dress, of period music and period artefacts. Jordan has said that the book 'gave me an opportunity to reinvent that extraordinary mix-ture of paranoia and paralysis, madness and mysticism that was the Ireland I grew up in in the 'fifties.' (*Production Notes*, undated, unpaginated). On the other hand, the somewhat stylised visuals and mannered acting styles under-mine the potential recognition effect offered by the deployment of brand names. One could also argue that the casting of Stephen Rae in the dual roles of Da Brady and the adult Francie (he also delivers the voice-over), combined with the film's 'contemporary' shooting style suggest a continuity between the past and the present, that the old ways which Ireland is so hurriedly either rejecting or relegating to nostalgia may not have vanished entirely.

As Pierre Sorlin notes, 'an historical period cannot be pictured if audiences do not feel disposed … to take an interest in it' (1980: 44). The success of *Michael Collins* at home and the proliferation of narratives set in Ireland of the 1950s suggest a common desire amongst Irish audiences and filmmakers to revisit these two key periods, of Independence and the last days of the old, nationalist order. As we have seen, the more recent historical films have replaced that almost hysterical sense of the burden of history with a new confidence that the events of the past may be put behind us. The alternative approach to depicting Irish history on film has been to envisage it with nostalgia, to represent Irish life in the mid-twentieth century as a time of innocence and, indeed, to persist in seeing Irish life in the present as little altered from those halcyon days. It is to these films that the next chapter is devoted.

9

FROM HISTORY TO HERITAGE

Defining the Irish heritage film

In the previous chapter, we saw how Irish historical narratives have dominated contemporary cinema, and that the view of the past most commonly proposed by these films has been one of trauma, which may or may not be overcome. The alternative to such works has been what I term here the Irish heritage film. This is a cycle of productions that is associated with the 1990s and has in common a nostalgic, edenic view of Ireland; such films are set primarily in the 1950s but also describe an Ireland of the present distinguishable by its 'pastness'.

In order to define such a cinema it is useful to borrow some of the critical terminology that has been produced in similar debates in Britain. For instance,

> The image of the past in the heritage films has become so naturalized that, paradoxically, it stands removed from history; the evocation of pastness is accomplished by a look, a style, the loving recreation of period details – not by any critical historical perspective. The self-conscious visual perfectionism of these films and their fetishization of period details create a fascinating but self-enclosed world. They render history as spectacle, as *separate* from the viewer in the present, as something over and done with, complete, achieved.
>
> (Higson, 1993: 113)

Higson's analysis is in turn indebted to Fredric Jameson's influential description of postmodernism as arising out of a post-industrial culture and characterised by nostalgia and pastiche (Jameson, 1988). We may also see such films reflecting a crisis in historicity described by Eric Hobsbawn thus:

> The destruction of the past, or rather of the social mechanisms that link one's contemporary experience to that of earlier generations, is one of the most characteristic and eerie phenomena of the late twentieth century. Most young men and women at the century's end grow up in a sort of permanent present lacking any organic relation to the public past of the times they live in.
>
> (1995: 3)

As we have seen in the previous chapter, although a number of Irish 'Big House' films exist, these differ distinctly from the comparable English examples (notably the films of Ismail Merchant and James Ivory) that in turn have come to define that heritage cinema. The Irish heritage films draw on a quite different tradition, one distinguished by rural pastoralism.

In an interview in *Film Ireland*, David Kavanagh, Director of the European Script Fund, was asked how Irish scripts compared with their European counterparts. He replied that whilst the quality was high, 'It's still the case that we persistently get 1950s rural coming-of-age stories ... you don't very often get urban dramas or projects written but not based in Ireland' (Flynn, 1995: 50). Although that moment now seems to have passed, this formula describes many of the films discussed here: *Into the West* (Mike Newell, Ireland, 1992), *War of the Buttons* (John Roberts, GB/France, 1994), *Broken Harvest, All Things Bright and Beautiful* (Barry Devlin, GB/Ireland, 1994), *Moondance* (Dagmar Hirtz, Ireland/Germany, 1994), *Circle of Friends, The Run of the Country* (Peter Yates, Ireland, 1995), *The Secret of Roan Inish* (John Sayles, USA, 1993). A second category includes the following rural dramas: *Hear My Song, The Playboys, Waking Ned, The Closer You Get* (Aileen Ritchie, GB, 2000). These are variations on the kind of rural romp/romantic comedy that are an inheritance of the British tradition of displacing onto Irish dramas a fantasy of innocence, a Celtic whimsy, that is only otherwise located in Scottish narratives (*Whisky Galore* [Alexander Mackendrick, GB, 1959], *Local Hero* [Bill Forsyth, GB, 1983]). To this list we might also add *Dancing at Lughnasa* (Pat O'Connor, Ireland/GB/USA, 1998), a film whose original content was overlaid with a veneer of sentimentality and pastoralism that conspicuously destabilised its social critique. It is no coincidence that many of these films were part financed by British television and their aesthetic is largely televisual. They also bear many similarities to the long-running BBC financed *Ballykissangel* (Barton, 2000a).

The Irish heritage films demonstrate the difficulty for a young national cinema of breaking with the dominant paradigms of representation that it has inherited, particularly within a mainstream environment. They specifically illustrate the interplay between tourism and representation within certain Irish cultural productions. R.W. Riley has speculated about the effects on tourism of using recognisable locations as film settings, citing, amongst others, the example of the small town where *Fried Green Tomatoes at the Whistle Stop Café* (John Avnet, USA, 1991) was set, which tourists visited in response to the associations of community and strong friendships viewing the film evoked in them (Riley, 1995). That this has been the experience of Avoca, the village in which *Ballykissangel* is set is evident to anyone who visits the locality (Barton, 1999: 42).

There is certainly a close connection between heritage tourism and the heritage film. Heritage tourism is a distinct branch of tourism, offering the consumer a cultural experience that is simultaneously escapist and pedagogic. As David Brett notes, 'the promotional literature of heritage exhibitions and parks transfers the language of tourism from travel in space to travel in time' (1996: 162). It is not even necessary to visit the idealised settings such productions evoke: 'When viewing movies, consumers become vicariously attracted without leaving the security of home and without the "hard sell" impressions inherent in paid advertising' (Riley, 1995: 454). These films thus satisfy the demands of the up-market television tourist and of the Irish tourist trade which, in the absence of a Mediterranean climate, has had to promote Ireland as a 'feel good' location with an Arcadian landscape. The similarities between the gaze of the tourist and the film/television viewer are obvious, sharing the desire for the discovery of lost moments, and the need to narrativise experience. In *Widows Peak* Edwina Broom's (Natasha Richardson) first glimpse of the local scenery mirrors Sean Thornton's arrival in Innisfree: 'Oh my,' she gasps looking over the misty lakeland, adding in a subsequent scene, 'I never dreamed, I had no idea ... that Ireland was like this. I'm so glad I came here. It's perfect.' Here the tourist's gaze is assimilated into the diegesis. Clearly, in an industrial climate of 'downsizing' and 'downshifting' this idyllic Ireland of the fifties, sixties and earlier is both comfortably close (physically and temporally) and safely 'other'. As the production designer for *The War of the Buttons* explained:

> Although it is a contemporary piece looking at contemporary values in terms of the sense of community that still exists around Cork, we wanted to keep some of the timeless elements in the story without turning it into a period piece. The way we dealt with it practically was to take away anything that was obtrusively modern and not to replace it with anything that was obtrusively period. It's still going to have all the charm without being over-sentimentalised. But the area itself proved ideal in this respect. If you look at any of the villages around Cork you actually wouldn't know at what point you were in the last fifty years. It has stayed timeless and it's glorious as a result.
>
> (*Production Notes*, undated, unpaginated)

David Brett (1996) convincingly argues that heritage tourism is simply an extension of the Victorian traveller's search for the sublime and the picturesque. Similarly, the process whereby the centre controls and consumes representations of the periphery remains the same. These works do not originate from within the communities they depict and, indeed, as the local Irish language cinema demonstrates, this is far from the self-image such areas have established on film.

The centrality of children and young people to many of the narratives reinforces the theme of innocence. In many cases, the children and young adults are caught up in old enmities and old traditions from which they largely manage to escape, holding out a promise for their future, our present. At a deeper level, this strategy of rendering as Ireland forever Tír na nÓg (Land of Youth) indicates these films' failure to break with the paradigms of colonial representation with its infantilising tendencies; the heritage filmmakers seem happy to plunder with impartial regard from imperialist and revivalist representations. Both *Into the West* and *The Secret of Roan Inish* are works that might be categorised as children's films though it is debatable whether they were conceived as such. Both feature children as their protagonists and depend on magical intervention to resolve their central dilemmas. They are distinguished by a deep investment in whimsy and both refuse to differentiate between history and legend. In each case, the crisis with which the children have to engage is triggered by their culture's abandonment of tradition, something that can only be resolved by recourse to other-worldly intercessionaries. The two films link the sea with themes of rebirth – in *Into the West,* Ossie (Ciarán Fitzgerald) is rescued from the Atlantic by a mystical mother figure from under the water; the young Fiona (Jeni Courtney) in *The Secret of Roan Inish* effects the return of her baby brother from the selkies (seal people) in a scene that equally carries resonances of the biblical story of Moses. Magic, it seems, is routine in mythical/modern Ireland; it is also rendered here as a benevolent force.

In terms of gender, the use of historical settings enables such works to portray women in traditional roles. Their small victories conceal more conventional aspirations – single mother, Tara (Robin Wright) abandons her fierce independence for life with an interesting, handsome stranger, Tom

Figure 9.1 Into the West. Ciarán Fitzgerald (Ossie Riley), Ruaidhri Conroy (Tito Riley). Courtesy of the Irish Film Archive of the Film Institute of Ireland and Little Bird.

(Aidan Quinn) in *The Playboys* and Benny (Minnie Driver) tames Jack (Chris O'Donnell) in *Circle of Friends*. Indeed, the latter is particularly disappointing, given that in the original story (Maeve Binchy, 1990), Benny's triumph is to turn her back on marriage and embrace a career.

Yearnings for older, more conventional gender relationships characterise *The Run of the Country*. Like a number of the films in the genre, the overall mood of nostalgia is dominated by the central character, Danny's (Matt Keeslar) recollection of his mother as an intensely idealised figure. She is nurturing and protective, shielding him from his father's (Albert Finney) violence (which, it is hinted at, is caused by sexual frustration: as she cannot have more children, they cannot have sex). This claustrophobic oedipal relationship with the absent or 'castrated' mother figure is the central *topos* of Connaughton's writing. In the earlier *A Border Station* (1989), for instance, which in many ways prefigures *The Run of the Country*, the young boy still sleeps with and suckles his mother. This extract is typical of the tenor of both books:

> How did she always smell so sweet, ripe and warm? How was she always soft and why was his father always hard? She was honey, he was water. She was milk, he was skim. She was straw, he was stubble. She was hay, he was thistle. She was feathers, he was bone. And he himself was in between the two of them; wanting to be like her but knowing he looked like him. His reflection in the mirror on the tea-room wall spelt it out. 'Spitting image of your father!' Pictures were words.
>
> (Connaughton, 1989: 48)

The Run of the Country opens with Danny's mother's funeral and she is remembered in a series of flashbacks, generally baking or carrying out other domestic work. This in turn becomes an impossible ideal against which no woman can measure up. Danny's first sexual encounter is with another teenager who 'picks him up' in the local dancehall. Despite his fantasies about sex, he is filled with horror when she 'lures' him into the back seat of a car/ modernity. He refuses her advances and the film clearly labels her as a dangerous 'loose' woman. His second encounter with a young woman is with Annagh Lee (Victoria Smurfit). The fact that she is a creature of nature is reinforced by her name which is also the name of a local river. Their relationship is initiated through a common love of poetry and consummated against the background of an idyllic lakeside setting.

It is at the point where she becomes pregnant that the film departs most significantly from the novel. In the latter, there is no mention of an abortion and Annagh Lee simply miscarries. This devastates Danny and, after her family sends her to Canada, he resolves to emigrate to New York to try to join up with her again. His father agrees with his decision to emigrate, commenting, 'A border hems you in, narrows your view. I'm glad you're going' (ibid., 246). In the film, her decision to have the abortion estranges them and after the miscarriage there is no suggestion that they will be reunited. In the final moments, Danny is reconciled with his father, it is implied, because Annagh Lee no longer is an issue; in fact it is to his father that Danny expresses his disenchantment with her, 'The thing that hurts most is Anna not wanting the baby'. The insertion of the proposed abortion may be read as a criticism of contemporary Irish womanhood's damaging embrace of modernisation, a theme which is echoed in another Shane Connaughton-scripted film, *Oh Mary, this London* (Suri Krishnamma, GB, 1994) which follows two friends who accompany a pregnant woman (the film suggests that, whilst this is not a triangular relationship, either could be the father) to London for an abortion. The abortion leaves her dislocated and mentally unstable and the film ends in tragedy. The only solution to modernity is to expel it, by removing the female from the story after punishing her, through the pregnancy, the miscarriage, the anger of her family and the loss of her boyfriend. By deciding not to emigrate to America but instead to go to college in Dublin, *The Run of the Country* is suggesting that the disgusted hero is properly abandoning matters of the flesh for matters of the mind.

The representation of Irish as exotic Celtic 'other' is expressed at a number of levels and may be contrasted with those films that emphasise the inherently violent tendencies of the Irish. It is particularly important for viewers, both within Ireland and without, weaned on a diet of news images of rioting and violence in Northern Ireland, that these films offer an alternative image of the Irish: the Irish of the heritage films have no axe to grind with the British, in fact they borrow some of the more familiar British screen actors to play their central roles – most notably Albert Finney. The landscape too has been re-tamed, its Gothic threat removed. Ruins are no longer signifiers of a disputed history but quaint relics presented for the heritage gaze. In general, the films are edited in an unobtrusive fashion, favouring long establishing shots, usually of the countryside, and cut to the rhythm of a rearranged traditional music soundtrack. Interiors, where featured, are meticulous reconstructions of the small country cottage of the day. As Keith Tribe argues:

> This history is ... recognised as Truth by the viewer not by virtue of the 'facts' being correct, but because the image looks right. The recognition effect 'that's the way it was' is a product not of the historicity of the plot, but of the manipulation of the image.
>
> (1977/78: 16)

It could be argued that if veracity of image falsely guarantees veracity of fact, then the reproduction of an acknowledged unstable/false image (the Irish stereotype) should undermine our reception of these films, preventing a 'straight' reading. This is potentially the case in *Hear My Song* and *Waking Ned* whose foregrounding of performance and excessive use of stereotypes invite an ironic reading. On the other hand, the negative reception particularly of the latter film in the local press counters this point, certainly from an indigenous perspective. Equally such films converge with the notion of Ireland as simulacrum, alluded to at the end of Chapter 5. The fact that *Waking Ned* was filmed on the Isle of Man (for tax benefits) enhances its sense of functioning as a representation of a representation, its 'reality' drawn not from any sense of Irish life as it is lived but as it has appeared in cinema, notably in *The Quiet Man* and other such fictions.

Where films such as *Michael Collins* are identifiable by their post-colonial imperative, the process in Edward Said's words of rescuing 'the suppressed native voice from colonial history' (1994: 302), the heritage films betray a quite different agenda. In a few instances, however, history comes face to face with heritage, as directors attempt to confront the past on a narrative level whilst adhering to the visual aesthetic of the heritage film. An example of these is Maurice O'Callaghan's 1994 production, *Broken Harvest*, a re-working, like *Caoineadh Airt Uí Laoire*, of the story of Art O'Leary. Through the use of flashbacks, the film covers a period from the Civil War through to the present day. The bulk of the action negotiates the playing out of a tangle of enmities against the backdrop of 1950s rural Ireland. The narrator, Jimmy O'Leary's (Darren McHugh) father, Arthur (Colin Lane) fought on the opposite side of the Civil War to his best friend's uncle, Josie McCarthy (Niall O'Brien). The two men were also rivals in love for the woman who is now Jimmy's mother. An example of how the film attempts to have it all ways and succeeds in none is the scene in the village school where the schoolmaster, Master O'Donnell (Jim Queally) is teaching his giggling and uninterested class, who have already heard this once too often, about the origins of the Civil War. Given the overall construction of the film, it would seem that the purpose of this interlude is to coach the audience (possibly with an eye to the international market) on the historical facts. Yet for an Irish viewer of that generation this scene recalls the relentless and romanticised instruction in the history of Irish Independence imposed by the educational system of the time. Compare this to the history class in *Our Boys* where the Brother teaches the group of boys, 'Now Brian Boru was a fine handsome man. All the women in Ireland were after him. But he was intent on the High Kingship.' The latter film establishes a series of associations around the Brothers – of physical cruelty, of anachronism, of emotional poverty – so that we are now encouraged to question the official interpretation of history (through the cult of the romanticised male hero) as perpetuated by the religious system.

Broken Harvest embraces its historical paradigms with a strenuous lack of subtlety. No scene is complete without a reference to the fallout from the Civil War. Aware of the historical resistance to this material, the film offers us the visual palliative of a loving recreation of the villages and countryside of pre-modern Ireland. The other theme that is central to *Broken Harvest* is one that is common to a number of Irish historical films – the tension between primitivism and modernism. The moment of catharsis in these films is often associated with the shock of the new – in *The Playboys* it is the arrival of the village's first television set – or its converse, the abandonment of modernity.

In *Hear My Song*, a film that updates many of the themes of the ballad films of the 1930s, the central character, Micky O'Neill (Adrian Dunbar) travels back to Ireland, back in time, to find the 'real' tenor, Joseph Locke. When he and his companion reach the borders of the West in their anachronistic Morris Traveller, they pitch camp and park their car, leaving the lights on which duly causes the battery to go flat. The camera watches them go into their tent (back to the womb, to be reborn) as in the foreground the lights of the car dim and extinguish, signalling the eclipse of modernity. The next morning they wake up and as Fintan (James Nesbitt) fries trout (or the salmon of knowledge) Mickey stretches and looks out over the view that magically (they have invoked the help of the fairies) produces Josef Locke.

Hear My Song, like so many of these works, takes its protagonists on a journey that is also a trip from the modern to the 'present in the past'. This dialogue between the old and the new reflects not just a tourist fantasy but a local ambiguity about the effects of modernisation. As Paul Ricoeur has noted, 'every culture cannot sustain and absorb the shock of modern civilization. There is the paradox: how to become modern and to return to sources; how to revive an old, dormant civilization and take part in universal civilization' (1965: 277). The signs are that the heritage cycle has come to an end; from a local perspective this may mean that it has fulfilled its function of

Figure 9.2 Hear My Song. James Nesbitt (Fintan O'Donnell) and Adrian Dunbar (Micky O'Neill).

acting as a palliative to the 'shock of the new' and that Irish fictions are now more concerned with engaging with a new, cosmopolitan, urban Ireland. The end was certainly signalled in advance with the release of *The Butcher Boy* and we may also note in this respect the demise of *Ballykissangel* and the RTÉ rural soap opera, *Glenroe*. The decision by the Film Board to abandon mid-budget filmmaking in favour of micro-budget productions will almost certainly be the nail in the coffin of this particular genre, unsuited as it is to digital camerawork and the aesthetics of 'poor cinema'.

On the other hand, the international success of recent high-profile films such as *Angela's Ashes* and *The Magdalene Sisters* that draw on coming-of-age themes (although expressed in both these instances as traumatic narrative) suggests that Ireland has become identified by its past and that this is its most recognisable generic mode of expression. That both these films were made by British directors indicates that the traumatising of the Irish past has widespread resonances. In other words, the sense of despoilment such narratives carry with them has much greater effect in the context of a country that had heretofore epitomised innocence and childlike naivety than had they been applied to the dominant long-modern cultures of Britain or America. In this manner, Ireland's recovered history is metonymic for a universal loss of innocence, displacing its function as locus of heritage nostalgia.

10

NORTHERN IRELAND

The Troubles and the peace process in indigenous and non-indigenous filmmaking

In Neil Jordan's *Angel* an artist, in this case, a saxophone player, is drawn into the violent conflict that has become known as the Troubles. Danny (Stephen Rea) witnesses the death of a young mute woman to whom he has just made love when the dance hall he has been playing in is blown up by unidentified paramilitaries in a dispute over protection money. With just one clue, that one of the men involved wears an orthopaedic shoe, he sets outs to avenge her death. The dance hall is named the Dreamland and the further Danny goes on his quest, the more it seems that he is leaving his previous quotidian existence behind him and entering a metaphysical dream world, signalled in the film through the use of night time colours, and coincidental occurrences. The film never identifies the paramilitaries or makes it clear whether their allegiance is to republicanism or loyalism – all, it is suggested, are the same. In one particularly oneiric sequence, the band performs in a mental hospital; as the notes of the saxophone are first heard, the inmates silently move into the room in which Danny is playing, gradually filling it; in another, close to the film's ending, a crowd gathers to witness the laying on of hands by the 'seventh son of a seventh son', a child blessed with supernatural gifts. Just as he will later do in *Company of Wolves* (GB, 1984) and *In Dreams* (USA, 1999), Jordan invites the viewer to abandon the rational world and enter, with his protagonists, a dream that will soon descend into nightmare, one peopled by psychic children, regretful killers and unexpected agents of retribution.

Like so many narratives about the Troubles, *Angel* is indebted visually and thematically to Carol Reed's *Odd Man Out*, a film that also contains a character who is an artist. Lukey (Robert Newton) is determined to paint the IRA man on the run, Johnny (James Mason) as he is dying, to catch a man as he is passing from one world into the next. In the end, we do not see his painting, and Lukey, we suspect, will never fulfil his ambitions. Belfast, in Reed's expressionistic drama, is also a dream/nightmare space. The film is shot predominately at night and, as Johnny travels through its bombed, post-war cityscape, the snow falls on him and on his surroundings, transforming it into a fairytale universe whose whiteness belies its menace. A child appears like an angel to Johnny as he hides in a cellar, and as he slowly moves towards his lover, who will also preside over his death, two children again look out towards him, this time without seeing him as he passes under their window. John Hill has critiqued Reed's a-historical, resigned approach to Ireland's political violence, seeing in the film's fatalistic words, 'we're all dying', an overarching failure to raise questions of agency and motivation (1987: 152–60).

Hill's response to *Angel* was to see in Jordan's work exactly those deficiencies he had pinpointed in *Odd Man Out*. In contrast with Richard Kearney who argued that the film 'enables the viewer to delve beneath the ideological clichés of political violence to its unconscious hidden dimension (1988b: 183), Hill countered that 'if the film's use of a decontextualising aesthetic strategy necessarily undermines the "legitimacy" or rationale of political violence, so it also adds to the legitimacy of the state by de-politicising its activities as well' (1987: 180). These conflicting interpretations of the one film throw into relief the dilemma of any artist who chooses to become involved in representing Irish political violence. On the one hand, there is the temptation to interpret it as an age-old conflict, whose reason for being has long been forgotten and which has devolved into a set of mutually destructive rituals. The Troubles in this case become the backdrop to the exploration of the existential hero, one who must undergo a series of ritual trials in order to come to a better understanding of self, and by extension humanity. It further leads to a confirmation of Tom Nairn's much-quoted comment that the politics of Northern Ireland are explained away as a 'myth of atavism' (Nairn, 1981: 222–4) and in turn to the 'two tribes' interpretation of Loyalist-Republican sectarianism. Violence in such films is seen as endemic to the human condition and, when it is not curtailed by the rational constraints of a normally functioning civic society, then it will erupt in a manner that is as destructive to those who wield it as those who are at its receiving end. Northern Irish society, by virtue of its being locked in these age-old grievances, is thus in some sense retarded and pre-modern, a kind of universal id where the unrestrained impulses of humanity are free to circulate.

This vision of Northern Irish society as being backward belongs to a specific and, again much discussed, tradition of representing the Irish as prehensile. Drawing on the work of L.P. Curtis Jr (1997), and Liz Curtis (1984) Martin McLoone reminds us that a certain section of British society represented by the Victorian cartoonists in *Punch* and later by political satirists from the tabloid newspapers drew associations between Irish violence and the behaviour of primitive man in his most apelike form (the pronoun is used deliberately – Irish women were represented as fair maidens of extraordinary virtue) (2000: 60–2). In the age of Darwinism, any threat to the civilising benefits of imperialism was rationalised as an expression of primitive regression and the Irish were portrayed in such cartoons as dark, simian monsters. That this was an experience shared by the Irish in America in the early to mid-nineteenth century has been chronicled by Noel Ignatiev (1995) who suggests that the immigrant Irish actively participated in racist policies in order to establish their difference from the country's black population.

The earlier depictions of the Irish as low in the evolutionary ladder are part of a discourse of colonialism that equally intersects with class-based prejudices. Such hostile depictions come from outside the native culture and work to reify a conceptual framework. Indeed, as we have seen in Chapter 3, not all representations of the Irish by the British belonged to this discourse and Irish characters were equally vulnerable to sentimentalising or, at least, being viewed as the embodiment of all that spontaneity that was so desired but seen to be so lacking in the British persona.

Much of the argument for the development of a native industry has rested on the assumption that this would function as a corrective to earlier stereotyping of the Irish by those working from within different and often hostile cultures. This accounts for the sense of disappointment shared by most writers on the representations of the Troubles who have generally agreed that Irish filmmakers have simply appropriated the paradigms laid down and perpetuated by non-indigenous cinemas. For critics coming out of a Marxist tradition, in particular, lack of attention to the economic conditions that have led to the Troubles has been compounded by a refusal to analyse them historically.

Coming from a different perspective, Brian McIlroy has proposed that representations of the Troubles have been weighted in favour of the republican point of view (1993, 1998, 1999). Loyalism has either been presented negatively or not at all. His is undoubtedly a valid opinion and one borne out by the small amount of films that deal with the Protestant or Loyalist cause. One reason for this, as McIlroy suggests, is that 'the Calvinist influence on Northern Ireland's Protestants of all stripes has made notions of culture difficult to flourish' (1998: 13). Against this, as he proceeds to note, Northern Irish Protestants have long worked in television and have contributed to fiction writing of all kinds as well as to the visual arts. Certainly loyalists lack the appeal of the underdog and have not benefited from the culture of sentimentality discussed above in relation to Irish Catholicism. Film critic, Alexander Walker, echoes this critique:

> The movies ... have made the perception of Northern Ireland much worse than it should be. Most of them were written to a republican agenda and some of them in fact included Sinn Féin/IRA propaganda which to an Ulster person like myself was very obvious but which was calculated to appeal easily and credulously to other people in other countries.
>
> (*As Others See Us: The Movies*, UTV, 1998)

Walker later suggests that much of the blame for this must be laid at the hands of the Irish-American audience and the films that cater for it. In fact, the British film tradition has been on occasion equally culpable, producing several 'crime thriller' narratives set against a backdrop of the Troubles.

Two such British films, *Hennessey* (Don Sharp, GB, 1975) and *Hidden Agenda* (Ken Loach, GB, 1990) seem to wish to emulate the techniques of Costa-Gavras, that is, to make a thriller that satisfies generic expectations whilst addressing specific political issues. The first is the story of a reluctant terrorist, the eponymous Hennessey (Rod Steiger) who, having witnessed the deaths of his daughter and child when a British soldier falls over and his gun starts firing at random, decides to blow up the Queen. The second is allegedly a dramatisation of the 'shoot-to-kill' policies of the 1980s, though with its stock characters of the genre – a strong-willed former television journalist, Ingrid (Frances McDormand) drawn in through the death of her boyfriend and co-civil rights worker, Paul Sullivan (Brad Dourif), a salt-of-the-earth police investigator only ever referred to by his surname, Kerrigan (Brian Cox), a mystery informant/double agent, also only known by his surname, Harris (Maurice Roëves), corruption at the top, a missing tape containing incriminating evidence and shadowy terrorists[2] – the film never manages to deal in any depth with the issues that seem to interest it. It is also surprisingly anglo-centric, more concerned with critiquing Thatcherism than British policies on Northern Ireland.

Of the two British films, *Hennessey* is certainly the most interesting, more for what seems to struggle under its surface than what it actually articulates. For a start, it plays on the classical 'hawk and dove' dichotomy that underlies so many Troubles narratives. This configuration pits the man of violence against the man of peace (again, the gender usage is not accidental since women played quite a different role in these dramas) – thus, in *The Gentle Gunman*, brother is set against brother as one, Terence (John Mills) renounces his membership of the IRA in favour of peace, whilst the other, Matt (Dirk Bogarde) embraces violence. The audience's sympathies are directed towards Terence, just as they are directed towards Fergus (Stephen Rea) in *The Crying Game* and Malachy (Ross McDade) in *This is The Sea*. In *Hennessey*, however, the dove must become a hawk in order to avenge the deaths of his family. As Hennessey makes his way slowly towards his day of reckoning, he is pursued by his best friend and brother-in-law Sean Tobin (Eric Porter) and the Scotland Yard detective, Hollis (Richard Johnson) who has been wounded during a tour of duty in Belfast. Like so many Northern Irish narratives, the film makes little pretence of illuminating the history or politics behind the events but its refusal to demonise its killer/protagonist suggests that it concedes that he is at some level justified in seeking revenge on the symbol of British imperialism for the death of what are certainly innocent victims. The film also is also wary of the British military presence in the North although principally on the grounds that the coloniser is becoming contaminated by the colonised: 'You were a good officer,' Hollis' superior, Rice (Trevor Howard) tells him, 'until you went to Belfast and Tobin went after you. The violence over there has corrupted you. You could find no answer to their methods except counter violence and now it's part of you. You're hooked just like they are.'

On a purely technical level, the film makes extraordinary usage of footage of the Monarch opening Parliament, even down to a cut-away (cut from the British theatrical version but included in American video release) in which she appears to react to Hollis and Hennessey scuffling in the gallery.

The IRA freedom fighter has also enjoyed an extended life in mainstream American cinema, although his (and, again, they are invariably male) position has had to be carefully negotiated so as not to appear to endorse terrorism. The romantic revolutionary of John Ford's oeuvre belongs most properly in Ireland where he is safely distant. Once the IRA man arrives in America or territories within the American influence then he represents a potential threat to democracy. Studios have had to bear in mind that overt sympathy for the IRA would alienate one of their key European allies, Britain, whilst support for 'the cause' would appeal to the Irish-American audience as it has been traditionally defined (that is, Catholic and Republican).

The ubiquity of the revolutionary Irishman in John Ford's cinema was recognised by the filmmaker whose work was devoted to deconstructing and reinventing the Fordian Western, Sergio Leone. In *A Fistful of Dynamite* (aka: *Giù la Testa, Duck, You Sucker, Once Upon a Time – the Revolution*, Sergio Leone, 1971, Italy) the Mexican peasant-revolutionary Juan (Rod Steiger), encounters IRA man Sean Mallory (James Coburn); impressed by Sean's skills with dynamite, Juan tries to persuade him to join him in realising his dream of robbing the Mesa Verde Bank. The attempt ends in disaster and then tragedy when Colonel Guttierez (Antoine Domingo) massacres Juan's children and father. Juan himself is betrayed by the revolutionary leader Dr Villega (Romolo Valli) who is collaborating with Guttierez. In a sequence of flashbacks, Sean remembers his own early years in the IRA, returning again and again to his friendship with another man, who, like Villega, would be broken by torture and betray him, causing him to flee his lover and country. The flashback sequences in Ireland are intensely and self-consciously sentimental. The Ennio Morricone soundtrack is fleshed out by a female chorus, singing 'Sean, Sean' over an Ireland that combines the rural primitivism of *The Quiet Man* with interiors constructed to recall *The Informer*. The Mexican Revolution itself is shot as if it were Second World War imagery, with the national army looking and behaving like Nazis. Mallory functions within the film as the catalyst for Juan's transformation from cynical bandit to vengeful revolutionary, and the Mexican willingly draws on the Irishman's superior technical and strategic experience to pursue his own ends. *A Fistful of Dynamite* recognises the Fordian, even the wider Hollywood, romance with the IRA and the figure of the Irish revolutionary, suggesting that such representations arise out of a history of idealised images. Mallory, like so many of Leone's heroes, is simultaneously an artifice and a flesh-and-blood character, a parody of a man of action, and a man of action.

More recently, Hollywood's divided allegiances have resulted in the foregrounding of the renegade IRA man, the hawk rather than the dove, in USA fictions. Such characters – Sean Miller (Sean Bean) in *Patriot Game* (Phillip Noyce, USA, 1992), Ryan Gaerity [*sic*] (Tommy Lee Jones) in *Blown Away* (Stephen Hopkins, USA, 1994) – are fanatical lunatics, prone to outbursts of nationalistic invective, delivered in Gaerity's case in an incomprehensible accent. By proposing that these men are loose cannons working outside the moral codes and ideology of the IRA, the films are able to reference a real terrorist organisation (crucial to this genre) whilst simultaneously disavowing it.

The remarkable casting of Richard Gere as an IRA paramilitary in *The Jackal* (Michael Caton-Jones, USA, 1997) where as Declan Mulqueen his special skills in undercover operations are harnessed by the FBI in order to outwit international terrorist the Jackal (Bruce Willis), suggests the gradual rehabilitation of the IRA men in such fictions. Mulqueen is not mad or particularly bad and has all the makings of a decent family man, even if his partner of choice is a retired female terrorist, Isabella (Mathilda May). Likewise, Brad Pitt's appearance as IRA man Frankie McGuire in *The Devil's Own* (Alan J. Pakula, USA, 1997) would make it seem that the IRA has benefited from a new respectability in the wake of the Peace Process. McGuire is no peace lover and, like so many of these narratives, has joined the fight out of personal reasons (the killing of his father by loyalists) rather than any considered political opinions, yet Pitt invests his role with the same kind of charm that Gere attempts, leading to criticism of both actor and film for being pro-IRA (Brooks, 1997: 3). In Britain the film met with a barrage of tabloid and conservative hostility, stoked by the news that Princess Diana had taken under-age Prince Harry to this 'IRA Film' (Harvey, 1997: 1).

Ultimately, it is futile to seek any kind of reflection on the Troubles in what are essentially generic movies that rely on the cinematic history of their signifiers considerably more than on any kind of need to explore history or politics. Instead we need to look within indigenous Irish filmmaking practices to discover alternative viewpoints on these issues. This has necessarily been complicated by the almost complete absence of a local Northern Irish filmmaking tradition. The advent of Channel 4 television provided some funding in the 1980s that resulted in a small number of films (all with contemporary themes) being completed. As a consequence of a combination of increased Arts Council funding, the BBC's Extending Choice policy (which encouraged greater regional autonomy) and UK lottery funds, the late 1990s witnessed the first sustained period of local filmmaking. Many of these draw on a vein of black comedy associated with Northern Ireland and characteristic of the works of novelists such as Colin Bateman and Robert MacLiam Wilson. At the same time, the key films about the Troubles (all those discussed below with the exception of *Divorcing Jack* [David Caffrey, GB/France, 1998]) have been made by filmmakers from the Republic of Ireland, Great Britain or the USA.

Brian McIlroy and Alexander Walker's reservations about the representation of loyalists on screen are given credence by two recent feature films both arising out of books by writers from Northern Ireland: *Nothing Personal* (Thaddeus O'Sullivan, Ireland/GB, 1995, from *All Our Fault*, Daniel Mornin, 1991), and *Resurrection Man* (Marc Evans, GB, 1997, from *Resurrection Man*, Eoin McNamee, 1994). Both films draw on the activities of the so-called 'Shankhill Butchers', a gang of loyalists who were responsible for random tortures and killings of Catholics in Belfast in the 1970s and both identify their loyalist protagonists with gangsterism.[3]

Of the two, *Resurrection Man*, a critical and commercial failure, is undoubtedly the most offensive. Set in 1975, the opening credits read, 'The streets are in turmoil. Murder is commonplace in a divided city where gangsters draw boundaries in blood', the words appearing on the screen as if shot out of a typewriter. As the credits roll, we see Victor (Stuart Townsend) emerging in slow motion out of his family home and walking towards the camera in a sequence which will later turn out to be his final moments before his death. To heighten this sense of determinism, in an early flashback we see the young Victor transfixed by Cagney's on-screen death in *The Public Enemy* (William Wellman, USA, 1931). The Hollywood gangster genre is again invoked when Victor's mother (Brenda Fricker) greets him with a hand slapping routine reminiscent of Cagney. Further she is played as the archetypal doting mother who can see no wrong in her son, 'I know nothing about no killings. Them's all lies to me', and only his Catholic father recognises that Victor is 'nothing but a wee shite'. The film progresses through a series of increasingly bloody and sadistic killings, largely of random victims, as Victor establishes his place in the turf wars. He is shadowed throughout by the wife-beating, hard-drinking journalist Ryan (James Nesbitt) for whom obtaining the story is a career move, although it will also give Victor the publicity he is seeking. For Victor, killing is a sadistic pleasure which also provides sexual excitement. Typically, in terms of the gangster genre, this is expressed in ambiguity about his own sexual tendencies. Homosexuality is here equated with perversion and symbolically enacted through Victor's weapon of choice, the knife, whilst religion is associated with the fundamentalist preacher and neo-Nazi, McClure (Sean McGinley). In both films, Belfast is represented as a post-industrial space.[4] The suggestion is that the extortion of 'protection' money has supplanted other industries to produce a new economy. Violence is its (il)legal tender, the State all but absent.

Resurrection Man is shot in the style of a Tarantino-influenced postmodern gangster blood bath with Victor's attacks cut to the beat of *Tiger Feet* and other popular songs chosen for their function as ironic counterpoint to the action. This referencing of the gangster genre is a frequent fictional device in novels and films about the Troubles and has been seen to coincide with the Thatcher government's policy of labelling paramilitaries criminals (McLoone, 2000: 62–4). However, it also draws on a popular discourse that itself criminalises both loyalists and republicans. Reports of drug-related 'punishment beatings' meted out by vigilantes of both allegiances often to teenage boys, the colourful life of renegade loyalist leader, 'Mad Dog'

Johnny Adair, successive bank robberies, not to mention rumours about counterfeit video duplicating and other illegal activities have all accrued to the image of the various underground organisations who represent the paramilitary spectrum. This highlighting of an often brutal community 'policing' plays a significant part in this as well as undoubtedly drawing on real situations. At the same time, the strength of the gangster is counterpointed against the weakness of the State.

Why, for instance, do individuals such as Kenny (James Frain) and Ginger (Ian Hart) patrol their loyalist neighbourhood in *Nothing Personal* and what does this say about the relationship between the State institutions and its citizens? The first of the feature films to fictionalise the Shankhill Butchers, *Nothing Personal* was directed by Thaddeus O'Sullivan, maker of the earlier *December Bride* (GB, 1990) and the later Dublin gangster film, *Ordinary Decent Criminal. Nothing Personal* concerns the activities of vigilantes Kenny and Ginger and Catholic lone father, Liam (John Lynch) through the course of one night in Belfast. Both parties are caught up in riots on either side of the 'Peace Line' after which Liam begins a lone odyssey across Belfast that inevitably leads him to Ginger and Kenny. At the end of the film, Kenny sets Liam free after torturing him, but as he returns to his children, a young boy aims his stolen gun to shoot at the loyalists and is wrestled down by Liam's daughter, Kathleen (Jeni Courtney), whom he inadvertently shoots dead. Kenny shoots Ginger and the army in turn fire on the car he

Figure 10.1 Nothing Personal, courtesy of the Irish Film Archive of the Film Institute of Ireland and Little Bird. James Frain (Kenny) and Ian Hart (Ginger).

is in, mistakenly believing they are under attack. Kenny and the driver are killed, and in the final moments of the film both Kenny's and Kathleen's burials are held in the same cemetery.

O'Sullivan has said in interview that:

> That state and that history are what we all know about Ulster Protestantism. I wanted to go beyond that, to show the reality and potential of the people in the bars and the streets. It seems to me they have much more to offer than their political leaders. It's the latter we see and hear all the time, not the people whose views they're supposed to be representing.
>
> (Leahy, 1996, 20).

However, instead of focusing on the people in the streets and the bars, the film's concern is with its central gangster hero. The visual representation of Belfast similarly draws closely on the conventions of the gangster film's city, superimposing a generic space upon a real space (even the fact that the film was shot in Dublin detracts from its claims to realism). In common with the heroes of the classic gangster genre, Kenny (unlike Victor), has many sympathetic qualities. He seems to be ideologically motivated; when he swears in the young boy Tommy (Ruaidhri Conroy) who is awe-struck by Kenny's authority within the community (and his consequent success with women), he makes him repeat, to the faint strains of Elton John singing 'Candle in the Wind', 'We defend Ulster by going on the attack, we get the information on those cunts and we kill them because they deserve killing, it's as simple as that. Our first loyalty is to each other ...' whilst accompanying his words with his customary ironic smile. In comparison, Ginger is an irredeemable psychopath who justifies his bloodlust through recourse to loyalist rhetoric. After setting alight a Catholic rioter, he shouts out 'Sure I love it, I never had so much friggin' fun ... We have to make their life so friggin' miserable that they get down on their hands and knees and crawl across the fucking border'. His uncontrollable behaviour is an embarrassment to his chief, Leonard (Michael Gambon) who orders Kenny to dispose of his sidekick – hardly a just representation of ordinary loyalists.

In the scene that lends the film its title, Kenny and Liam face each other, Liam bound to a chair having been beaten by Kenny's men. Kenny reminds him that the beating was 'nothing personal' and begins to reminisce about the summer they shared on Liam's father's farm sheltering from German attack. The film fails to develop this theme but it is one of a number of mirroring devices that establishes the similarities between the two 'tribes'. Indeed, O'Sullivan goes to some pains to move from the Catholic to the loyalist side of the barricades and back, though the decision to square Liam, a gentle paterfamilias, off against two fanatical gangsters somewhat skews the equation.

Joe Cleary has noted that 'in the case of Northern Ireland, many of the most popular and generically recurrent narratives about the conflict adopt the form of a romance that straddles the political divide' (2002: 110). This, he adds, generally proves to be unworkable – 'whether they be heterosexual or homoerotic, however, one of the most striking features about these romances is the frequency with which they come to nought' (ibid.: 112). As we have seen, in earlier dramas, the love-across-the-divide structure was generally positioned to be between an Englishman and an Irish woman and could end either in harmony (*This Other Eden*) or tragedy (*Ryan's Daughter*). Although this motif still recurs, notably in Cathal Black's *Love and Rage* in which, drawing on the story of James Lynchehaun[5] it is reversed to portray the rape of the English settler woman by the native countryman, in the 1980s and 1990s it became more commonly applied to internal divisions, recurring in any number of films including *Cal* (Pat O'Connor, GB, 1984), *This Is the Sea* (Mary McGuckian, Ireland/USA/GB, 1996), *Bogwoman* (Tom Collins, GB/Ireland/Germany, 1997) and *Titanic Town* (Roger Michell, GB/Germany/France, 1998). It is applied to internal divisions within the Republican movement in *The Boxer* and to sectarianism in the Republic in the historical film, *A Love Divided*.

In *Nothing Personal*, a tentative romance occurs between Liam and Ann (Maria Boyle Kennedy), Kenny's estranged wife. She thus provides a further link between the homo-social relationship between Liam and Kenny but all hope for any kind of symbolic union is abandoned by the film's denouement. O'Sullivan employed a similar structuring device in what remains one of the most thoughtful films about Northern Ireland, the period drama, *December Bride*.

December Bride can be distinguished from the other films discussed in this chapter not just because of its formal allegiances but because of its conscious re-working of the conventional indices of Ulster Protestant identity. O'Sullivan has likened his film to the work of the Scandinavian filmmakers:

> I didn't want the film to look in any way Irish or British, in terms of its casting, the way it was written, the look of it, the framing of it, the colour of it, anything ... I also wanted to position the film in a Northern European context, visually and culturally – the Presbyterian thing you get in Scotland or Scandinavia.
>
> (Floyd, 1991: 27)

The film, set at the turn of the century and spanning the lifetime of one generation, borrows both its ethos and much of its story line from the original novel by Sam Hanna Bell (Pettitt, 2001: 9–28). The Echlin family take in two local women, Martha (Brenda Bruce) and her daughter Sarah (Saskia Reeves), as servants. On their way back from a trip to one of the nearby islands to fetch a ram, their boat capsizes and when Echlin senior (Geoffrey Golden) realises that there are too many of them to hold on to the overturned boat, he lets go so that the others might survive. After his death, Martha moves out but Sarah stays on with the two brothers, Hamilton (Donal McCann) and Frank (Ciaran Hinds) and has two children. It is not clear who is the father of either. Less content with the situation than his brother, Frank goes out courting at the Twelfth of July celebrations but is shunned by the community as a consequence of his irregular domestic situation. When he tries to see a woman, a shadowy group of men beat him up, leaving him crippled. As a coda to the action, 18 years later, Sarah's daughter (Dervla Kirwan) finally persuades her mother to marry so that she in turn can marry and 'have a name'. However, in the final wedding sequence, we are left unsure as to which brother Sarah weds.

From its opening sequences, *December Bride* suggests that rituals are central to human and animal survival. The collective gathering of the kelp on the shoreline, the trip to the island for the ram, the carrying of the water jug out into the fields, the lighting of the lamp in the evening, are, we know, repeated from year to year; further, they carry a visual reminder not just of Bergman but of the Irish School, in particular the paintings of Paul Henry and Jack Yeats. Overlaid on these natural, cyclical rituals are the traditions of the Orange Order, expressed through the recurring figure of the Lambeg drummer on the skyline and ultimately through the Twelfth of July celebrations. Whilst it could be argued that the beat of the drums echoes and blends with nature, the intervention of the Orangemen in another aspect of the natural order, Frank's courtship, suggests more a clash than a sense of harmony. This dissonance between the natural and the man-made is reinforced through the contrasting shots of the Minister, Sorleyson's (Patrick Malahide), garden with its neat rows of potatoes and the dark, shallow expanse of earth in which the Echlins' crop is planted. In the case of the Minister, however, nature triumphs over ritual as he moves from preparing a parable for his sermons about man's cultivation of the garden to one about the inevitability of nature's growth, an evolution which parallels his failure to persuade Sarah to baptise her first child and ultimately ends in his unwanted caress of her cheek. Even within the Echlin household, living in its precarious Utopia, rituals are not without their difficulties. There is a constant, underlying tension between Hamilton's reluctant occupation of his role as head of the household (which had been natural to his father) and Sarah's assumption of her role as matriarch which enables her to break out of the cycle of service for which she chides her mother. It is in her own inherent sectarianism that the differences are most explicitly realised, in particular through Hamilton's acceptance of their neighbour's Catholicism which is anathema to the otherwise apparently iconoclastic Sarah. Whilst Sarah has shown only contempt for the rituals of Presbyterianism ('all botched on the inside, but smooth to the eye, like lazy work'), she is still reluctant to acknowledge the Catholic observance of fasting on Friday and strenuously objects to the brothers relocating the Catholic family to her mother's old house.

It is only the Echlin brothers who appear to be immune to the traditional bigotry of the Northern Irish tradition and resilient against the demands of orthodox religion. 'It's our way and it works', Hamilton informs Sorleyson when he tries to persuade them to conform. The brothers' negation of accepted familial mores coincides with their denial of the loyalist ethic. By submitting to Sarah's will, and through a number of visual hints, they are seen to be feminised. O'Sullivan establishes this on a visual plane through the brothers' intimate contact with the child and through their pleasure in Sarah's company, typically in the scene where they are glimpsed through a window dancing around the kitchen. This positions them outside the 'macho' loyalist ethic:

> The threat of violence has long been part of the rhetoric of unionist politicians ... Another assumption in many quarters is that being a loyalist is about being a man, and a 'real man' at that! There is no room for the 'wimpish' type of individual, the 'namby pamby' or gays.
>
> (Douglas, 1994: 13)

What the film must ultimately admit is that it is not possible to live in splendid isolation; and that conformity is as in-built in the younger generation as it was in the old; as Sarah caustically remarks to her daughter, 'Youse young ones are all for marrying now; all for convention'. The closing off of options is echoed by the closing off of the causeway. According to O'Sullivan:

> That's a theme we used throughout: arrival and departure over causeways which are covered by water. And as soon as people arrive, the gap closes behind them. We tried to make that work in terms of the brothers' relationship with the community; it's a visual echo of that.
>
> (Floyd, 1991: 27)

Merely setting the film in a rural landscape is a marker of *December Bride's* exceptional nature. As Martin McLoone discusses, part of its originality lies in its association between Presbyterianism and the land:

> The insertion of Orange drums and a devout Presbyterian community into the Irish landscape is a reminder that the industrial workers of Belfast are only part of the Protestant story and the romantic nationalism of Catholic Ireland is only part of the story of Irish landscape.
>
> (2000: 209)

He further makes the comparison between the use of landscape in this and *The Quiet Man*, in particular drawing attention to the bonnet race which in *The Quiet Man* is the device which will ultimately unite the lovers and in *December Bride* leads directly to Frank's beating as if, 'a wholly different people have wandered into a recognisably Irish film' (ibid.: 210–11).

Ultimately, the film offers no solutions to the cultural and religious conflict of Northern Ireland. By altering the ending of the original novel (in which Sarah resignedly marries Hamilton, Frank being dead) to her grim arrival at the altar accompanied by both brothers, the film suggests that if you cannot live without traditions, you can (perhaps) rise above them.

One of the notable drawbacks to the 'two tribes' analysis of the political situation has been the almost complete elision of the British position. Westminster has allowed itself to be represented as honest broker in a battle between two sides of warring fanatics. Why those fanatics should have arrived at that point is considered to be a matter in the so far distant past as to be unworthy of consideration. The part played by the British government and its forces in the recent Troubles has also been carefully elided from the record.

One film that has sought to return the British role in Irish affairs into popular discourse is Jim Sheridan's *In the Name of the Father*. Loosely based on Gerry Conlon's book, *Proved Innocent* (1990), the film covers a time span from the Guildford bombing of 1974 to the release of Conlon and his co-accused in 1989. Whilst drawing on the source material of Conlon's description of his imprisonment and the reported facts of the case, Sheridan's film is a problematic re-working of the docudrama format. This 'tampering' with the facts (the Conlons did not share the same cell but were often in separate prisons, solicitor Garth Peirce (whose name is misspelt 'Gareth' in the credits of *In the Name of the Father*) only entered the case at a late stage, the court case was not heard in the manner portrayed and much of the legal groundwork was covered by Alistair Logan, Charles Burke was not an elderly tramp but someone Conlon met in a hostel) caused some anger amongst critics particularly in Britain where most of the reviews contained reports of the film's inaccuracies. *In the Name of the Father*'s detractors did not just include the conservative British media but also Robert Kee, Mary Holland and Mary Kenny. Where Sheridan saw the film's emphasis on the father/son relationship with its religious resonances (in the re-titling of the film) as symbolic, to much of the British press this focus on the personal and the recourse to melodrama opened up a space to critique its veracity. *In the Name of the Father* was also criticised by the Maguire family (the Maguire Seven were accused of conspiring to help the Guildford Four) who claimed not to have been consulted in its making and who objected to being shown at the same trial as the Guildford Four (another inaccuracy). The battle over the film's authenticity was carried as far as its posters; those intended for an American audience carried a sub-heading claiming that the film was 'a true story', and when around one hundred of these turned up outside British cinemas, a complaint was registered with the Advertising Standards Authority and the posters were replaced with others reading 'Based upon a true story'. Before the film's release, there were threats by the Surrey police to sue the filmmakers and their case was taken up by some of the British press who claimed that the film would incite anti-British feeling. According to the *Mail On Sunday*, 'When the Noraid collection box is rattled in the bars and pubs of America's East Coast cities – New York, Boston,

Philadelphia – the hate *In the Name of the Father* is generating will ensure that it returns full' (Stern and Davis, 1994: 49). The *Mail On Sunday* also objected to an icon of British theatre appearing in Sheridan's production, announcing, 'Sorry, Emma [Thompson]: You're crazy to do this film' (Keane, 1993, 33) before continuing to anticipate a similarly 'naive' American reaction to the film. In the end, although the American reviews of the film were largely favourable, the film did unexceptionable business, taking $24m in its first four months (Dean, 1994: 14).

The focus of *In the Name of the Father* is the father/son relationship. Through the course of the film, Gerry moves from a rejection of all parental authority (in his role of petty thief) to a brief capitulation to the authority of the British police (when he is cradled by the police officer [Dixon/Corin Redgrave] under interrogation), to his admiration for the IRA leader Joe McAndrew (Don Baker) and subsequent disenchantment when McAndrew sets alight the sympathetic prison officer, to eventual reconciliation with his own father whose place he takes (in campaigning for their release) after the death of Giuseppe (Pete Postlethwaite; the name is misspelt 'Guiseppe' in the film's credits). The rejection of the bad father for the good is also an ideological trajectory, the point where Gerry abandons his (misplaced, the film suggests) admiration of IRA tactics. The prison offers Gerry a surrogate family within which to make his oedipal passage. The Jamaicans become his brothers and, in the scene following Giuseppe's

Figure 10.2 In the Name of the Father. Daniel Day-Lewis (Gerry Conlon) and Emma Thompson (Garth Peirce). Courtesy of the Irish Film Archive of the Film Institute of Ireland and United International Pictures.

170

death, where we see hundreds of flaming paper tributes floating down from the prison windows in the darkness, the communality of prison life is stressed.

As I have argued elsewhere (Barton, 2002: 63–98), mainstream filmmaking practices are generally unable to analyse political issues in any great depth and rely on conveying ideological points of view through their symbolic human relationships. This has inevitably brought them into collision with the expectations of theorists whose positions we have seen articulated in relation to avant-garde cinema. Whilst it is easy to dismiss the political efficacy of *In the Name of the Father* (and one must concede that the film *is* compromised by its 'inaccuracies'), it does, as the British press acknowledged, make a very strong overall point about the potential injustices for Irish citizens being tried by the British court system. This it achieves through its central father-son relationship and the emotional potency of its story-telling techniques. It is not a campaigning film, nor is it a pro-IRA film, though as Brian Neve suggests, 'The overall effect is political, in the sense that Sheridan's film countered whispering campaigns from official circles that were designed to cast doubt on the overturning of the Guildford Four convictions in 1989.' (1996: 86). Whilst the film offers a strong element of closure, in this case it can easily be understood as a parable, a warning of further potential injustices and its meaning extends beyond its final moments.

What Gerry discovers from his father's death and his encounter with McAndrew is that constitutional resistance is more effective and more humane than individual acts of violence. Thus, he pursues his case through the courts with the aid of Garth Peirce and achieves victory along the kind of lines his father would have approved of. There are of course flaws in this type of argument in that it could be said that the Guildford Four were 'lucky' to have their case resolved by the judiciary and that other similar victims have been less fortunate. As the film suggests in its closing titles, those who perpetrated this injustice have not been punished and, thus, the larger question, of the ability of the British establishment to deal fairly with the Irish, remains hinted at but not fully explored.

The event that has come to bear the weight of contemporary history in the context of the role of the British army in Northern Ireland is Bloody Sunday. Most people are by now well familiar with the broader outline of what occurred on 30 January 1972. On that day, paratroopers from the Parachute Regiment in Derry killed 13 men and wounded 17, all it appears unarmed, during a civil rights march. A further victim died later. It remains to be established beyond doubt who fired the first shot and, given the investment by so many opposing sides in the history of this atrocity this seems unlikely to occur, but the army insisted that they were fired on and retaliated. Local witnesses, the families of the dead and those involved with the march have all asserted that the army were the first to shoot; they suffered no fatalities. In the wake of Bloody Sunday, the then British Prime Minister, Edward Heath, announced the establishment of a tribunal into the shootings to be headed by Lord Widgery. This much-discredited investigation concluded that the balance of the blame lay with the organisers of the march and that, whilst some soldiers could be accused of reckless firing, overall no culpability ought to be attached to the British command. In 1998, an enquiry under Lord Saville reopened the investigation because of pressure from local interests and in the light of new forensic evidence.

To mark the thirtieth anniversary of Bloody Sunday, two films were broadcast on television, of which one, Paul Greengrass' *Bloody Sunday* (GB/Ireland, 2001), also received a limited theatrical release in Ireland before becoming a critical success in the United States where it gained a cinema release. The second film, Jimmy McGovern's *Sunday* (Channel 4, 2002) was the more conventional of the two, focusing on one family and playing out the events in the highly melodramatic fashion with which McGovern is associated. Greengrass had a career in investigative television journalism and docudrama to his name before making *Bloody Sunday*, having worked on BBC's World in Action and had written and directed the programme investigating the death of black London teenager, Stephen Lawrence, *The Murder of Stephen Lawrence* (ITV, 1999). *Bloody Sunday* draws on the book, *Eyewitness Bloody Sunday* (edited by Don Mullan and John Scally, 1977), for much of its detail.

Greengrass shoots *Bloody Sunday* as a news item or cinema-vérité documentary, making use of digital cameras to come in close to characters' faces, to swing rapidly from event to event, to catch incidental moments as if off-camera, and to give an impression of filming under pressure, with loss of focus, overlapping sound and indistinct dialogue. 'Real life' characters make appearances including MP Bernadette Devlin and journalist Eamonn McCann. The publicised casting of a former SAS officer, Simon Mann, as Colonel Wilford of the parachute regiment, added to the film's claims to authenticity and it was widely read as such: 'Bloody Sunday has a terrifying authenticity: handheld cameras are jostled as crowds flee, soldier's eye viewpoints reveal movement that might be interpreted as almost anything and usually attracts fire. The confusion, fear, chaos and hatred are captured convincingly' (Kehoe, 2002: A8).

Like so many films about the Troubles, the accompanying publicity referenced Gillo Pontecorvo's *The Battle of Algiers* (Algeria/Italy, 1965). In fact, the film achieves little in the way of even-handedness other than including in its characters a young soldier who senses that a wrong is about to occur but is powerless to intervene or rectify it later. By 'omitting' to have a camera on the spot when the first shot is fired, the answer to the question of who initiated the slaughter remains elusive. At the same time, the film is evidently sympathetic towards the nationalist community, portrayed conventionally as family-oriented and socially deprived. The casting of James Nesbitt, an actor best known for sympathetic television roles, as the Civil Rights leader, Ivan Cooper, is a further sign, if one were needed of the film's sympathies and Greengrass also manages to slip in a 'love across the divide' relationship between a young Catholic-Protestant couple. The wild shooting of these unarmed men and women becomes metonymic for the lack of restraint shown by an army whose leaders apply the standards of an Imperial age to modern conflict. The young men of Derry are 'yobbos' and 'hooligans' as far as the paras are concerned, 'It's the end of our tour, let's teach them a fucking lesson', one calls out to approval from his mates.

Despite nods to understanding the position in which these ill-educated, hyped-up troops found themselves, *Bloody Sunday*'s thrust is to establish a certain 'truth', namely the culpability of the British army, the central issue being investigated by the Saville Inquiry. This it achieves largely through its formal devices, in particular its camerawork and editing, as much as by way of its content, its inner narrative. Its faux-documentary format further allows it to place itself within a tradition of influential television documentaries that have over the years exposed many of the British miscarriages of justice in Northern Ireland, most famously in this case Peter Taylor's *Remember Bloody Sunday* (BBC, 1992).

In *Televising Terrorism*, Schlesinger *et al.* distinguish four main ways of talking about terrorism:

- the 'official perspective': 'the set of views, arguments, explanations and policy suggestions advanced by those who speak for the state ... the official perspective removes terrorism from the political arena by stressing its essential criminality' (1983: 2).
- the 'alternative perspective': these views:

  do not offer a fundamental challenge to the official claims made for a legitimate use of the means of violence, they do question the implications of excessive repression for the rule of law and democratic rights [and advocate] ... strategies of political change and social engineering designed to defuse the violence and tackle its causes.

  (ibid.: 16–17)

- the 'populist perspective': argues for a civilian 'on the ground' response to terrorism (ibid.: 24–7).
- the 'oppositional perspective': 'justifies the use of violence in the pursuit of political ends [by terrorists]' (ibid., 27).

The authors further distinguish between 'open' and 'closed' viewpoints ('based on whether the programme deals with one or more viewpoints' [ibid.: 32]) and 'tight' and 'loose' programmes (based on whether interpretation is closed off or opened up [ibid.]).

The majority of the films under discussion here roughly reflect the alternative, liberal perspective whilst also, in several cases, illustrating the intransigency of the official perspective. Their viewpoints tend to be 'closed' and to a large extent they are 'tight'. There has been a tendency, however unconsciously, to internalise the official perspective, particularly through depicting paramilitary groups as criminals/gangsters and through the focus on human interest stories (a feature of 'official' news stories). On the other hand, to many of those from within the official perspective, these films with their perceived justification of paramilitarism, represent the ideas of the oppositional perspective.

Bloody Sunday ends with a shot of a line of young men queuing to sign up to join the paramilitaries. Having discredited the 'official perspective', it, unusually for most films about the Troubles, comes close to endorsing the 'oppositional perspective'. It may not actually suggest that a paramilitary response is an appropriate one, but it does at least explain its origins in a sympathetic manner.

This tentative move towards legitimising terrorist activity beyond the fictional parameters of the personal revenge narrative that conventionally was associated with Troubles fictions is indicative of *Bloody Sunday*'s positioning within a post-ceasefire discourse[6] and is comparable to the similar trajectory within the generic American thrillers already mentioned. It is easier to explore the roots of recent IRA paramilitary activity when that activity is now viewed as less of a threat. The two loyalist/gangster films, however, have their origins in pre-ceasefire novels (the later, *Resurrection Man*, was published in 1994, so its genesis is pre-ceasefire) and express no interest in seeking a political rationale for their central characters' killings.

The inevitable outburst of vilification from the British conservative media accompanied the screening of *Bloody Sunday* on television. A reading of the response of the local press, however, reveals a sense that Greengrass' film offered itself to participants and viewers as a therapeutic narrative, enabling them to revisit and work through the trauma of 30 years ago ('A Kind of Closure', *Derry Journal*, www.derryjournal.com/bloodysunday, accessed 18 December 2002). Similarly, the director proposed that by bringing together the many extras from both the area and the army, a sense of closure and, even reconciliation, emerged during the making of the film (Greengrass, 2002).

The dilution of political tensions caused by the Peace Process and various ceasefires of 1994 onwards has been reflected in the emergence of a new set of cinematic narratives, a 'Peace Process Cinema'. Some such as *The Boxer* are directed at those elements within the nationalist community who have not made the move towards constitutional nationalism (Barton 2002, 99–123). Others, for instance *With or Without You* (Michael Winterbottom, GB/USA, 1999) conspicuously divest the Northern Irish city and landscapes of their conventional signifiers, replacing the rundown city streets, the Saracens, and the ever-hovering helicopters with a new vision of Belfast as a glass and chrome space of pleasurable consumption.[7] *With or Without You* aspires to be, as its DVD jacket screams in a quotation from a lesser-known publication: 'sexy, sassy and irresistibly Irish!' Another route has been to replicate on screen the gallows humour of local writers such as Colin Bateman and Robert MacLiam Wilson. The production of indigenous short films and the occasional feature has been characterised by this particularly local brand of comedy, resulting in works such as the feature, *Divorcing Jack,* and a plethora of short films, amongst them, *The Pan*

Loaf (Seán Hinds, Channel 4, 1994) and *The Cake* (Jo Neylin, BBC, 1995). This surreal, often absurd vision of life in Northern Ireland also informs the television series *Give My Head Peace*. The latter

> parodies theatrical, film and television genres, which carry a subversive, satirical charge, aimed at ridiculing the pervasive jargon of the peace process and media representations of the Troubles, which are seen largely to be imposed from outside, and the dominant ideologies of the two main political communities, which are demonstrably inadequate to the demands for peaceful transformation (rather like the residual discourse of the Catholic Church in the Republic, failing to keep pace with the emergent ideas of the laity).
>
> (Pettitt, 2000: 198)

Black humour further distinguishes the comedy *The Most Fertile Man in Ireland* (Dudi Appleton, GB/Ireland, 1999), *An Everlasting Piece* (Barry Levinson, USA, 2000) scripted by local Belfast writer, Barry McEvoy, who also takes the lead role, and *Wild About Harry* (Declan Lowney, GB/Ireland, 2000).

Except for its commitment to scenes of graphic violence, *Divorcing Jack* is typical of this cycle of films. Based on the novel of the same name by Colin Bateman who adapted it for screen, it concerns the misfortunes that befall cynical, hard-drinking journalist, Dan Starkey (David Thewlis), when the woman with whom he is having an affair is murdered, apparently uttering the words 'divorcing Jack' as she dies. With Black-American journalist, Charlie Parker (Richard Gant) in tow, Starkey must rescue his wife, confront the candidate for first Prime Minister of Northern Ireland and elude the various paramilitaries in pursuit of him.

The film proposes a view of the Troubles as orchestrated on all levels by trigger-happy men distinguishable primarily by their excessive bloodlust, and of politics as anarchic and corrupt. As the nurse who by night doubles as a 'nun-o-gram' muses, 'It's chaos out there, but then it always has been'. Caffrey's production references a Belfast that is both familiar and surreal; its early scenes suggest that it will linger on the new urban chic of the post-industrial city but this illusion of normalcy is shattered by the graphic death of the young woman in her garage-apartment. In the manner that comedy is wont, it both establishes and disavows the viability of its central premise, that in a society with such deeply riven sectarian divisions, the violence of the past will always irrupt into the present.

Divorcing Jack is perhaps the most pessimistic of the films mentioned here; both short films, *The Pan Loaf* and *The Cake*, envisage in their moments of catharsis some kind of progression. In the former, two students leave a party to buy a loaf of bread. Traversing late-night Belfast, they move through the geography of sectarianism. Initially cocky Finbar (Conor Grimes) wilts at the idea of purchasing the eponymous commodity from a late-night loyalist venue but his companion advises him to pass himself off as a persecuted Russian Christian. The loyalist shopkeeper (Ian McElhinney) is not to be misled, 'A persecuted Protestant Christian or a persecuted Catholic Christian?' he leans over and enquires. As the two young people take possession of their loaf, a group of men moves into the shop from a back room. Utterly fazed, the twosome act upon Gwen's (Emma O'Neill) exhortation to 'run like fuck'. Once they have left, the shopkeeper and his cohorts can return to what they were interrupted in doing, namely watching pornographic videos on the television in the corner. Drawn together by their shared experience, Gwen and Finbar return to the party. In its design, *The Pan Loaf* is indebted to the expressionistic tradition associated with *Odd Man Out* whilst *The Cake* boasts a visual garishness more common to comic books. In the latter film, a young Catholic woman is putting the touches on a highly ornamental cake as the Twelfth of July celebrations take place around her (mixed) neighbourhood. Looking down at her from the wall are the icons of traditional Catholicism, the Pope and John F. Kennedy; as she glances at them they wink at her. She makes her way through the revelry, encountering en route a drunken bandsman (Tim Loane) who propositions her through his slurred and fast receding consciousness. Once in the Orange Lodge she presents her cake to the three men who have commissioned it. In an exchange carried out with the measured tones of heightened performance, they pronounce themselves dissatisfied with her work, in particular with the amount of green (nationalist) grass on the decorative icing. The conversation proceeds from absurdity to absurdity as they forget her name and in turn produce a rabbit from a hat and streams of red, white and blue bunting. Symbols it seems have magical properties and substitute for reality. Back home, the woman happily eats the cake, breaking down the green icing and decapitating the figure of the Orangeman perched on it. Just as the French consumed croissants in order to demean the symbol of their Turkish enemies, so Josephine (Lorraine Pilkington) reduces the artefacts of Orangeism to mere matter.

Perhaps the most charming of the recent short films to emerge from Northern Ireland is the Academy Award-nominated *Dance Lexie Dance* (Tim Loane, BBC, 1996). In this short drama, a recently bereaved father and daughter live together and, whilst he is out at work, she discovers Riverdance, the highly successful Irish dancing show that rendered Irish dancing simultaneously sexy and part of global consumer culture. After she has practised her moves in slippers, Laura (Kimberley McConkey) announces to her father that she wants to learn Irish dancing. 'But we don't dance', he protests in deference to his Protestant upbringing. 'We can start' she replies. Symbolically, the film illustrates its theme of bridging divides – between father and daughter, Protestant and Catholic traditions, life and death – by the device of the boat Lexie (B.J. Hogg) steers across the Foyle to and from his home and job, itself in a mixed workplace. Finally, Laura performs in a Féis (dancing competition) in honour of which the boat is decked out in red, white and blue bunting. The film eschews a triumphant victory in favour of a quiet moment of solace in which father and daughter lay to rest the memory of her mother and he takes his first dancing lesson from his child.

The emphasis on a feminine subjectivity in these and other short films, notably Dublin-based director Stephen Burke's *After '68* (Ireland, 1993) is a welcome corrective to the insidious machismo of many Troubles fictions with their almost pornographic vision of violence. These films appear to be in search of a new visual and narrative aesthetic for Northern Ireland, one that will both acknowledge and distance itself from the trauma of the Troubles and of life in the wake of the Peace Process. To date, the filmmaker who has most consistently sought to reinvent Northern Ireland on film, although in a non-fiction tradition, is John T. Davis.

Born in 1947, Davis attended art college and became attracted to the medium of film. Making his name with the punk documentary, *Shell Shock Rock* (Holywood Films, 1979) and progressing though his love-affair with the marginal spaces of American culture, *Route 66* (Central Television, 1986) and *Hobo* (BBC, 1991), his fascination with American and Northern Irish evangelism in *Dust on the Bible* (Channel 4, 1989) and *Power in the Blood* (BBC, 1989), Davis made his most personal film, *The Uncle Jack* (Channel 4/RTÉ, co-directed with Sé Merry Doyle) in 1996. Davis' work has been described as 'visual poetry' (McCracken, 1999) and is infused with a sense of being both inside and outside of the culture he is observing: 'To him Ireland is a unique location, a kind of peripheral state of the USA where the attitudes and the people differ greatly from those of European countries' (O'Brien, 2001: 169). Not all, by any means, of Davis' many films have concerned Ireland but those that have, have divested the figure of the Ulster Protestant from its associations with fanatical bloodlust or bowler-hatted repressiveness and replaced that imagery with one that draws connections between the American bible belt and Northern Irish fundamentalist belief. The men and women in the loyalist clubs that the American missionary-preacher, Vernon, visits in *Power in the Blood* appear to fall into an almost convulsive state on hearing his words, betraying an emotional vulnerability that is apparently utterly spontaneous.

In Davis' films objects shimmer in the sunlight as they move into the camera's viewfinder; alternately, he lingers on neon lighting and rain-washed night time streets. In *Dust on the Bible*, a film devoted to Northern Ireland's evangelical street preachers, a voice-over prophesises fire and brimstone as apocalyptic views of black clouds massing in an evening sky fill the screen. His is a world of entropy and decay, compassionately observed. Until the making of *The Uncle Jack*, his subjects – the hobos whom he joined as they rode the railcars of mid-America, the fundamentalist missionary in *Power in the Blood* – were allowed to speak at length about themselves or declaim from the Bible. In *The Uncle Jack*, however, he turned the camera on himself as he documented the work of his uncle, John MacBride Neill, foremost architect of Northern Ireland's cinemas until the decline of cinema-going. As Ted Sheehy has written, 'his other films all have subjects which are like manifestations of Davis himself in a celluloid parallel universe. They show how he might have turned out had life bitten him differently' (1996: 17). Forcing himself to confront his own sense of guilt at having dismissed his favourite relative when the latter became so obsessive that his mental health broke down and he was institutionalised, Davis takes a journey though his life that opens out to become a meditation on culture, identity and family. It takes in a history of the North's short-lived filmmaking tradition ('the Hollywood dreams of Northern Ireland') centred around Richard Hayward whose film *Devil's Rock* (Ireland, 1938) was shot in his uncle's most glorious cinema, the Tonic. It is about privilege – the Uncle Jack and his mother came from a well-off Irish family – and prejudice, his father, whom Jack belittled, came from the other side of the tracks. It was these 'narrow certainties of Northern Ireland' that caused Davis' flight to America and which he tries to tease apart in this film. Most of all, *The Uncle Jack* is about his own ageing and his recognition of his parents' and uncle's later lives.

Davis has said about the film, 'It's foolish to say it's a documentary, it's an experimental art film or something. Everything in it is designed, constructed or deliberate – there's no documentary reality. The story is abstract, it's a film in the mind' (ibid.). The intertwining of the personal and the political, the sense that the history of Northern Ireland might in some way reflect a greater metaphysical condition lies at the heart of the film that opened this discussion. In Davis' films, this desire to forge connections between the Protestant cultures of Northern Ireland and an equally marginalised and dispossessed American evangelism bespeaks a similar ambition to render that community less discursively isolated. On the other hand, few films do attempt to negotiate the quite specific historical and political reasons for the Troubles even if, in varying ways, they raise questions about legitimacy and the motives for violent confrontation. The very specific challenge that now faces filmmaking in and about Northern Ireland is to move beyond the tired paradigms of Troubles cinema and invent a new set of narratives that correspond to the wider experience of the inhabitants of that geographical space.

11

INCLUSION, EXCLUSION, CONCLUSION

The regions and the margins in contemporary Irish film-making

The decade since the re-establishment of the Irish Film Board in 1993 witnessed the first sustained period of indigenous filmmaking since the inauguration of the State. Some of the debate over the extent of its achievements, specifically in terms of the quality rather than the quantity of films produced, has echoed through the earlier chapters of this part of the book. It is certainly disappointing that the foremost auteurs of Irish film culture still remain Neil Jordan, Jim Sheridan and, to a lesser extent, Pat O'Connor, whose reputations were made before 1993. These filmmakers do not rely on Film Board support, using their international standing to draw instead on American studio funding. Furthermore, many of those directors, actors and technicians who have emerged from Ireland in the 1990s have migrated into British, American and mainland European filmmaking where, it appears, the opportunities are greater. The extent of this trend was demonstrated by the line-up of 'Irish' film premieres at the Dublin International Film Festival of 2003 where, of the seven features, three had no Irish content. In the same year, Neil Jordan released his latest film, *The Good Thief* (GB/France/Ireland, 2002), a remake of *Bob Le Flambeur* (Jean-Pierre Melville, France, 1955). The Irishness of *The Good Thief* was limited to the appearance of identical twins with dubbed Irish accents as minor criminals. A further cause for concern has been the absence of any 'crossover' successes. None of the small films made in Ireland during the 1990s broke into the mainstream as *My Left Foot* and *The Crying Game* had done; nor has there been any equivalent *Trainspotting* (Danny Boyle, GB, 1995), *The Full Monty* (Peter Cattaneo, GB, 1997) or *Billy Elliott* (Stephen Daldry, GB, 2000). By and large, their core audience has been Irish, with few of the productions achieving notable success in overseas markets; whilst this suggests that their address has, therefore, been primarily a local one, a condition of a national cinema, their performance in the home market has also been in many instances unremarkable (see the Appendix).

Judging films by their success or failure in the marketplace is, of course, a yardstick of only limited usefulness. Many of the films that were spurned by cinemagoers were warmly reviewed in the media and highly regarded within the industry. A notable such case was Martin Duffy's *The Boy From Mercury* (GB/France/Ireland, 1996). Centred around Duffy's characteristically otherworldly boy protagonist (Duffy has also made *The Bumblebee Flies Anyway* [USA, 2000] and *The Testimony of Taliesin Jones* [GB/USA, 2000]), the film invests the well-worn coming-of-age drama with a sense of intense familiarity through its invocation of the artefacts and mannerisms of the 1950s whilst its creaking sci-fi plot and use of overly-bright colours renders that period simultaneously fantastical. Like so many of his contemporaries, Duffy associates childhood pleasures with imported popular culture, here the weekly episodes of *Flash Gordon* shown at the local cinema. At the same time, his Ireland is a constricted place, haunted by death and one which its youngest inhabitants dream of leaving.

That Duffy's film fitted into no discernible category, functioning neither as children's film or otherwise, left it susceptible to a market more used to generic Hollywood fare. The extent to which it has been either advisable or necessary to conform to dominant cinema practices has been an issue that has most often been decided by budgetary limitations. Few filmmakers in Ireland have been able to access the kind of capital that would enable them to make Hollywood-standard entertainment and have tended instead to adapt themselves either to the style favoured by British and Irish television or the European art cinema circuit. Thus productions such as *Ailsa* (Paddy Breathnach, Ireland, 1994) and *All Souls Day* (Alan Gilsenan, Ireland, 1997), again films that under-performed at the box office, overtly positioned themselves within the aesthetic of the European art film. In each case, the films are distinguishable by a solipsistic exploration of masculine identities, something that we have already seen characterised many of the films of this period.

Other directors actively confronted the less salubrious aspects of Irish society, exploring and celebrating its marginalised members and repositioning its inhabitants within local and international concepts of identity. It is with these films that this book will conclude and with the proposal that Irish cinematic culture is now a much richer constituency than it was before the 'boom' of the 1990s and that future filmmakers may fruitfully develop this achievement.

The production of Irish-language films has, as we have seen, largely been the preserve of Bob Quinn and is part of his cinema of subversion. The Film Board and other bodies have long applauded the notion of an indigenous language cinema, yet the potential audience for such a practice is so limited that finance and expertise have militated against its evolution. To date, the most sustained work of Irish-language drama is the soap opera, *Ros na Rún*, produced for the Irish-language television channel, TG4. As Ruth Lysaght has argued, the makers of this programme have shown a determination to portray a Gaeltacht (Irish speaking area) that is distinguished by its modernity and its vibrancy.[1] TG4 has facilitated some documentary filmmaking, including the challenging *An Scéalaí Deireanach? (The Last Storyteller?)* (Desmond Bell, Ireland, 2002), a work that also received Film Board funding. Bell's 'creative' documentary reflects many of the concerns of the fiction filmmakers discussed here, namely a desire to engage with traditional culture within a contemporary format.[2] The same ambition marks one of the few feature films made for TG4, *An Focal Scoir* (*The Last Word/Le Dernier Mot* [Sebastien Grall, Ireland/France, 1999).

An Focal Scoir is a French-Irish co-production and, rather than conceal its dual funding, it foregrounds it. The film was shot in Schull (County Cork) and Paris and concerns two teenagers, Irish Cynthia (Laura Brennan) and French Nicolas (Lorant Deutsch); the two are pen friends and the film opens as Cynthia is making a short video to send Nicolas. Cynthia's father (Macdara O'Flatharta) is not too happy with the friendship, blaming what he sees as his daughter's increasing 'weirdness' on her contact with Nicolas. Cynthia, who dresses as a latter-day hippy, and Nicolas are Buddhists and swap ideas and writings on their shared interest. When Cynthia arrives in Paris a series of comic misunderstandings takes place, although all is satisfactorily resolved by the dénouement. *An Focal Scoir* is imbued with a teenage sensibility and an astute eye for teenage attitudes. Cynthia and her friends self-consciously smoke cigarettes as they march over the hillside from school, their conversations revolve strictly around boys and they regard their parents with contempt. Their home is a far remove from traditional representations of the west of Ireland and community life is viewed as more global village than rural idyll.

The growing body of Irish-language short films similarly articulates a desire to move away from revivalist/tourist representations of the west of Ireland, where most Gaeltacht communities are to be found. Funded primarily by the Film Board through initiatives such as *Oscailt* and *Lasair*, and exhibited at festivals and on TG4, the films reflect the *súil eile* (another perspective) tagline attached to TG4. Works such as *An Leabhar* (*The Book*) (Robert Quinn, Ireland, 2000) and *Tá Schumacher ar a Bhealach* (*Schumacher is on the Way*) (Brian O'Tiomain, Ireland, 2002) invest their seabord settings with, in the former, a bright metropolitan look and an absurdist plot about secret cabals and random violence, and, in the latter, an expectant father who obsesses about Formula One racing. Meanwhile, Kester Dyer's *Padraig Agus Nadia* (*Padraig And Nadia*) (Ireland, 2002) is one of the first Irish films to explore an interracial love affair. The experience of immigration is given comic treatment in another Irish-language short, *Yu Ming is Ainm Dom* (*Yu Ming is My Name*, Daniel O'Hara, Ireland, 2003) about a young Chinese man arriving in Ireland, having prepared himself by learning not English, but Irish. Lysaght notes that whilst such films appear to step outside the traditional themes of Irish narratives, they both recognise and mock their cinematic and cultural inheritance (2003: 37). Such is certainly the case in *Lipservice* (Paul Mercier, Ireland, 1998), a hilarious parody of the Leaving Certificate Irish oral exam. Set in a disadvantaged Dublin school, the film parades a succession of charming students, of whom few have the faintest grasp of their native tongue, in front of an increasingly bemused examiner (Sean

McGinley). In line with many short Irish films that view Ireland more as a figment of the imagination than a real location, James Finlan's *Éireville* (Ireland, 2002) recasts Irish history as a science fiction drama in the mode of Godard's *Alphaville* (France/Italy, 1965). A totalitarian State, in thrall to a dead patriot, Patrick von Pearsemann, whose brain has been wired to the computer, Dev 69, the country lives in the past tense and only recognises the digits 1, 9, 6 (after 1916).

If the *Oscailt* and *Lasair* films have been notable for their refusal to relegate Irish-language culture to the cinematic margins, so other works in the 1990s have removed issues of social marginality from the preserve of the avant-garde and 'poor cinema' and attempted to relocate them within mainstream filmmaking practices.

In his account of the lives of Dublin's criminal underworld, Paul Williams noted in 1998 that:

> Crime causation tells us as much about the fundamentals of our society and indeed, ourselves as any other study. It illustrates social dysfunction – in other words the failure of our systems of education, welfare, employment and justice. Crime is about the gulf between the haves and the have nots. The vast majority of our criminal population grew up in deprivation, on the wrong side of a social and economic boundary wall. Behind this wall exists a sub-culture where the norms of the middle class mean little ... In the midst of

Figure 11.1 Eireville. Michael O'Sullivan (Lemmy Cúramach) and Siobhán O'Kelly (Natasha von Tuairise). Courtesy of James Finlan; photography by Colm Hogan.

Ireland's unprecedented economic boom, we are creating the next
generation of criminals, as the socio-economic boundary grows
higher and more impregnable.

(1998: 11–12)

Williams ascribes the rise in gangland crime to the economic boom of the
1960s that in turn gave way to the drug trade of the 1980s and 1990s and
was facilitated by the increased availability of firearms in the wake of the
outbreak of the Troubles. Until the murder of journalist Veronica Guerin
in 1996, the response of the gardaí was 'slow and inadequate' (ibid.: 10) and
the gangland bosses began to think of themselves as 'untouchable and above
the law' (ibid.). The fear of an impregnable crime world over which the
police had little control marks out two minor crime films of the 1980s,
The Courier (Joe Lee/Frank Deasy, GB/Ireland, 1987) and *Taffin*
(Francis Megahy, GB/USA, 1987). Partly a showcase for two rising Irish
stars, Gabriel Byrne and Pierce Brosnan respectively, and, in the case of the
former, Ireland's emerging independent rock scene (the soundtrack features
Hothouse Flowers, Something Happens and U2), both films attempt to
address visually and thematically questions of drug scams and planning corruption in a new, modernising Ireland. *The Courier*, in particular, makes
much of Dublin's evolving high-rise cityscape, its traffic jams, and a sense
of seediness, accentuated, in this case, by the criminal, Val's (Byrne) 'perverse' sexuality. In the latter, set in a small village just outside of Dublin, the
locals hire vigilante, Mark Taffin (Brosnan) to protect their interests when a
shady business conglomerate seems set to develop the local playing fields to
house a chemical plant. Both films explicitly link corruption, modernisation
and business development in scenes where the master criminal expresses his
sense of mastery in a high rise office with windows overlooking and dominating the city and its inhabitants below.

Aesthetically, attempting to work from within a genre cinema that had no
local roots hampered *The Courier* and *Taffin*. The representation of Dublin
as a corrupt city did have some ontological history, dating back to the plays
of Séan O'Casey and Ford's *The Informer*; it re-emerges in a number of films
of this period, including *Pigs* and, most bizarre of all the 1980s' works, *The
Fantasist* (Robin Hardy, Ireland, 1986), a sex crime drama. Yet, the gangster
and vigilante have little place in this history, belonging most properly to the
Hollywood tradition but also familiar from a number of contemporary
British thrillers, to which *The Courier* and *Taffin* are indebted. Where the
American examples are informed by a (de-)mythologising imperative, envi-
saging the gangster/vigilante as 'tragic hero' (Warshow, 1970), a figure
from the dark underside of America's expansionist dreams and bearer of a
recalcitrant ethnicity, the British equivalents have been more concerned with
'exposing the flip side of working-class respectability and male gentility'
(Chibnall and Murphy, 1999: 2). The opprobrium for crime expressed by
the classic British gangster films has trickled down into the Irish productions, opening them up to a conservative reading that proposes the necessity
for a stronger police/State.

The dual assassinations of Veronica Guerin and, earlier in 1994, of the Dublin criminal known as The General, opened up a floodgate of Irish crime films, generally inspired by one or other event. These include: *The General* (John Boorman, Ireland/GB, 1998), *When the Sky Falls* (John MacKenzie, Ireland/USA, 1999), *Ordinary Decent Criminal, Veronica Guerin* (Joel Schumacher, USA, 2003) and the television film, *Vicious Circle* (David Blair, BBC, 1999). Gangster activity also inspired *I Went Down, Saltwater* (Conor McPherson, Ireland/GB/Spain, 1999), *Sweety Barrett* (Stephen Bradley, Ireland, 1998) and the television series, *Making the Cut* (RTÉ/ BBC, 1997) whilst criminality and drug-dealing are at the heart of *Flick* (Fintan Connolly, Ireland, 1999). Most, although not all, of these films are set in Dublin, a city that had by now gained a modest televisual sense of self, largely through the ongoing RTÉ soap opera, *Fair City*.

Many of these films emulate the post-Tarantino Hollywood gangster cycle, already noted in relation to *I Went Down* and the Northern Irish gangster films and are more interested in exploring aspects of masculinity, whilst toying with alternative cinematic methods of portraying the Irish cityscape and landscape, than with addressing those issues of social exclusion listed by Williams (above). *The General,* on the other hand, fuses echoes of Hollywood (the jewel heist, the camaraderie of the all-male group) with the focus on class and conscience of the British tradition. Such a melange befits a director whose filmmaking career has straddled Britain and Hollywood and whose best-known works, *Point Blank* (USA, 1967), *Deliverance* (USA, 1972) are dedicated to the exploration of singular, obsessive masculinity. Boorman has lived in Ireland since the 1970s and has written of his central character, Martin Cahill's (Brendan Gleeson) characteristic gesture of denying even his identity, that this was:

> honed in surviving the oppression of two colonising powers, the English and the Church. A role is assumed, a cover story concocted and the play-acting conceals a contempt for authority, a rage perceived at injustice, a ferocious cunning, a sense of perpetual celebration, a dark brutality – in fact, the pagan characteristics of a Celtic chieftain.
>
> (*Production Notes*, undated: 20)

The director further describes his fascination with Cahill and proposes that his and the public's mutual obsession with the criminal probably, 'drew on something archetypal from the deep past, a relish and envy for the freedom of one who dares to defy the might of society' (ibid.: 20–1).

Shooting the film in saturated colour and then transferring it to black and white (both versions have been screened, although the black and white one should be regarded as the 'official' print), enhanced Boorman's relocation of Cahill from contemporary Dublin to a mythic Celtic past. The result is a work that seems to pull in two ways at once, one dictated by the fuzzy Celticism of its director, and the other by the source material, Paul

Williams' eponymous biography of Cahill (1995, revised 1998), which articulates a strong critique of the society that produced Cahill whilst reminding the reader of its subject's brutality. The film is more antagonistic than the book to the Catholic Church, cited here as abusive and morally bereft, and lampoons the gardaí, whose country accents mark them out, as they do in a number of Irish films, as figures of fun. Gleeson plays Cahill with some sympathy and without the sense of danger that Brosnan or Byrne might have brought to the part. On the other hand, his performance and accent root the gangster within a very specific social milieu, the Dublin of corporation flats, pool halls and narrow, warren-like alleyways into which, like a rat, he may escape.

A comparison with the 'disguised' version of the Cahill story, Thaddeus O'Sullivan's *Ordinary Decent Criminal*, in which the Cahill character, here named Michael Lynch, was played by Kevin Spacey, his wife by Linda Fiorentino and two of his henchmen by Scottish actors Peter Mullan and David Hayman, illustrates the difficulties that arise when actors who are not conversant with the background to the plot are used in central roles. Spacey's accent has reduced local audiences to unsolicited laughter and further destabilises a film that seems to have some difficulty in deciding whether it is a 'serious' thriller or postmodern parody.

The benefits of using a local cast were demonstrated in an earlier attempt to bring another disadvantaged group into the larger Irish cinematic narrative, the 1996 film, *Trojan Eddie* (Gillies MacKinnon, GB/Ireland). The so-called Travellers have formed the most marginalised grouping in Irish society since before Independence. Descendants of Famine dispossessed, they have pursued an itinerant existence around Ireland for many generations, stopping at official 'halting sites', on roadsides and, nowadays, in those spaces that are still open to them. Largely ostracised by the 'settled' community, their exclusion from Irish cinema is a reflection of their wider positioning within the State. In the few films that they appear, whether as disruptive presences – *The Field* – or romantic, pre-modern nomads – *Into the West* – the films' narratives have confirmed their marginality. Even Joe Comerford's opaque fiction, *Traveller* (GB, 1982), whilst featuring members of the travelling community, imposed on them a narrative that did not originate from within their native culture. Two documentaries made in the 1990s – *Southpaw* (Liam McGrath, Ireland/GB, 1999) and *Traveller* (Alan MacWeeney/John T. Davis, RTÉ, 2000) made some gesture towards addressing, and in the case of the former, celebrating the lives of today's Travellers. *Southpaw* told the story of the boxer, Francie Barrett, who represented Ireland in the 1996 Atlanta Olympic Games and of his life after his victory, with sporting achievement offering Barrett status within the discourse of the national. In *Traveller* MacWeeney set out to discover what had happened to the Travellers he had photographed on the Cherry Orchard Halting Site in 1965. In the latter film, the resistance of Travellers to representation from outside is symbolised by a photograph of a young woman pulling a torn plastic bag across her face; it is she whom MacWeeney most hopes, but fails, to find. *Trojan Eddie* brought together several generations of Irish actors: Richard Harris as the Traveller king, John Power; Stephen Rea as his 'townie' (non-Traveller) huckster; Brendan Gleeson as Power's son, Ginger; Séan McGinley as the feckless Raymie who runs off with Power's wedding money, and Stuart Townsend as Dermot who runs off with Power's bride, Kathleen (Alison McGuckian). Based on a script by playwright, Billy Roche, the film mediates the viewer's access to the travelling community through the eponymous Trojan Eddie, who, like most of the film's viewers, is also excluded from the wider group. Herein lies the film's reversal of convention – in this narrative, it is the non-Traveller who is the outsider. Traveller life is represented as rich in tradition yet MacKinnon refuses to romanticise it. The King's 'Tinker's Wedding' is equal parts ancient and kitschy, his wooing of the much younger Kathleen mocked by the singer (Dolores Keane) when she serenades the couple with a ballad entitled *Love Makes a Fool of You*. His young wife may long for a settled life ('people think that Travellers don't like beautiful things, but we do. And they think we don't feel the cold as well, but that's not true either') but she does not speak for the whole community. The camp is seen to divide along lines of kinship, the McDonaghs rallying around their son when Power tries to separate him from Kathleen, and come together in its public rituals of bare-knuckle fighting. The camera picks out and then loses individual faces, hinting at their transitory lifestyle, allowing them to wander in and out of frame, yet never presuming to view them from the 'inside'. Details of locale are left unclear, the film suggesting that relationships between people take pre-eminence over relationships with place.

Issues of exclusion unite the films discussed so far in this chapter. Indeed, this is a theme that has been mobilised by a range of narratives in the 1990s, noticeably in those youth films that have chosen to scrutinise the underside of the Celtic Tiger. A slew of such works, *Crush Proof, Accelerator, Disco Pigs, On the Edge* have explored issues of youth and disaffection in the context of a society that is unable to deal with social disadvantage or accommodate non-conformity. *On the Edge* is made by one of the most distinctive directors to have emerged out of the recent Irish production boom. John Carney, with his filmmaking partner, Tom Hall, has been responsible for the elegiac *November Afternoon* (John Carney/Tom Hall, Ireland, 1996) a film that is as indebted to John Cassavetes as to Woody Allen. Shot on video and in black-and-white, it was one of the earliest films to view Dublin as a modern capital – even if in this instance the light veneer was to reveal hidden traumas; this was followed by another chamber-piece, *Just in Time* (Ireland, 1996), and the disturbing rape/therapy drama, *Park* (John Carney/Tom Hall, Ireland, 1999). Carney is also responsible for the RTÉ series, *Bachelor's Walk*, and *On The Edge*. Both it and Kirsten Sheridan's *Disco Pigs* focus on late teenagers, both include central performances by Cork actor, Cillian Murphy, and both express a sense of extreme unease over what it means to grow up in modern Ireland. Sheridan (daughter of Jim), like Carney has a distinctive cinematic vision and her debut feature demonstrates an ambition

Figure 11.2 On the Edge. Stephen Rea (Dr Figure). Courtesy of the Irish Film Archive of the Film Institute of Ireland and United International Pictures.

to move beyond the conventional visual signifiers of Irishness and, also like Carney, to locate her characters within an international youth culture marked by its sense of anomie.

On the Edge begins with the death of Jonathan Breech's (Murphy) father, proceeds to the boy's attempted suicide and explores his experience of psychiatric hospital. Jonathan's alienation is not a consequence of social deprivation – most of the young inmates of the hospital appear to come from financially comfortable backgrounds – but of an inability to connect with the hedonistic lifestyle of Celtic Tiger Irish culture. Rachel (Tricia Vessey), with whom he forms a tentative relationship in the hospital, mutilates herself for sexual gratification, and his friend Toby (Jonathan Jackson), blames himself for the death of his brother in a car he was driving. The hospital, under the benevolent, if somewhat ineffectual, leadership of psychiatrist Dr Figure (Stephen Rea) becomes a surrogate home, an asylum in every sense from the madness without. By refusing to make strange the behaviour of the hospital's inmates, the film opens up the question as to which side of the wall 'normality' is to be found on. The teenagers in the hospital are considerably more sympathetic and sensitive than their contemporaries 'outside'. On each occasion when they come into contact with other social groups, in the pub and in the bowling alley, the encounters turn into conflicts. On the other hand, the party they organise for themselves and the day patients in Rachel's family home when her father is away is virtually indistinguishable from any other such suburban social event.

In both films, adults are of little help. In *On The Edge* they appear only on the margins of the story, specifically in Rachel's father's case as helpless and ill-attuned to the needs of his daughter. Even surrogate father, Dr Figure, turns out to be unable to prevent the film's final tragedy, and any hope that resides in a kind of salvation for Jonathan and Rachel comes from Jonathan's assumption of responsibility for her.

In *Disco Pigs* it is made somewhat more explicit that the children, especially Runt (Elaine Cassidy), come from dysfunctional families. Born on the same day, Runt and Pig (Cillian Murphy) speak their own language, are prone to extremes of violence and believe that they will become king and queen within their own fairytales. They define themselves as outside the symbolic order through their refusal to speak conventional English, instead communicating in a language that has not evolved beyond a form of baby talk. Theirs is a separate linguistic space that marks their refusal to grow up and participate in the repressive rituals of the symbolic order. Like children they believe in a fairytale world, yet when Pig develops sexual yearnings and Runt discovers the pleasures of shared female companionship, their own world comes under threat from their unwished-for development.

To find yourself on the margins of society is, particularly in *On the Edge*, a marker of individuality; yet these individuals themselves yearn for a sense of connectedness that has, it seems, vanished from Celtic Tiger Ireland. Jonathan's healing begins at the moment when the outpatients are watching *Singin' in the Rain* (Stanley Donen/Gene Kelly, USA, 1952) and unselfconsciously join hands with him and each other. In these people, most of them older than him, he retrieves a feeling of community that his family has not been able to offer him, and that he has not found in his previous 'on the edge' lifestyle of clubbing and drug-taking. The difference between the two films is that Carney's assumes that its central characters are 'normal' and it is the rest of the world that is strange, whilst there is no mistaking the dysfunctionality of Sheridan's teenage protagonists. The equally disadvantaged Marky (Darren Healy) is as much their victim as that of the social order, a point spelt out in the scene where the schoolteacher mocks his reading difficulties. The film discourages audience identification with either Pig or Runt, leaving them equally alienated from the other individuals in the filmic text and the audience.

Questions of exclusion and belonging also inform the growing body of films, including *2by4*, that focus on the young Irish diasporic community, located invariably in New York. Throughout the 1990s, these have tended to be low-budget works – *Gold In the Streets* (Elizabeth Gill, USA/Ireland, 1997), *Beyond the Pale* (George Bazala, USA/Ireland, 1999), *Exiled* (Bill Muir, USA/Ireland, 1999) – that have highlighted the difficulties the 'naive' Irish face on arrival in a culture indifferent to their problems. In 2003, Jim Sheridan released his (by Irish standards) big budget version of that encounter, *In America* (Ireland/USA, 2003).

Set in 1982, the year of the release of *E.T.*, Sheridan's film is an indulgent reworking of his own family's history, here the death of a child (echoing the loss of Sheridan's own brother, Frankie, in childhood) and the consequent (fictional) decision to emigrate America, something that Sheridan and his wife themselves did in 1981. *In America* could be argued to bring full circle a number of the themes arising out of the exile narratives discussed during the course of this book. Sheridan himself has said that the film is about 'getting away from the death culture' that is so prevalent in Ireland and expressed so repetitively in Irish literature (Public Interview, Irish Film Centre, 7 March 2003). Ireland is associated with a trauma in the past that can be worked through by contact with the modernity of American society. If this was the experience of the early cinematic immigrants of the 1920s, it is then reversed in *The Quiet Man*, and revived here. Thematically, the film is held together through its referencing of *E.T.*, the film that nearly causes the family to lose all their money when Johnny (Paddy Considine), gambles it on winning an *E.T.* doll for Ariel (Emma Bolger), his youngest daughter. If *The Quiet Man* was E.T.'s introduction to American life, now the Extra-Terrestrial opens up American culture for the newly arrived Irish family. The final image from Spielberg's film is also the point of cathartic release when Ariel can 'let go' her dead brother and leave the death culture behind. Cinema has now replaced Catholicism as a validating belief system.

What remains of the structures of Catholicism become intertwined with a kind of generalised spirituality. Like the earlier immigrant films, integration into American culture is symbolised through acceptance of inter-ethnic rela-

Figure 11.3 In America, courtesy of Fox Searchlight Pictures. Samantha Morton (Sarah Sullivan).

tionships, here expressed through the children's encounter with the black artist, Mateo (Djimon Hounsou). Culturally, the film suggests, strong links unite the Irish family and Mateo; symbolically, he must die to 'save' them. After his death (from AIDS), it turns out that he has willed them the money that will pay the hospital costs for the birth of their baby.

Ultimately, *In America* is a celebration of the Irish-American encounter and the strength of the family unit. Where so many Irish films of the 1970s onwards ended with the disintegration of the family, Sheridan argues for its durability, a prognosis aided rather than defeated by modernity. *In America* is also a personal reflection on the opportunities America offered its director; it is a home movie (Christy [Sarah Bolger], the elder sister views her family through a camcorder) that foreign finance, in this case American, has allowed him to make and exhibit to a worldwide audience, an analogy, if you like, for the evolution of Irish national cinema.

It is salient to conclude with an example taken not from cinema but advertising. In a recent advertisement, two young people make contact across a crowded pub. She slips a phone number into his pocket before leaving the premises. Just as she exits, he makes the call on his mobile. Her face lights up only to register instant disappointment when, for the first time, she hears his voice – he speaks in an unadulterated rural accent. The message is that, beset by such a social drawback, a man ought to use his text-messaging facility. This book has described Ireland and its cinema in evolution. It has traced a passage from an ideology of the rural as the 'real' Ireland, homeland of immigrant dreams and symbol of a nationalist invest-ment in cultural purity to a new, post-Troubles, post-Catholic, urban space where the rural lingers on in the unrefined tones of occasional policemen and other bearers of comic relief. It is a story of a slowly evolving artform, that now seems to be splitting into multiple modes of address. As it changes, so it does not quite leave the 'old' Ireland behind but concedes that its place is increasingly problematic. A liberation for some, a betrayal for others, Irish cinema is fragmented, contradictory and increasingly eclectic. By sifting through not only its canonical works but also its lesser-known moments, we can locate in it an ever-increasing ambition to address issues of the national, the individual and the global, to antagonise us and to entertain us, a measure indeed of the contemporary nation.

APPENDIX

Viewing figures, where available, for films with part or complete Irish financing, Republic of Ireland and Northern Ireland (theatrical); RTÉ viewing figures (1993–2000)

Title (date of theatrical release)	Theatrical take; viewing figures*	RTÉ viewing figures	Share (%)
About Adam (2000)	£IR538,270 = 168,209		
Accelerator (1999)	£IR328,759 = 102,737		
Agnes Browne (1999)	£IR551,603 = 172, 316	435,000	36
Ailsa (1995)	£IR1,300 = 429	86,000	19
All Souls Day (1997)	£IR3,328 = 1,040	81,000	9
All Things Bright and Beautiful (1993)	n/a	246,000	36
The American (1998)	n/a	50,000	15
Angela's Ashes (2000)	£IR2,205,593 = 689,248		
Beyond The Pale (1999)	n/a	24,000	17
Bogwoman (1997)		46,000	22
The Book That Wrote Itself (1999)	n/a	24,000	8
Borstal Boy (2000)	£IR89,017 = 27,818		
The Boxer (1998)	£IR800,000 = 261,438	438,000	39
The Boy From Mercury (1996)	£IR6,457 = 2,348	468,000	45
Broken Harvest (1994)	£IR80,000 = 27,304	1. 230,000	37
		2. 172,000	36
The Butcher Boy (1998)	£IR1.1m = 359,477	605,000	49
Circle of Friends (1995)	+/- £IR1.4m = 462,046	634,000	49
The Closer You Get (1999)	£IR157,533 = 49,229		
Country (2000)	£IR15,547 = 4,858		
Crush Proof (1998)		230,000	17
Dancing at Lughnasa (1998)	£IR653,714 = 213,632	558,000	47
The Disappearance of Finbar (1997)	£IR17,296 = 5,405		
Drinking Crude (1997)	n/a	170,000	38
Exiled (1999)	n/a	44,000	12
Flick (2000)	£IR12,675 = 3,961		

Title (date of theatrical release)	Theatrical take; viewing figures[*]	RTÉ viewing figures	Share (%)
Frankie Starlight (1995)		402,000	31
A Further Gesture (1997)	£IR3,048 = 953	251,000	31
The General (1998)	£IR1,372, 396 = 448,495	646,000	52
Gold in the Streets (1997)	£IR10,387 = 3,246	449,000	38
High Boot Benny (1993)		314,000	46
I Went Down (1997)	£IR600,000 = 187,500	427,000	40
In the Name of the Father (1994)	£IR2.4m = 819,113	572,000	48
Korea (1995)	£IR40,000 = 13,201		
The Last Bus Home (1997)		48,000	9
Last of the High Kings (1996)	£IR240,000 = 87,273		
The Last September (2000)	£IR26,253 = 8,204		
A Love Divided (2000)	£IR614,930 = 192,166	657,000	57
The Magdalene Sisters (2002)			
A Man of No Importance (1994)	£IR60,000 = 20,478	378,000	33
The Matchmaker (1997)	n/a	214,000	34
Michael Collins (1996)	£IR4m = 1,454,546	837,000	49
The Nephew (1998)	£IR287,102 = 93,824		
Night Train (1998)			
Nora (2000)	£IR96,870 = 30,271		
Nothing Personal (1995)	£IR70,000 = 23,102	571,000	43
November Afternoon (1996)		65,000	17
On the Edge (2001)			
Ordinary Decent Criminal (2000)	£IR225,704 = 70,533	543,000	43
Park (1999)	n/a	49,000	25
The Run of the Country (1995)	£IR170,000 = 56,106	1. 505,000	48
		2. 408,000	35
Saltwater (2000)		495,000	39
Separation Anxiety (1997)	n/a	51,000	19
Snakes and Ladders (1998)	£IR9, 054 = 2,959	108,000	19
Some Mother's Son (1996)	£IR750,000 = 272,727	375,000	44
The Sun, The Moon and the Stars (1996)	£IR2,899 = 1,054	474,000	36
Sweety Barrett (1999)	£IR57,195 = 17,873	260,000	20
This is My Father (1999)	£IR508,184 = 158,806	675,000	47
Trojan Eddie (1996)	£30,000 = 10,909	370,000	34
When Brendan Met Trudy (2000)	£IR744,478 = 232,649		
When the Sky Falls (2000)	£IR204,776 = 63,993		
Words Upon the Window Pane (1995)	£IR2,100 = 693	137,000	25

Sources: *INPRODUCTION, Screen International*, RTÉ.
*Admissions are calculated as per average ticket price listed in *European Audiovisual Observatory Statistical Yearbook*, 1999: 94; 2000: 109. These are: 1993: £2.57, 1994: £2.93, 1995: £3.03, 1996: £2.75, 1997: £3.20, 1998: £3.06; I have estimated: 1999: £3.20 and 2000: £3.20; figures are converted from ECUs.

NOTES

1 IRISH CINEMA – NATIONAL CINEMA?

1 In her report on cinema statistics in the Irish Free State of 1936, T.J. Beere claims a figure of only six visits per annum for every man, woman and child in the State compared with an average of 22 visits per head per annum in Britain (Beere, 1936: 96). She also argues that reports of long cinema queues do not reflect the prosperity of the cinemas, and they were 'as a rule only in respect of the cheaper-priced seats. There may often be a queue outside and many empty seats inside'. (ibid.: 97)

2 The size of the queues, therefore, we can assume to reflect the high proportion of lower-income customers. More recent statistics, however, place Irish cinema-goers at the upper end of the European average list. In the period 1995–2001, they topped that list; internationally (excluding Asia), the Israelis had the highest attendance followed by the Americans and Canadians (*European Audiovisual Observatory Yearbook* [2002] 3: 38).

3 Resources have regrettably not permitted me to consider Irish-Australian cinematic representations in this publication.

4 See John Hill, *Cinema and Northern Ireland*, London: BFI Publishing, forthcoming.

5 See my introduction to Barton, R. and O'Brien, H. (eds) *Keeping it Real*, Wallflower Press, forthcoming.

2 A SILENT REVOLUTION

1 Now O'Connell Street.

2 It is unclear exactly which period Bailey is describing but it appears to have been pre-1910.

3 The term 'newsreel' is applied retrospectively to these films and was not in use at the time. 'Actualities' refers to short items, footage of events that were usually of local interest without being newsworthy; 'topicals' had news value.

4 In the case of the Easter Rising, the British newsreels were only reflecting a shared antipathy towards the brief military action: 'Initial popular response to the Rising was general fury and disgust at the human and material wastage. Rebels were roughed up on active service by enraged women and pelted with tomatoes after surrendering.' (Fitzpatrick, 1989: 198–9) If the Easter Rising of 1916 had little national support, the executions of its leaders led to a wave of revulsion in Ireland and in the United States that was to translate into political support for Sinn Féin, the Republican party (despite their having little to no involvement with the Rising). This was heightened by continuing resistance to the notion of British conscription and by the entry of the US, with its commitment to Republicanism, into the World War in April 1917.

5 His name is variously spelt Macnamara and MacNamara.

6 Not only do the separate accounts of Olcott's career vary on this, they also disagree on numbers of films made and their years of production.

7 The historical figure, Rory O'Moore, was associated with the 1641 Rising but the film seems to be set during the 1798–1803 period of the United Irishmen and Robert Emmet (Rockett, 1996: 252).

8 For synopses of these films, see Rockett, 1996: 6–7.

9 In fact, Ulster Protestant opposition to Home Rule within the core six counties was virulent and united. In 1913, the Ulster Volunteer Force was set up and in 1914 it was illegally armed. Sectarianism was rife particularly within urban areas and amongst the thriving industrial workforce. The mass slaughter of Ulster regiments during the Battle of the Somme in 1916 was to cement the commitment of the Protestant community to the cause of Empire just as it was to act as a reminder for many years to come of Britain's debt to the Province.

3 CONTESTED IMAGES

1 The Eucharistic Congress was an event of enormous significance. It enabled the State to invite the wider world in to Ireland to witness its stability and legitimacy as well as providing the public with an opportunity for mass street celebrations; it brought forward the establishment of a high power transmitter in Athlone so that the new national radio station, 2RN (to Erin) could be widely received. As well as being a remarkably colourful and international event, it also allowed de Valera 'to baptize his synthesis of republicanism and Catholicism, reminding the papal legate, in his feline way, that he was a loyal son of Rome' (Lee, 1989: 177).

2 Censorship was avoided by bodies like the University College Dublin Dramatic Society, the Dublin Little Theatre Guild and the Irish Film Society who screened art films such as *The Cabinet of Dr. Caligari* (Robert Wiene, Germany, 1919) free of charge and on a membership-only basis.

3 This forms part of a lengthy and poignant exchange of letters in the *Mail* on the subject of the 'modern girl'. Seen by some to be an example of the defacing of nature by modernity, others viewed her as awesomely desirable. The modern girls themselves complained bitterly about the inability of the Irish male to act in a romantic manner and to commit himself to marriage. This letter provoked a deluge of shocked responses as well as some notes expressing agreement. For an analysis of women's memories of cinema-going in the 1940s and 1950s, see Byrne, H. (1997) 'Going to the Pictures: The Female Audience and the Pleasures of Cinema', in Kelly, M.J. and O'Connor, B. (eds), *Media Audiences in Ireland*, Dublin: University College Dublin Press; for other reminiscences of cinema-going, see McBride, S. and Flynn, R. (eds) (1996) *Here's Looking at You, Kid! Ireland goes to the Movies*, Dublin: Wolfhound.

4 Press accounts refer to this film as 'Gallipoli'. It is almost certainly, however, *Tell England* which was also known as *The Battle of Gallipoli*.

5 Virtually any general overview book on Irish literature, cinema or the visual arts will deal in some way or another with the relationship between Irish cultural nationalism and artistic production in this period. Brown (1985), Gibbons (1996), Kiberd (1996) and Lloyd (1993) are all recommended for their own distinctive interpretations of this movement; for its relevance to Irish cinema, see McLoone (2000).

6 US title: *Dawn Over Ireland*.

7 For the real names of these actors who appeared under pseudonym, see Rockett, 1996: 11).

8 This emphasis on the War of Independence as a local event is in fact more faithful to its history than later fictions that claim it was a national struggle. Much of the country saw little action though Kerry was at the heart of the armed resistance.

9 Elizabeth Butler Cullingford very interestingly traces the motif of the captive British soldier through a number of Irish narratives, including Brendan Behan's *An Giall* (The Hostage) (1958) and Neil Jordan's *The Crying Game* (GB, 1992). See Cullingford (2001).

10 Also known as *West of Kerry, Eileen Aroon* and in the United States as *Men of Ireland*. For details of the various versions of the film see Rockett, 1996: 16–17.

11 For a listing of Irish actors in Hollywood, see my entry in the forthcoming, *Journeys of Desire: European Actors in Hollywood* (eds) Phillips, A. and Vincendeau, G. London: BFI Publishing (forthcoming).

12 aka *Bucket of Blood*.

13 US title: *Norah O'Neale*. The only extant copy of this film seems to be a condensed version (lodged in the Irish Film Archive). It runs at around 30 minutes and simply depicts the love triangle of Fitzgerald, Norah O'Neale and Nurse Otway. It contains one of my favourite lines of Irish cinema dialogue: 'You know what, you're a very satisfactory woman to look at.'

14 US title: *River of Unrest*.

15 Burke was born in England of Irish origin.

16 Families departing for America were given a communal send-off similar to the ritual of mourning with music, song and drinking that was known as an American wake.

17 In the 1930s Irish sound recordings were mostly made in Britain by EMI and Decca, published in London and then sold back to the then Free State. It was not until 1935 that Sean Lemass introduced a sound recordings tax and local operations slowly began.

18 He changed his name to Lucan in honour of the then small village (now a suburb) outside Dublin where he first courted the much younger Kitty McShane.

19 *Abie's Irish Rose* was released twice in 1928, first as a silent film, then in sound with some edits. It was remade in 1947.

20 This is already an unlikely scenario given that the landlord system was pretty much abolished by the 1920s. Rather than referencing reality, it draws on certain stock melodramatic situations inherited from popular theatre and other entertainment forms of the nineteenth century.

21 This does not reflect a general social reality; Kerby Miller suggests that girls enjoyed greater social freedom in America but that domestic service was 'a nearly universal part of the life cycle for young married girls', and 'Irish-American women's work was often hard and poorly paid' (Miller, 1985: 318, 407).

22 For a detailed look at some of these films as well as earlier productions, see Curran (1989) and Rockett, K. (1987) 'The Irish migrant and film' in P. O'Sullivan (ed.) *The Creative Migrant*, London and Washington: Leicester University.

4 NEGOTIATING MODERNISATION

1 I am indebted to Neville Keery for sharing with me his recollections of the Film Society and only regret that space constrictions prohibit me from doing justice to their work.

2 See O'Flynn, S. 'Black and White and Collar Films' in Barton, R. and O'Brien, H. *Keeping it Real*, Wallflower Press, forthcoming.

3 My thanks to Mel Doherty for showing me his copy of the film and explaining the background to its production.

4 During the inter-party government of 1948–51, the politically inexperienced but idealistic Dr Noel Browne was appointed Minister for Health. In 1952 he announced the implementation of free natal and postnatal care for mothers and free medical care for all children under 16. This was not to be means-tested. The so-called 'Mother and Child scheme' fell foul of the medical profession who suspected that they would lose income, and the Church hierarchy who feared that non-Catholic doctors might instruct Irish women on gynaecological issues. Both parties vehemently objected to the absence of a means-test and in the ensuing debacle, Browne was forced to resign.

5 Sherry was a member of the Irish Film Society.

6 In real life Agar and Temple were married.

7 For a discussion of this practice see my entry in *Journeys of Desire, European Actors in Hollywood* (forthcoming).

8 aka *Three Leaves of a Shamrock.*

9 The films produced by Emmet Dalton in what became 'Emmet Dalton Productions' were *Sally's Irish Rogue* (George Pollock, Ireland, 1958); *The Big Birthday* (1959); *Home is the Hero* (1959); *This Other Eden* (1959); *Boyd's Shop* (Henry Cass, Ireland, 1960); *Lies My Father Told Me* (Don Chaffey, Ireland, 1960); *The Webster Boy* (Don Chaffey, Ireland, 1961); *The Devil's Agent* (John Paddy Carstairs, Ireland, 1962).

10 *The Rising of the Moon* was partly shot in Limerick. According to one local description, Ford and Killanin met their match when the women whom they were using as extras rebelled against their low wages, hard buns and the provision of tea rather than porter. Only the intervention of a curate from a nearby parish who threatened the rebels with excommunication saved the day (Malone, J. undated: 30).

11 Kennedy, of Irish-American background, was the film's big-name actor.

12 For a detailed analysis of *This Other Eden*, see Farley (2001).

5 IRISH INDEPENDENTS

1 The appropriation of the conventions of early cinema by the avant-garde is discussed by Rod Stoneman in his article, (1981) 'Perspective Correction', *Afterimage* 8/9: 50–63.

2 For a discussion of the contemporary reception of the poem, see L.M. Cullen, 1993, '*Caoineadh Airt Uí Laoghaire*, The Contemporary Political Context', *History Ireland* 1, 3: 23–7.

3 This could be seen as a borrowing from earlier British films about Ireland or a separate formulation in response to the idealisation of the peasantry by official nationalist history.

6 THE SECOND FILM BOARD YEARS

1 US title: *Waking Ned Devine.*

2 For an analysis of the spread of cinemas and the potential for greater 'arthouse' penetration, see Connolly, N. and Dillon M. (2001) *Developing Cultural Cinema in Ireland*, Dublin: The Arts Council/The Irish Film Board/Enterprise Ireland/The Northern Ireland Film Commission.

7 THE DEFLOWERING OF IRISH CINEMA

1 Graham does not address issues of masculinity.

2 Murphy refers to her primary sources as 'diaries'; technically, this is incorrect. A Carmelite Brother, Luke Cullen, transcribed Anne Devlin's account of her

involvement in Emmet's abortive rising and her time in prison after he befriended her. He also supported her to the best of his means when she was destitute (after the death of her husband). The manuscript was transcribed with some additional material and published by John Finegan under the title *Anne Devlin, Patriot and Heroine* (1992 [2nd edition], Dublin: Elo Publications). It was the first edition (published 1968) that Pat Murphy used.

3 At the turn of the century in Italy, an 11-year-old child, Maria Goretti, was murdered by a young man who had tried to rape her. As she resisted, he stabbed her repeatedly with a stiletto. In 1947 she was beatified by Pope Pius XII and in 1950 she was canonised.

4 See also Elizabeth Butler Cullingford, 'The Prisoner's Wife and the Soldier's Whore: Female Punishment in Irish History and Culture' in Barton, R. and O'Brien, H. (eds) *Keeping it Real*, Wallflower Press, forthcoming.

5 Following the Gibraltar shootings of March 1988 when a group of IRA suspects was shot dead in what was to be highly contentious circumstances, the film's makers were asked to withdraw their interview with Mairead Farrell, one of the victims of the shooting. They were also requested to make a number of other changes including cutting out the footage of a woman who had been shot in the face by a rubber bullet, which they reluctantly acceded to. By the time the programme was ready for airing, new legislation, forbidding the broadcasting of interviews with terrorists, suspected or otherwise, and their supporters, made the showing of the documentary completely impossible (it was aired much later in Channel 4's 'Banned' season).

6 Actually, gay relationships were naturalised in films about Ireland as early as 1977 with the inclusion in *The Purple Taxi* (*Le Taxi Mauve*) (Yves Boisset, France/Ireland/Italy, 1977) of two comfortably camp basket weavers in the West of Ireland pub frequented by Boisset's sexually voracious cast of characters.

8 ANOTHER COUNTRY

1 This may be read as a reference to the fate of Elizabeth Bowen's own home, Bowen's Court, which was bought by a local timber merchant for its trees and the house left to fall into ruin. In fact, the home in *The Dawning* is more a large country house than a palatial family pile; however, its characters are otherwise presented as typical of the Anglo-Irish gentry.

10 NORTHERN IRELAND

1 These allegations were first raised in 1982 against the RUC. John Stalker, Deputy Chief Constable of Manchester, was appointed to investigate the claims but subsequently suspended on grounds which were later declared void (the so-called Stalker Affair). Colin Sampson of the West Yorkshire Police replaced him and disciplinary action was taken against a number of RUC officers. The character of Harris in *Hidden Agenda*, according to the scriptwriter Jim Allen (in Murphy and Gogan, 1990: 16), was based on Colin Wallace, a Northern Irish civilian, who, as army press officer, was responsible for disseminating 'disinformation' to the press and may have been wrongly accused of the murder of antiques dealer Jonathan Lewis in 1981 as part of a campaign to discredit him. However, the fictional character equally suggests Captain Robert Nairac who was kidnapped and killed by the IRA in 1977 whilst working undercover for the SAS. In the same interview, Allen explains that they had initially sought the co-operation of Stalker but were put off by his lawyers; they made former British intelligence officer, Fred Holroyd, technical adviser and also showed the script to Colin Wallace.

2 John Hill has suggested that the early death of the civil rights activist and the obvious typecasting of Kerrigan are deliberate strategies to undermine generic expectations (1997: 135); however, this begs the question as to whether audiences will read the film this way or as a failed thriller.

3 Stephen Baker has convincingly argued for a reading of *Resurrection Man* as a vampire film, situating it within a loyalist self-image of vampirism in Barton, R. and O'Brien, H. (eds) *Keeping it Real* (Wallflower Press, forthcoming).

4 In fact, *Nothing Personal* was filmed in Dublin and *Resurrection Man* in England.

5 The screenplay is loosely based on James Carney's book, *The Playboy and the Yellow Lady*, about the events that also inspired Synge for his creation of Christy Mahon in *The Playboy of the Western World*.

6 The IRA declared a ceasefire on 31 August 1994. On 13 October of that year, the Combined Loyalist Military Command also went on ceasefire. In February 1996 the IRA brought its ceasefire to an end with the planting of the Canary Wharf bomb but restored it in summer of 1997. The Belfast Agreement (Good Friday Agreement) was signed in April 1998.

7 See, McLoone, M. 'Topographies of Terror and Taste: The Re-imagining of Belfast in Recent Cinema' in Barton, R. and O'Brien, H., *Keeping it Real*, Wallflower Press, forthcoming.

11 INCLUSION, EXCLUSION, CONCLUSION

1 See Lysaght, R. 'Pobal Sobail: Ros na Rún, TG4 and Reality' in Barton, R. and O'Brien, H. (eds), *Keeping it Real*, Wallflower Press, forthcoming.

2 See Bell, D. 'Telling Tales: Narrative, Evidence, and Memory in Contemporary Documentary Film Practice' in ibid.

BIBLIOGRAPHY

Adams, B. (2002) *Denis Johnston, A Life*, Dublin: The Lilliput Press.

Adams, M. (1968) *Censorship: The Irish Experience*, Alabama: University of Alabama Press.

Alba, R.D. (1990) *Ethnic Identity, The Transformation of White America*, New Haven and London: Yale University Press.

Allen, K. (2000) *The Celtic Tiger*, Manchester and New York: Manchester University Press.

Althusser, A. (1971) *Lenin and Philosophy and Other Essays*, London: New Left Books.

Anderson, B. (1983) *Imagined Communities: Reflections on the Origins and Spread of Nationalism*, London: Verso.

Backus, M.G. (1999) *The Gothic Family Romance*, Durham and London: Duke University Press.

Bailey, P. (1986) 'Introduction', in P. Bailey (ed.) *Music Hall: The Business of Pleasure*, Milton Keynes: Open University Press.

Bailey H. and O'Shea, T. (1996) 'A Limerick Apprenticeship', in J. Kenny (ed.) *The Limerick Anthology*, 278–81.

Barsam, R. (1988) *The Vision of Robert Flaherty*, Bloomington and Indianapolis: Indiana University Press.

Barton, R. (1997) 'From History to Heritage: some recent developments in Irish Cinema', *The Irish Review* 21: 41–56.

—— (1999) 'Going There Saw the Movie . . .', *Film Ireland* 72: 42.

—— (2000a) 'The Ballykissangelization of Ireland', *Historical Journal of Film, Radio and Television* 20, 3: 413–26.

—— (2000b) 'Portrait of a Lady', *Film Ireland* 75: 12–15.

Barton, R. (2002) *Jim Sheridan: Framing the Nation*, Dublin: Liffey Press.

Beere, T.J. (1936) 'Cinema Statistics in Saorstát Eireann', *Statistical and Social Inquiry Society of Ireland Journal* 89th session: 83–106.

Bell (1921) 'Knock-na-gow' (review) *Variety* 30 September: 35.

Bergfelder, T. (2000) 'The Nation Vanishes: European co-productions and popular genre formulae in the 1950s and 1960s', in M. Hjort and S. MacKenzies (eds) *Cinema and Nation*, London and New York: Routledge.

Bew, P. (1996) 'When Jordan shot Collins', *The Sunday Times* Section Three, 10 November: 6.

Bhabha, H.K. (1990) 'DissemiNation', in H. K. Bhabha (ed) *Nation and Narration*, London and New York: Routledge.

Black, G.D. (1994) *Hollywood Censored: Morality Codes, Catholics, and the Movies*, Cambridge: Cambridge University Press.

Blaisdell, G. (1914) 'Irish History on the Screen', *The Moving Picture World*, 20 August: 1,245.

Brady, C. (ed.) (1994) *Interpreting Irish History, The Debate on Historical Revisionism*, Dublin: Irish Academic Press.

Breathnach, R. (1959) 'The Future of Irish Films', *Scannán*, 4,1: 4.

Brett, D. (1996) *The Construction of Heritage*, Cork: Cork University Press.

Brennan, T. (1990) 'The national longing for form', in H. K. Bhabha (ed.) *Nation and Narration*, London and New York: Routledge.

Brooks, R. (1997) 'IRA Films Beset by Troubles Amid Sniping in Hollywood', *The Observer* 13 April: 2, 3.

Brown, T. (1981; 2nd edn 1985) *Ireland A Social and Cultural History, 1922–1985*, London: Fontana Press.

Bunreacht na hÉireann (Constitution of Ireland) (1937), Dublin: Government Stationery Office.

Byron, R. (1999) *Irish America*, Oxford: Oxford University Press.

Cairns, D. and Richards, S. (1991) *Writing Ireland: Colonialism, Nationalism and Culture*, Manchester: Manchester University Press.

Censorship of Films Act 1923, Government Stationery Office.

Chibnall, S. and Murphy, R. (1999) 'Parole Overdue: Releasing the British crime film into the critical community', in S. Chibnall and R. Murphy (eds) *British Crime Cinema*, London and New York: Routledge.

Cleary, J. (2002) *Literature, Partition and the Nation State*, Cambridge and New York: Cambridge University Press.

Connaughton, S. (1989) *A Border Station*, London: Abacus.

Cowie, E. (ed.) (1978) 'Notes From a Discussion with the Film-maker' (uncredited interview with Thaddeus O' Sullivan), *Catalogue British Film Productions 1977–1978*, London: British Film Institute.

Cullingford, E.B. (2001) *Ireland's Others*, Cork: Cork University Press.

Curran, J.M. (1989) *Hibernian Green on the Silver Screen*, New York, Westport Connecticut, London: Greenwood Press.

Curtis Jr, L.P. (1971, revised edn 1997) *Apes and Angels*, Newton Abbot: David and Charles.

Curtis, L. (1984) *Ireland: The Propaganda War*, London and Sydney: Pluto Press.

Dean, J. (1994) 'The Far Side – American Letter', *Film West*, 18: 14–15.

Devane, R.S. (S.J.) (1942) 'Brollach', *Scannán* 6: 3–5.

Dooley, R.B. (1957) 'The Irish on the Screen: 1', *Films in Review* 3, 5: 211–17.

Douglas, S. (1994) 'Loyalism: Male, Macho and Marching?', *Irish Reporter* 14: 13.

Downing, T. (1979–80) 'The Film Company of Ireland', *Sight and Sound* 49, 1: 42–5.

Dwyer, M. (1981) 'Political Award?', *In Dublin* 126: 10–11.

—— (1997; first published 1982) '10 Days that Shook the Irish Film Industry', *Film West* 30: 24–8.

Dyer, R. (1997) *White*, London and New York: Routledge.

Eagleton, T. (2000) *The Idea of Culture*, Oxford: Blackwell.

Edge, S. (1995) 'Women Are Trouble, Did You Know That, Fergus?', *Feminist Review* 50: 173–86.

Editorial (1959) 'Change of Name', *Scannán* 4, 1: 3.

Elsaesser, T. (1993) 'Images for Sale: The 'New' British Cinema', in L. Friedman (ed.) *British Cinema and Thatcherism*, London: UCL Press.

—— (1996) 'Subject Positions, Speaking Positions', in V. Sobchack (ed.) *The Persistence of History*, New York and London: Routledge.

Falsetto, M. (1999) *Personal Visions: Conversations with independent film-makers*, London: Constable.

Fanon, F. (1967) *The Wretched of the Earth* (translated by Constance Farrington), Harmondsworth: Penguin.

Farber, M. (1971) *Negative Space*, New York: Prager.

Farley, F. (2000) *Anne Devlin*, Trowbridge: Flicks Books.

Farley, F. (2001) *This Other Eden*, Cork: Cork University Press.

Fehlman, G. (1991) 'An Historical Survey', in J. Genet (ed.) *The Big House in Ireland*, Dingle/ Maryland: Brandon/Barnes & Noble.

Fielder, M.K. (1985) 'Fatal Attraction: Irish-Jewish Romance in Early Film and Drama', *Eire-Ireland* 20, 3: 6-18.

Fitzpatrick, D. (1989; reissued 2001) 'Ireland since 1870', in R.F. Foster (ed.) *The Oxford History of Ireland*, Oxford: Oxford University Press.

Floyd, N. (1991) 'Interview with Thaddeus O'Sullivan', *Time Out*, 6 February: 27.

Flynn, R. (1995) 'Our Man in Nirvana', *Film Ireland* 47: 49–51.

Foster, C. (2000) *Stardust and Shadows, Canadians in Early Hollywood*, Toronto: Dundurn Press.

Foster, R. (2001) *The Irish Story*, London: Allen Lane, The Penguin Press.

Foucault, M (1980) *Power/Knowledge*, Gordon, C. (ed); trans: C. Gordon, L. Marshall, J. Mepham, K. Soper, New York, London, Toronto, Sydney, Tokyo, Singapore: Harvester Wheatsheaf.

French, B. (1978) *On the Verge of Revolt*, New York: Frederick Ungar.

Gabriel, T.H. (1989) 'Third Cinema as Guardian of Popular Memory: Towards a Third Aesthetics'; in J. Pines and P. Willemen (eds) *Questions of Third Cinema*, London: BFI Publishing.

Gallagher, T. (1986) *John Ford: The Man and His Films*, Berkeley: University of California Press.

Gibbons, L. (1987) 'Romanticism, Realism and Irish Cinema', in K. Rockett, L. Gibbons and J. Hill, *Cinema and Ireland*, London and Sydney: Croom Helm.

—— (1992) 'On the Beach', *Artforum*, 31, 2: 13.

—— (1996) *Transformations in Irish Culture*, Cork: Cork University Press.

—— (2002) *The Quiet Man*, Cork: Cork University Press.

Giles, P. (1991) 'The Cinema of Catholicism: John Ford and Robert Altman', in L. Friedman (ed.) *Unspeakable Images, Ethnicity and the American Cinema*, Urbana and Chicago: University of Illinois Press.

Glancy, H.M. (1998) 'Hollywood and Britain: MGM and the British "Quota" Legislation', in J. Richards (ed.), *The Unknown 1930s: An alternative history of the British cinema 1929–39*, London and New York: I.B. Tauris.

'Golly Gosh' (1935) 'Letter', *Dublin Evening Mail*, 26 February: 3.

Graham, C. (2001) *Deconstructing Ireland*, Edinburgh: Edinburgh University Press.

Graham, I. (1995) 'An Irishman in Hollywood', *Film Ireland* 45: 24–6.

Greene, G. (1993) 'Riders to the Sea', in D. Parkinson (ed.), *Mornings in the Dark, The Graham Greene Film Reader*, Manchester: Carcanet.

Greengrass, P. (2002) 'Making History', *The Guardian* (G2), www.guardian.co.uk (accessed 18 December 2002) 11 January.

Grene, N. (1999) *The Politics of Irish Drama*, Cambridge: Cambridge University Press.

Hannigan, M. (1989) 'Reefer and the Model' (review), *Circa* 43: 30–1.

Harper, S. (1994) *Picturing the Past*, London: BFI Publishing.

Harvey, M. (1997) 'Under-Age Storm as Diana Takes Harry to IRA Film', *Daily Mail*, 23 June: 1, 5.

Higson, A. (1993) 'Re-presenting the National Past: Nostalgia and pastiche in the Heritage Film', in L. Friedman (ed.) *British Cinema and Thatcherism*, London: UCL Press.

—— (1996) 'The Heritage Film and British Cinema', in A. Higson (ed.) *Dissolving Views*, London and New York: Cassell.

Hill, J. (1987) 'Images of Violence', in K. Rockett, L. Gibbons and J. Hill *Cinema and Ireland*, London and Sydney: Croom Helm.

—— (1999) *British Cinema in the 1980s*, Oxford: Clarendon Press.

—— (2000) 'The Banning of *Ourselves Alone*', *Historical Journal of Film, Radio and Television* 20, 3: 317–33.

Hobsbawm, E. (1995; first published 1994) *Age of Extremes*, London: Abacus.

hooks, b. (1994) *Outlaw Culture*, New York and London: Routledge.

Hurst, B.D. (undated), Untitled autobiography, lodged in the British Film Institute library.

Ignatiev, N. (1995) *How the Irish Became White*, London and New York: Routledge.

Inglis, T. (1998, revised edn; first edn 1987) *Moral Monopoly, The Rise and Fall of the Catholic Church in Modern Ireland*, Dublin: University College Dublin Press.

Innes, C.L. (1993) *Woman and Nation*, Athens, Georgia: University of Georgia Press.

Jameson, F. (1988) 'Postmodernism and Consumer Society' in E. Kaplan (ed.) *Postmodernism and its Discontents*, London and New York: Verso.

Johnston, C. (1981) 'Maeve', *Screen*, 22, 4: 54–71.

Jordan, N. (1996) *Michael Collins*, London: Vintage.

Keane, D. (1993) 'Sorry, Emma: You're crazy to do this film', *Mail On Sunday*, 7 November: 33.

Kearney, R. (1988a) *Across the Frontiers, Ireland in the 1990s*, Dublin: Wolfhound Press.

—— (1988b) *Transitions*, Dublin: Wolfhound Press.

—— (2002) *On Stories*, London and New York: Routledge.

Kehoe, E. (2002) 'Bloody Sunday, Armageddon in Derry', *The Sunday Business Post*, 27 January: A8.

Kelly, M. (1978) letter (in response to Rockett, 1978), *Film Directions*, 1, 3: 15.

Kiberd, D. (1996, first published 1995) *Inventing Ireland*, London: Vintage.

Kickham, C.J. (1988, first published 1870) *Knocknagow*, Dublin: Anna Livia Press.

Kilroy, J.F. (1971) *The 'Playboy' Riots*, Dublin: Dolmen Press.

Kirby, P. (2002) 'Contested Pedigrees of the Celtic Tiger', in P. Kirby, L. Gibbons and M. Cronin *Reinventing Ireland*, London, Sterling Virginia: Pluto Press.

Kirkland, R. (1999) 'Gender, Nation, Excess', in S. Brewster, V. Crossman, F. Becket and D. Alderson *Ireland in Proximity*, London and New York: Routledge.

Leahy, J. (1996) 'Nothing Personal', *Vertigo*, 6: 18–21.

Lee, J.J. (1989) *Ireland 1912–1985*, Cambridge: Cambridge University Press.

Leerssen, J. (1996a) *Mere Irish and Fíor-Ghael*, Cork: Cork University Press.

—— (1996b) *Remembrance and Imagination*, Cork: Cork University Press.

Lloyd, D. (1993) *Anomalous States*, Dublin: Lilliput Press.

—— (1999) *Ireland After History*, Cork: Cork University Press.

Longley, E. (1994) *The Living Stream*, Newcastle Upon Tyne: Bloodaxe Books.

Lourdeaux, L. (1990) *Italian and Irish Filmmakers in America*, Philadelphia: Temple University Press.

Low, R. (1985) *Film Making in 1930s Britain*, London: George Allen & Unwin.

Lyons, F.S.L. (1985) *Ireland Since the Famine*, London: Fontana Press.

Lysaght, R. (2003) 'Súil Nua', *Film Ireland*, 90: 36–7.

McArthur, C. (1994) 'The Cultural Necessity of a Poor Celtic Cinema', in J. Hill, M. McLoone, P. Hainsworth, (eds.) *Border Crossing: Film in Ireland, Britain and Europe, Belfast and London*, Institute of Irish Studies/BFI Publishing.

McCracken, K. (1999) 'Poetic Documentary. The Films of John T. Davis', in J. MacKillop, (ed.) *Contemporary Irish Cinema: From* The Quiet Man *to* Dancing at Lughnasa, Syracuse: Syracuse University Press.

McCrum, R. (1992) 'The Gifts of the Gabbers', *The Guardian*, 12 December: 7.

McDonagh, J. (1976) 'Film Production in Ireland in the Early Days', in L. O'Leary *Cinema Ireland 1895–1976*, Dublin: Dublin Arts Festival.

McDonagh, M. (1997) *The Cripple of Inishmaan*, London: Methuen Drama.

McFarlane, B. (1999) *Lance Comfort*, Manchester and New York: Manchester University Press.

McIlroy, B. (1993) 'The Repression of Communities: Visual Representations of Northern Ireland during the Thatcher Years', in L. Friedman (ed.) *British Cinema and Thatcherism*, London: UCL Press.

—— (1994) 'British Filmmaking in the 1930s and 1940s: The Example of Brian Desmond Hurst', in W. Winston Dixon (ed.) *Re-Viewing British Cinema, 1900–1992*, New York: State University of New York Press.

—— (1998) *Shooting to Kill*, Flicks Books, Wiltshire, UK.

—— (1999) 'Challenges and Problems in Contemporary Irish Cinema: The Protestants', *Cineaste* xxiv, 2–3: 56–60.

MacKillop, J. (ed.) (1999) *Contemporary Irish Cinema: From* The Quiet Man *to* Dancing at Lughnasa, Syracuse: Syracuse University Press.

—— (1999) 'The Quiet Man Speaks', in J. MacKillop (ed). *Contemporary Irish Cinema: From* The Quiet Man *to* Dancing at Lughnasa, Syracuse: Syracuse University Press.

McLoone, M. (1999) '*December Bride*', in J. MacKillop (ed). *Contemporary Irish Cinema: From* The Quiet Man *to* Dancing at Lughnasa, Syracuse: Syracuse University Press.

—— (2000) *Irish Film, The Emergence of a Contemporary Cinema*, London: BFI Publishing.

Macnab, G. (2001) 'About Adam' (review) *Sight and Sound*, 11, 5: 38.

McWilliams, D. (1999) *The Bigger Picture*, Dublin: Film Makers Ireland.

Malone, J. (undated) 'John Ford and the Women of Limerick', *The Old Limerick Journal*, 15: 29–31.

Maltby, R. (1996) 'Censorship and Self-Regulation', in G. Nowell-Smith (ed.) *The Oxford History of World Cinema*, Oxford: Oxford University Press.

Meaney, G. (1993) 'Sex and Nation: Women in Irish Culture and Politics', in A. Smith (ed.) *Irish Women's Studies Reader* Dublin: Attic Press.

—— (1998) 'Landscapes of Desire: Women and Ireland on film', *Women: A Cultural Review* 9, 3: 237–51.

Miller, K.A. (1985) *Emigrants and Exiles*, New York and Oxford: Oxford University Press.

Mjoset, L. (1992) *The Irish Economy in a Comparative Institutional Perspective*, Dublin: National Economic and Social Council.

Monk, C. (1995) 'Sexuality and the Heritage', *Sight and Sound*, 5, 10: 32–4.

Morash, C. (2002) *A History of Irish Theatre, 1601–2000*, Cambridge: Cambridge University Press.

Montrose, L.A. (1989) 'The Poetics and Politics of Culture', in H. Aram Veeser, (ed.) *The New Historicism*, New York and London: Routledge.

Murphy, P. and Gogan, J. (1990) 'In the Name of the Law', *Film Base News*, September/October: 13–17.

Murray, C. (1997) *Twentieth-Century Irish Drama*, Manchester and New York: Manchester University Press.

Musser, C. (1991) 'Ethnicity, Role-Playing, and American Film Comedy: From *Chinese Laundry Scene* to *Whoopee* (1894–1930)', in L. Friedman (ed.) *Unspeakable Images, Ethnicity and the American Cinema*, Urbana and Chicago: University of Illinois Press.

Naficy, H. (1999) 'Framing Exile', in H. Naficy (ed.) *Home, Exile, Homeland*, London and New York: Routledge.

Nairn, T. (1981) *The Break-Up of Britain*, London: Verso.

Nandy, A. (1983) *The Intimate Enemy*, Delhi, Bombay, Calcutta, Madras: Oxford University Press.

Napper, L. (1997) 'A Despicable Tradition? Quota Quickies in the 1930s', in R. Murphy (ed.) *The British Cinema Book*, London: BFI Publishing.

Nash, C. (1997) 'Embodied Irishness', in B. Graham (ed.) *In Search of Ireland, A Cultural Geography*, London and New York: Routledge.

Neale, S. (1987) *Genre*, London: BFI Publishing.

Negra, D. (2001a) *Off-White Hollywood*, London and New York: Routledge.

—— (2001b) 'The New Primitives: Irishness in Recent US Television', *Irish Studies Review* 9, 2: 229–39.

Neve, B. (1996) 'Film and Northern Ireland: beyond 'the troubles'?' in W. Everett (ed.) *European Identity in Cinema*, Bristol: Intellect Publishing.

Nowell-Smith, G. and Ricci, S. (eds) (1998) *Hollywood and Europe: Economics, Culture, National Identity 1945–95*, London: BFI Publishing.

O'Brien, H. (2000) 'Projecting the Past: historical documentary in Ireland', *Historical Journal of Film, Radio and Television* 20, 3: 335–50.

—— (2001) 'Somewhere to Come Back to: The Filmic Journeys of John T. Davis', *Irish Studies Review* 9, 2: 167–77.

—— (2002) 'Culture, Commodity, and *Céad Míle Fáilte*: U.S. and Irish Tourist Films as a Vision of Ireland', *Éire-Ireland*, xxxvii: I & II: 58–73.

O'Conluain, P. (1953) 'Ireland's First Films', *Sight and Sound* 23, 2: 96–98.

O'Donovan, F. (1988; first published 1911) 'Aim of Irish Players', in E.H. Mikhail (ed.) *The Abbey Theatre, Interviews and Recollections* Basingstoke: Macmillan Press.

Ó Drisceoil, D (1996) *Censorship in Ireland, 1939–1945*, Cork: Cork University Press.

O'Faolain, N. (1996) 'Cinematic Revival of Classics helps form Community', *The Irish Times*, 25 November: 14.

O'Flaherty, L. (1971, first published 1925) *The Informer*, Northampton: John Dickens.

O'Flynn, S. (1996) 'Irish Newsreels: an expression of national identity?', in R. Smither and W. Klaue (eds) *Newsreels in Film Archives* Madison, Teaneck: Fairleigh Dickinson University Press/Trowbridge: Flicks Books.

O'Kelly, K. (1960) 'Ireland's Film Festival', *Scannán*, 5, 1: 8–10.

O'Leary, L. (1990) *Cinema Ireland, 1896–1950*, Dublin: The National Library of Ireland.

—— (1993, first published 1980) *Rex Ingram, Master of the Silent Cinema*, Pordenone/London: 12th Pordenone Silent Film Festival/BFI Publishing.

O'Regan, T. (1996) *Australian National Cinema*, London and New York: Routledge.

Peillon, M. (2002) 'Culture and State in Ireland's New Economy', in P. Kirby, L. Gibbons and M. Cronin (eds) *Reinventing Ireland*, London, Sterling Virginia: Pluto Press.

Pettitt, L. (1997) 'Pigs and Provos, Prostitutes and Prejudice', in E. Walshe (ed.) *Sex, Nation and Dissent in Irish Writing*, Cork: Cork University Press.

—— (1999) 'A Construction Site Queered: "Gay" Images in New Irish Cinema', *Cineaste*, xxiv, 2–3: 61–3.

—— (2000) *Screening Ireland*, Manchester: Manchester University Press.

—— (2001) *December Bride*, Cork: Cork University Press.

Petley, J. (1986) 'State of the Union', *Monthly Film Bulletin*, 53, 624: 4.

Phillips, G.D. (1998) *Exiles in Hollywood: Major European Film Directors in America, 1922–31*, London: Routledge & Kegan Paul.

Place, J.A. (1979) *The Non-Western Films of John Ford*, Secaucus: Citadel Press.

Power, E. (2001) 'Mae Galvin, first "leading lady" of Irish film', *Ireland's Own*, 4,777, 8 June: 31.

Power, P. (2000) 'Straight Shooter', *The Irish Times* (The Ticket), 17 January: 4–5.

Quinn, B. (2001) *Maverick*, Dingle: Brandon.

Rayns, T. (1977) 'Modernism', in J. Ellis (ed.) *1951–1976 British Film Institute Productions* (catalogue), London: BFI Publishing.

Richards, J. (1973) *Visions of Yesterday*, London: Routledge & Kegan Paul.

—— (1984) *The Age of the Dream Palace*, London, Boston, Melbourne and Henley: Routledge & Kegan Paul.

—— (1996) 'Ireland, the Empire and film', in K. Jeffery (ed.) *An Irish Empire?*, Manchester and New York: Manchester University Press.

Riley, R.W. (1995) 'Movie-induced Tourism', in A.V. Seaton (ed.) *Tourism, The State of the Art*, London: John Wiley and Sons.

Ricoeur, P. (1965) *History and Truth*, trans. Charles A. Kelbey, Evanston: Northwestern University Press.

Rockett, K. (1978) 'The Realism Debate and "Down the Corner"', *Film Directions*, 1, 2: 18-20.

—— (1980) 'Film Censorship and the State', *Film Directions*, 3, 9: 11-15.

—— (1987) 'Breakthroughs'; 'An Irish Film Studio' in K. Rockett, L. Gibbons and J. Hill, *Cinema and Ireland*, London and Sydney: Croom Helm.

—— (1991) 'Aspects of the Los Angelesation of Ireland', *Irish Communications Review*, 1: 18–23.

—— (1994) 'Culture, Industry and Irish Cinema', in J. Hill, M. McLoone and P. Hainsworth (eds), *Border Crossing, Film in Ireland, Britain and Europe*, Institute of Irish Studies/Queen's University Belfast/British Film Institute: Belfast and London.

—— (1996) *The Irish Filmography*, Dublin: Red Mountain Press.

—— (1999) 'Irish Cinema, the National in the International', *Cineaste*, xxiv, 2–3: 23–5.

—— (2000) 'Protecting the Family and the Nation: the official censorship of American cinema in Ireland, 1923–1954, *Historical Journal of Film, Radio and Television* 20, 3: 283–300.

—— (2001) 'From Radicalism to Conservatism: Contradictions within Fianna Fáil Film Policies in the 1930s', *Irish Studies Review* 9, 2: 155–65.

Rockett, K. and Collins D. (1980) 'Introduction to Film Censorship Statistics', *Film Directions*, 3, 9: 23–34.

Rockett, K., Gibbons, L. and Hill, J. (1989) *Cinema and Ireland*, London and Sydney: Croom Helm.

Rosenbaum, J. (1976) 'Coilin & Platonida', *Monthly Film Bulletin*, 43, 515: 248.

Rushdie, S. (1982) 'The Empire Writes Back with a Vengeance', *The Times*, 3 July: 8.

Said, E. (1994, first published 1993) *Culture and Imperialism*, London: Vintage.

Savage, R. (1996) *Irish Television, the Political and Social Origins*, Cork: Cork University Press.

Schlesinger, P., Murdock, G. and Elliott, P. (1983) *Televising 'Terrorism'*, London: Comedia.

Sheehy, T. (1996) 'The Windhover', *Film Ireland* 55: 16–17.

—— (2002) 'The Arts Council … and Film', *Film Ireland* 85: 36–8.

Sherry, P. (1944) 'Production in Eire', *Sight and Sound* 13, 51: 72–3.

Sheeran, P.F. (2002) *The Informer*, Cork: Cork University Press.

Shields, P. (2001) 'The Carney', *Film Ireland*, 82: 12–15.

Slide, A. (1988) *The Cinema and Ireland*, Jefferson, North Carolina and London: McFarland.

Smith, A.D. (1996) 'Memory and Modernity: Reflections on Ernest Gellner's theory of nationalism', *Nations and Nationalism* 2, 3: 371–88.

Sorlin, P. (1980) *The Film in History, Restaging the Past*, Oxford: Basil Blackwell.

Stern, C. and Davis, V. (1994) 'Hollywood has Put us in the Dock … This Torture Stuff is Pure Fantasy', *Mail on Sunday*, 2 January: 48–9.

Sutton, D. (2000) *A Chorus of Raspberries*, Exeter: University of Exeter Press.

Sykes, C. (1942) 'Brian Desmond Hurst', *The Screen*, June 1942: 3–4, 8.

Sullivan, M. (1997) '*The Visit*, Incarceration, and Film by Women in Northern Ireland: An Interview with Orla Walsh', *The Irish Review* 21: 29–40.

Swift, R. and Gilley, S. (1999) *The Irish in Victorian Britain*, Dublin: Four Courts Press.

Tansey, P. (1998) *Ireland at Work: Economic Growth and the Labour Market, 1987–1997*, Dublin: Oak Tree Press.

Tierney, M. (2001) 'Minister for Transport, Gerry Stembridge', *Film West*, 43: 14–17.

Tobin, F. (1984) *The Best of Decades, Ireland in the 1960s*, Dublin: Gill and Macmillan.

Tóibín, C. (2002) *Lady Gregory's Toothbrush*, Dublin: The Lilliput Press.

Tribe, K. (1977/78) 'History and the Production of Memory', *Screen*, 18, 4: 9–22.

Warshow, R. (1970) *The Immediate Experience*, New York: Atheneum Books.

Wilcox, H. (1967) *Twenty-Five Thousand Sunsets*, London, Sydney, Toronto: The Bodley Head.

Willemen, P. (1989) 'The Third Cinema Question: Notes and Reflections; in P. Willemen and J. Pines (eds) *Questions of Third Cinema*, London: BFI Publishing.

—— (1994) *Looks and Frictions*, London: BFI Publishing.

Williams, P. (1998) *Gangland*, Dublin: The O'Brien Press.

Wollen, P. (1982) *Readings and Writings*, London: Verso.

Zizek, S. (1993) 'From Courtly Love to *The Crying Game*', *New Left Review*, 202: 9–108.

Documentaries

As Others See Us: The Movies, UTV (Ireland, 1998).
Irish Cinema – Ourselves Alone, Poolbeg Productions (Ireland, 1995).
Short Story – Irish Cinema 1945–1958. BAC Films (Ireland, 1986).

INDEX